PRESIDENTIAL CANDIDATES:

CONTAINING

SKETCHES,

BIOGRAPHICAL, PERSONAL AND POLITICAL,

OF

Prominent Candidates for the Presidency

IN

1860.

BY D. W. BARTLETT.

NEW YORK:
A. B. BURDICK, PUBLISHER,
8 SPRUCE STREET.
1859.

W. H. TINSON, Stereotyper.

GEO. RUSSELL & Co., Printers.

PREFACE.

THE sketches in this volume vary in length and minuteness, not from a disposition, on my part, to withhold facts, but because a few of my subjects are too cautious to allow their private history to go before the public; nevertheless, the work contains full and accurate details of the private and public history of our "PRESIDENTIAL CANDIDATES"—not one of whom has any idea of the position I have assigned him.

In selecting candidates, of course, I have followed my own judgment—had I made use of everybody's, I might fill a dozen volumes. I have sketched *the prominent men* who have been named in connection with the Presidency in 1860. Messrs. Buchanan and Pierce I have passed over as men who have gone through a campaign—and through a Presidential term—and the people know them. It is the men who have not run the race for Presidential honors—the new men—of whom the public would learn something, or I have made a mistake in writing this book. The general reader will easily find in the volume the position of any candidate on the issues of the day; and possibly, beside, interesting personal details which show the character of the man.

THE AUTHOR.

CONTENTS.

PRESIDENTIAL CANDIDATES.

WILLIAM H. SEWARD.

The stranger who enters the hall of the United States Senate and casts his eye over the array of senators, will be not a little surprised, possibly somewhat amused, when William H. Seward is pointed out to him. Accustomed to think of Mr. Seward as one of the greatest men in the country, a first-class statesman, as well as orator—for he has *read*, not *heard*, his numberless speeches upon the subjects of the day—he expected to find a gentleman of imposing aspect, to discover the impressive appearance which awes the stranger, or the audience. But, instead of this, he finds a quiet man, sitting in his seat, listening with imperturbable calmness to every senator who chooses to speak, however dry, however provoking, however stupid. For Mr. Seward is well known to be *the best listener* in the Senate. This arises from his rigid politeness, if we may use the phrase, which will not allow him to refuse his ear and eye to any man who chooses to speak. There he sits, leaning back in his chair, a slender man, of average height, clad in simple black, with a singular face, grey eyes, grey hair, Roman nose, a second Wellington, ever in repose. Who ever saw William H. Seward excited? He is never to be provoked by friend or enemy, and is either devoid of all sensibility, or has a spirit which can triumph over, soar above, the common infirmities of poor human nature. We have seen Mr. Seward on two very trying occasions. One, when Mr. Hale, his friend and seat-mate, thought it his duty to severely criticise his vote on the army bill (this was in the winter of 1857–8), and in which criticism he was very personal. Mr. Seward sat composedly in his seat during the painful review of his brother senator, and rose to reply as pleasantly and as quietly as he ever did in his life.

On another occasion, when the Senate sat late in the night on the Cuban bill—last spring—Mr. Toombs made a fierce, and we must say disgraceful attack upon Mr. Seward, calling him, among other names, "a tuppenny demagogue." During the entire harangue by the Georgian senator, Mr. Seward twirled his spectacles, unconsciously, and in his reply was slow, freezingly cold, and never for a moment addressed or looked at Mr. Toombs. These facts show that Mr. Seward purposely refuses in public to allow himself to be angered by personalities or to offer there personalities. He guards constantly against the temptation to offend in this particular. He has often been accused by ardent Republicans of lacking courage, physical courage, and that he did not reply to the attacks of his southern enemies with sufficient spirit. It is a mistake to ascribe this conduct of Mr. Seward to cowardice. It is the result of deliberate thought in him—and if it is mistaken policy, then of course it is to be set down as a blunder, not a vice.

When Mr. Seward speaks, he again disappoints the stranger. There is no *manner*, none of the acts of the orator are to be seen. He leans against the top of his chair, and in an easy, conversational manner *talks* to the Senate, all the time swinging his spectacles to and fro as if at the fireside.

With his arms folded, and leaning back upon the lofty railing in the old Senate hall, we heard Mr. Seward deliver such startling sentiments as these:

"I think, with great deference to the judgments of others, that the expedient, peaceful, and right way to determine it, is to reverse the existing policy of intervention in favor of slave labor and slave States. It would be wise to restore the Missouri prohibition of slavery in Kansas and Nebraska. There was peace in the territories and in the States until that great statute of Freedom was subverted. It is true that there were frequent debates here on the subject of slavery, and that there were profound sympathies among the people, awakened by or responding to those debates. But what was Congress instituted for but debate? What makes the American people to differ from all other nations, but this—that while among them power enforces silence, here all public questions are referred to debate, free debate in Congress. Do you tell me that the Supreme Court of the United States has removed the foundations of that great statute? I reply, that they have done no such thing; they could not do it. They have remanded the negro man, Dred Scott, to the custody of his master. With that decree we have nothing here, at least nothing now, to do. This is the extent of the judgment rendered, the extent of any judgment they could render. Already the pretended further decision is subverted in Kansas. So it will be in every free State and in every free Territory of the United States. The Supreme Court, also, can reverse its spurious judgment more easily than we could reconcile the people to its usurpation. Sir, the Supreme Court of the United States attempts to command the people of the United States to accept the principles that one man can own other men, and that they must guarantee the inviolability of that false and pernicious property. The people of the United States never can, and they never will, accept principles so unconstitutional and so abhorrent. Never, never. Let the Court recede. Whether it recede or not, we shall reorganize the Court, and thus reform its political sentiments and practices, and bring them into harmony with the Constitution and with the laws of nature. In doing so we shall not only reassume our own just authority, but we shall restore that high tribunal itself to the position it ought to maintain, since so many invaluable rights of citizens, and even of States themselves, depend upon its impartiality and its wisdom.

"Do you tell me that the slave States will not acquiesce, but will agitate? Think first whether the free States will acquiesce in a decision that shall not only be unjust, but fraudulent. True, they will not menace the Republic. They have an easy and simple remedy, namely to take the government out of unjust and unfaithful hands, and commit it to those which will be just and faithful. They are ready to do this now. They want only a little more harmony of purpose and a little more completeness of organization. These will result from only the least addition to the pressure of slavery upon them. You are lending all that is necessary, and even more, in this very act. But will the slave States agitate? Why? Because they have lost at last a battle that they could not win, unwisely provoked, fought with all the advantages of strategy and intervention, and on a field chosen by themselves. What would they gain? Can they compel Kansas to adopt slavery against her will? Would it be reasonable or just to do it, if they could? Was negro servitude ever forced by the sword on any people that inherited the blood which circulates in our veins, and the sentiments which make us a free people? If they will agitate on such a ground as this, then how, or when, by what concessions we can make, will they ever be satisfied? To what end would they agitate? It can now be only to divide the Union. Will they not need some fairer or more plausible excuse for a proposition so desperate? How would they improve their condition, by drawing down a certain ruin upon themselves? Would they gain any new security for Slavery? Would they not hazard securities that are invaluable? Sir, they who talk so idly, talk what they do not know themselves. No man when cool can promise what he will do when he shall be inflamed; no man inflamed can speak for his actions when time and necessity shall bring reflection. Much less can any one speak for States in such emergencies."

The Senate Hall was crowded—the galleries packed with a dense throng of men and women, and the entire audience leaned forward to catch every one of the words we have quoted, the southern senators smiling scornfully, while some of them were speaking; yet the orator went on as smoothly, as easily, as if he were discoursing a passage of ancient history with a knot of tried friends, instead of dealing with great and living issues before an audience, half of whom, to say the least, were his bitter enemies, eagerly listening to convict him of any imprudent or unjust sentiment.

Mr. Seward is no orator as the word is ordinarily understood. He has little or no animation, no address, no impressiveness. It is *the thoughts*, *the ideas* of his speeches, which make them so powerful, so widely popular. Almost any one of his speeches *reads* better than it delivers. Mr. Seward, long ago, must have lost all ambition to become merely an orator—if he ever at any time indulged in such an ambition. He speaks not to the few hundreds who can hear his voice, as he well knows; but to millions outside the walls of the Capitol. And so he studies his speeches, makes them truly great, and worth reading by anybody and everybody, then commits them to memory, and recites them in the Senate that they may go with the official stamp upon them to the millions of readers in the free States.

Mr. Seward has long been popular in Washington —personally, we mean—even among his political enemies. When he came to Washington, it was with difficulty that he got a pew in one of the fashionable churches of the capital. Association with him was then thought to be contamination; but, long since, his hospitality, his high mindedness, and his charitable nature, have won for him not only the respect, but the love of many of the citizens of Washington, and some at least of the citizens of the far southern States. No man has more bitter political enemies than Mr. Seward, and no prominent man fewer personal enemies. Those who know him, esteem him highly, however severely they may condemn his political sentiments.

William Henry Seward was born in Florida, New York, May 16, 1801, and is now 58 years old. His ancestors were of Welsh extraction upon his father's side, and of Irish on the mother's side. His father was a physician in the State of New York, of good character and excellent abilities, and his mother was a woman of warm affections and a strong and cultivated intellect. The people of the little town of Florida, generally, were natives of New England, and the tone of society was what some would call Puritanic. In such a village, education and good morals were highly esteemed, and the young mind would be naturally impressed with the importance of great truths, of morality and humanity.

William Henry, while a boy, was noted in the village where he lived, and especially among his circle of family friends, as a great student. His intellect was thought to be precociously developed; but if such was the fact, none of the later effects which usually follow unnatural precocity showed themselves in Mr. Seward's career. He was also known, and is still remembered by his school-day friends, for that frankness, purity and gentleness of character which now distinguish him. As a boy he was pure, and a brother senator remarked of Mr. Seward in our hearing the other day, "He is the purest public man I ever knew!"

When nine years old, he was sent to school at an academy in Goshen, N. Y. At fifteen, the pale, thin, studious lad entered Union College at Schenectady, where he very rapidly distinguished himself by his application, his brilliant talents and the gentleness of his character and disposition. His favorite studies were rhetoric, moral philosophy and the ancient classics. He was a close and thorough student. He rose at four in the morning and sat up late at night. It was here that he acquired those habits of continuous mental toil which have characterized him since he came to public life.

Mr. Seward graduated from Union College with distinguished honors. Among his fellow-graduates were Judge Kent, Dr. Hickok, Professor Lewis, and other eminent men. Shortly after leaving college, Mr. Seward entered the law office of John Anthon, in the city of New York, where, as in college, his unusual devotion to his studies attracted the attention of his teachers and led his friends to prognosticate for him a brilliant future. He finished his legal studies with Judge Duer and Ogden Hoffman, in Goshen, and was admitted to the bar of the Supreme Court of New York at Utica in 1822.

In 1823, Mr. Seward took up his residence in the pretty village of Auburn, N. Y. which to this day is his "home," and will always be his abiding place. He became, in 1824 the law-partner of Judge Miller of Auburn and married his youngest daughter, Frances Adeline Miller. The fruits of this marriage were five children, one of whom died young, another took to the army, another to the law, and the remaining two are comparatively young.

Mr. Seward's personal appearance cannot be said to be prepossessing, yet there are fine points in his personal appearance. His ways are modest, his brow and eyes have, however, a sleepy aspect, which has been fostered by his habit of snuffing and smoking tobacco immoderately.

The first time we saw Mr. Seward was at his home—the pretty village of Auburn—beneath the roof of a mutual friend. His face struck us at first unpleasantly, for it seemed too lifeless and expressionless for a man with so much mind, so great an intellect; but in a few moments the clouds passed off and the clear vault of his intellect was open to the eye. His eye grew bright and the fascination of his conversation was at once felt. The compact brow expressed power, the eye genius, the lips force of character, the whole body stately dignity, as well as frankness. In his manners and conversation both in private and in public, Mr. Seward is one of the most natural of men. Nothing is forced or affected, but a pleasant negligence characterizes his manner.

Some men pass for great men because they are physically great and dignified, and because they utter few words and those in a sententious manner. Mr. Seward is not one of these dignitaries, but has won his greatness by *hard work*. He never was one of those brilliant geniuses who suddenly startle the world, but wrought out his reputation, and *earned* the honor which has been so freely accorded to him by his fellow-men.

In Auburn, Mr. Seward has long been personally very popular. His position is a happy one. He has moderate wealth—enough for all his wants—and there at least—however much his hospitality in the Capitol may savor of splendor—there he lives in plain, almost frugal style. He has for years been a member of the Episcopal church at Auburn.

Mr. Seward's father was a Jeffersonian Democrat, and he naturally accepted the politics of his father; but not long after he began to practise law, he left the Democratic party for the opposition. When the Missouri Compromise roused the North from its slumbers, he sided almost instinctively with the friends of freedom, and made several public speeches during the excitement against any compromise with slavery. In 1830, he was elected to the State Senate on anti-Masonic grounds. In 1833, he made the tour of Europe. One year later, he was nominated for governor of the State of New York by the Whig party, and was defeated. In 1838, he was again nominated to that office, and was elected by ten thousand majority. When his term had expired, he was again elected to the same honorable post. While governor of New York he made her respected and admired throughout the world. He used all his influence and power for the repeal of all State laws which in any manner countenanced the institution of negro slavery. The law which permitted a southern slaveholder to retain possession of his slave while travelling through the State, was repealed. A law was also passed which allowed a fugitive the benefit of a jury-trial, and prohibiting State officers from assisting in the recovery of fugitives, and also denying the use of the jails for the confinement of fugitive slaves under arrest. The Supreme Court pronounced most of these laws unconstitutional afterward. Another law was passed, chiefly through the influence of Mr. Seward, for the recovery of kidnapped colored citizens of New York.

Under the operation of this humane enactment, Solomon Northup, who for twelve years had been forced to toil upon a far distant southern plantation, was rescued and brought back to his friends. The story of his case was published afterward and had a very large sale.

To crown his official acts, Mr. Seward, just before retiring from his gubernatorial office, recommended the abolition of that law requiring a freehold qualification of negro voters.

The governor of Virginia made a requisition upon him for the surrender of certain parties accused of assisting slaves to escape from their owners. He refused to comply with the demand, upon the ground that the article in the Constitution authorizing a demand of fugitives from justice covered only such persons as were criminals by the laws of the several States and the civilized world. Aiding a slave to escape from his master, in his opinion, was no crime, and he did not feel it to be his duty to surrender the accused. A long controversy was the result of this bold decision, and retaliatory measures were tried by the State of Virginia, but Governor Seward remained firm to the end.

In 1847, Mr. Seward defended John Van Zandt, who was accused of aiding the escape of slaves from their master, at the bar of the Supreme Court of the United States. It was one of the most eloquent arguments he ever made, and he would not accept of a dollar's compensation for his great effort.

While riding once upon the banks of the beautiful Owasco Lake, the friend who was with us, pointed out a pleasant farmhouse as the scene, a few years before, of a terrible murder, and not far distant, in a lonely churchyard, we saw the graves of the victims. A negro of the name of William Freeman, at the age of sixteen, was sent to the State Prison for five years, for alleged horse-stealing. He declared his innocence of the charge, and it has since been admitted by those who tried him, that he was doubtless an innocent man; but, through the false swearing of the real thief, he was sent to prison. The injustice of his punishment, coupled with barbarous treatment while in prison, resulted in an idiotic insanity, and when, at last, he was set free, his term of imprisonment having expired, he went forth an idiot—a lunatic—with but one idea in his brain—that the outside world had most foully wronged him.

One night, without a spark of provocation, this wretched negro entered the house of a Mr. Van Nest and killed him, his wife, a child, and his mother, a woman of seventy. He was arrested the next day, and such was the terrible state of excitement in and around Auburn, that it was with great difficulty that the people were restrained from hanging the culprit up to the most convenient tree. The negro, idiot that he was, confessed the murder and laughed over it. This enraged the people still more, and they clamored for his blood. Mr. Seward had acquired much popularity in his arguments in criminal cases, and his neighbors became at once alarmed for fear he would defend the negro. He was absent then at the South, and such was the frantic state of the people of Auburn that his law-partners announced that he would not defend the case. But Mr. Seward was his own master still, and though he saw what the feeling was, and that the negro was sure to be brought in guilty, yet as the miserable man was friendless, he examined most carefully into the case and came to the deliberate conclusion that Freeman was insane. Hoping that other counsel would appear, he did not offer his services. The day of trial came, and the villagers hoped that no lawyer *dared* to defend the criminal. The indictment was read against him, and he was asked if he plead guilty or not guilty. The only reply he made was "Ha!" He was asked if he had counsel—"he didn't know." The poor wretch had no idea of what was transpiring, that he was upon his trial for life. At this juncture, Mr. Seward, who was present, was entirely overcome by his feelings, but he in a moment answered:

"May it please the court: *I shall remain counsel for the prisoner until his death.*" For two weeks, in the hottest of weather, he conducted the defence, without pay. He was subjected to insult from some of his old friends, and the feeling of the town was strongly against him. The well known John Van Buren was the District Attorney, and with the predetermination of the jury, of course a verdict of "guilty," was rendered. Mr. Seward's argument was one of the finest he ever made. Alluding to the unpopularity which he had brought upon himself by his course, he said:

"In due time, gentlemen of the jury, when I shall have paid the debt of nature, my remains will rest here in your midst with those of my kindred and neighbors. It is very possible they may be unhonored, neglected, spurned! But perhaps years hence, when the passion and excitement which now agitate this community shall have passed away—some wandering stranger—some lone exile—some *Indian*, some *negro*, may erect over them a humble stone, and thereon write this epitaph, 'HE WAS FAITHFUL.'"

An Appellate Court granted a new trial, but before it came on the criminal died. A post mortem examination revealed the fact that his brain was *one mass of disease, and nearly destroyed!* Mr. Seward was suddenly and unexpectedly set right again before the people, and was restored to the old place in their affections.

We have noticed this portion of Mr. Seward's life

because it effectually disposes of that cry raised against him by certain persons, that he is a demagogue. No demagogue defends the poor and forsaken, at the expense of personal popularity. He flatters the prejudices of the people and does not go across them to his own injury.

Mr. Seward was elected, in 1849, to the Senate of the United States, where he has remained to this day. His course is everywhere known. He was a Whig, and is of course warmly in favor of a Protective Tariff and other prominent Whig measures, though he subordinates them all to the great question of Human Freedom.

As a Whig, Mr. Seward was the friend of the slave. He opposed the famous compromise measures of 1850, struggled against the repeal of the Missouri Compromise — came slowly into the Republican movement, but when once in it, no man could excel him, and few equal, in hearty devotion to the party and its cause. From the first, he condemned the great American movement, and has lost popularity in some quarters for doing so. He is in favor of internal improvements and a homestead law, as his votes will show. He objects to any hasty, irritating attempts to buy or take Cuba—no insults—let everything be done fairly and gentlemanly; and, if the pear drops to the ground ripe, eat the fruit. *But no fruit-stealing, or buying at ruinous prices!*

A friend of Mr. Seward speaks of Mr. Seward's style in the following language:

"His rapid idealization, his oriental affluence, though not vagueness of expression, and the Ciceronian flow of his language, proceeding not from the heat of youth or the vapors of wine, but from the exceeding fertility of his imagination, combine to render him an interesting speaker. Yet his enunciation is neither clear nor distinct, and the tones of his voice often grate harshly upon the ear. He is not devoid of grace, however; he is calm and dignified, but earnest.

"His style is elegant rather than neat; elaborate rather than finished. It possesses a sparkling vivacity, but is somewhat deficient in energetic brevity. It is not always easy, for there is more labor than art; but if the wine has an agreeable *bouquet*, the connoisseur delights to have it linger. Like young D'Israeli, whose political position, in some respects, resembles his own, he has occasionally a tendency to restore declamation, a natural predilection perhaps for Milesian floridness and hyperbole, and, like Napoleon, a love for gorgeous paradoxes. But, in general, his words are well-chosen and are frequently more eloquent than the ideas. His sentences are all constructed with taste; they have often the brilliancy of Mirabeau, and the glowing fervor of Fox."

We must notice a few quotations from a very few

of Mr. Seward's most prominent speeches. At Detroit, Oct. 2, 1856, he spoke upon "The Slaveholding Class," to a mass convention, in which he first argued that the aggrandizement of the slaveholding class, to the detriment of the rest of the people of the country, is a perversion of the Constitution. He then, in a masterly style, gave a sketch of the condition of the country—showed the organization of the courts, of Congress, of the departments—all—all entirely in the control of the slaveholding class—and closed with the subjoined paragraphs:

"Mark, if you please, that thus far I have only shown you the mere governmental organization of the slaveholding class in the United States, and pointed out its badges of supremacy, suggestive of your own debasement and humiliation. Contemplate now the reality of the power of that class, and the condition to which the cause of human nature has been reduced. In all the free States, the slaveholder argues and debates the pretensions of his class, and even prosecutes his claim for his slave before the delegate of the Federal Government, with safety and boldness, as he ought. He exhorts the citizens of the free States to acquiesce, and even threatens them, in their very homes, with the terrors of disunion, if that acquiescence is withheld; and he does all this with safety, as he ought, if it be done at all. He is listened to with patience, and replied to with decorum, even in his most arrogant declamations, in the halls of Congress. Through the effective sympathy of other property classes, the slaveholding power maintains with entire safety a press and permanent political organizations in all the free States. On the contrary, if you except the northern border of Delaware, there is nowhere in any slaveholding State personal safety for a citizen, even of that State itself, who questions the rightful national domination of the slaveholding class. Debate of its pretensions in the halls of Congress is carried on at the peril of limb and life. A free press is no sooner set up in a slaveholding State than it is demolished, and citizens who assemble peacefully to discuss even the extremest claims of slavery, are at first cautioned, and, if that is ineffectual, banished or slain, even more surely than the resistants of military despotism in the French empire. Nor, except just now, has the case been much better even in the free States. It is only as of yesterday, when the free citizens, assembled to discuss the exactions of the slaveholding class, were dispersed in Boston, Utica, Philadelphia and New York. It is only as of yesterday, that when I rose, on request of citizens of Michigan, at Marshall, to speak of the great political questions of the day, I was enjoined not to make disturbance or to give offence by speaking of free soil, even on the ground which the Ordinance of 1787 had saved to freedom. It was only as of yesterday that Protestant churches and theological seminaries, built on Puritan foundations, vied with the organs of the slaveholding class in denouncing a legislator who, in the act of making laws affecting its interests, declared that all human laws ought to be conformed to the standard of eternal justice. The day has not even yet passed when the press, employed in the service of education and morality, expurgates from the books which are put into the hands of the young all reflections on slavery. The day yet lasts when the flag of the United States flaunts defiance on the high seas over cargoes of human merchandise. Nor is there an American representative anywhere, in any of the four quarters of the globe, that does not labor to suppress even there the discussion of American slavery, lest it may possibly affect the safety of the slaveholding class at home. If, in a generous burst of sympathy with the struggling Protestant democracy of Europe, we bring off the field one of their fallen champions, to condole with and comfort him, we suddenly discern that the mere agitation of the principles of freedom tend to alarm the slaveholding class, and we cast him off again as a waif, not merely worthless, but dangerous to ourselves. The natural and ancient order of things is reversed; freedom has become subordinate, sectional and local; slavery, in its influence and combinations, has become predominant, national and general. Free, direct and manly utterance in the cause of freedom, even in the free States themselves, leads to ostracism, while superserviceability to the slaveholding class alone secures preferment in the national councils. The descendants of Franklin, and Hamilton, and Jay, and King, are unprized—

—— 'Till they learn to betray,
Undistinguish'd they live, if they shame not their sires,
And the torch that would light them to dignity's way,
Must be caught from the pile when the country expires.'

"In this course of rapid public demoralization, what wonder is it that the action of the Government tends continually with fearfully augmenting force to the aggrandizement of the slaveholding class? A government can never be better or wiser, or even so good or so wise as the people over whom it presides? Who can wonder, then, that the Congress of the United States, in 1820, gave to slavery the west bank of the Mississippi quite up to the present line of Kansas, and was content to save for freedom, out of the vast region of Louisiana, only Kansas and Nebraska! Who can wonder that it consented to annex and admit Texas, with power to subdivide herself into five slave States, so as to secure the slaveholding class a balance against the free States then expected to be ultimately organized in Kansas and Nebraska? Who can wonder, that when this annexation of Texas brought on a war with Mexico, which ended in the annexation of Upper California and New Mexico, every foot of which was free from African slavery, Congress divided that vast territory, reluctantly admitting the new State of California as a free State, because she would not consent to establish slavery, dismembered New Mexico, transferred a large portion of it to slaveholding Texas, and stipulated that what remained of New Mexico, together with Utah, should be received as slave States if the people thereof should so demand? Who can wonder that the President, without any reproof by Congress, simultaneously offered to Spain two hundred millions of dollars for the purchase of Cuba, that it might be divided into two slaveholding States, to be admitted as members of the Federal Union, and at the same time menaced the European Powers with war should they interfere to prevent the consummation of the purchase? Who can wonder that, emboldened with these concessions of the people, Congress at last sanctioned a reprisal by the slaveholding class upon the regions of Kansas and Nebraska, not on the ground of justice or for an equivalent, but simply on the ground that the original concession of them to freedom was extorted by injustice and unconstitutional oppression by the free States? Who can wonder that the slaveholding class, when it had obtained the sanction of Congress to that reprisal, by giving a pledge that the people of those territories should be perfectly free, nevertheless, to establish freedom therein, invaded the territory of Kansas with armed forces, inaugurated an usurpation, and established slavery there, and disfranchised the supporters of freedom by tyrannical laws, enforced by fire and sword, and that the President and Senate maintain and uphold the slaveholding interests in these culminating demonstrations of their power, while the House of Representatives lacks the power, because it is wanting in the virtue, to rescue the interests of justice, freedom, and humanity? Who can wonder that federal courts in Massachusetts indict defenders of freedom for sedition, and in Pennsylvania subvert the State tribunals, and pervert the *habeas corpus*, the great writ of Liberty, into a process for arresting fugitive slaves, and construe into contempt, punishable by imprisonment without bail or mainprize, the simple and truthful denial of personal control over a fugitive female slave, who has made her own voluntary escape from bondage? Who can wonder that in Kansas lawyers may not plead or juries be empannelled in the Federal Courts, nor can even citizens vote, without first swearing to support the Fugitive Slave Law and the Kansas and Nebraska act, while citizens who discuss through the press the right of slaveholders to domineer there, are punished with imprisonment or death; free bridges, over which citizens who advocate free institutions, may pass, free taverns where they may rest, and free presses through which they may speak, are destroyed under indictments for nuisances; and those who peacefully assemble to debate the grievances of that class, and petition Congress for relief, are indicted for high treason?

"Just now, the wind sets with some apparent steadiness at the North, and you will readily confess therefore that I do not exaggerate the growing aggrandizement of the slaveholding class, but you will nevertheless insist that that aggrandizement is now and may be merely temporary and occasional. A moment's reflection, however, will satisfy you that this opinion is profoundly untrue. What is now seen is only the legitimate maturing of errors unresisted through a period of more than thirty years. All the fearful evils now upon us are only the inevitable results of efforts to extinguish, by delays, concession, and compromises, a discussion to which justice, reason and humanity, are continually lending their elemental fires.

"What, then, is the tendency of this aggrandizement of the slave interests, and what must be its end, if it be not now or speedily arrested? Immediate consequences are distinctly in view. The admission of Kansas into the Union as a slave

State, the subsequent introduction of slavery, by means equally flagrant, into Nebraska, and the admission of Utah with the twin patriarchal institutions of legalized adultery and slavery, and these three achievements crowned with the incorporation of Cuba into the Republic. Beyond these visible fields lies a region of fearful speculation—the restoration of the African slave trade, and the desecration of all Mexico and Central America, by the infliction upon the half-civilized Spanish and Indian races dwelling there, by our hands, of a curse from which, inferior as they are to ourselves, they have had the virtue once to redeem themselves. Beyond this last surveyed, lies that of civil and servile wars, national decline and—RUIN !

"I fear to open up these distant views, because I know that you will attribute my apprehensions to a morbid condition of mind. But confining myself to the immediate future which is so fearfully visible, I ask you in all candor, first, whether I have ever before exaggerated the aggrandizement of the slaveholding class. Secondly, whether the movement that I now forbode is really more improbable than the evils once seemed, which are now a startling reality.

"How are these immediate evils, and whatever of greater evils that are behind them, to be prevented? Do you expect that those who have heretofore counselled compromise, acquiescence, and submission, will change their course and come to the rescue of liberty? Even if this were a reasonable hope, are Cass, and Douglass, and Buchanan, greater or better than the statesmen who have opened the way of compromise, and led these modern statesmen into it? And if they indeed are so much greater and so much better, do you expect them to live forever?

"Perhaps you expect the slaveholding class will abate its pretensions, and practise voluntarily the moderation which you wish, but dare not demand at its hands. How long, and with what success, have you waited already for that reformation? Did any property class ever so reform itself? Did the patricians in old Rome, the noblesse or the clergy of France? The landholders in Ireland? The landed aristocracy in England? Does the slaveholding class even seek to beguile you with such a hope? Has it not become rapacious, arrogant, defiant? Is it not waging civil war against Freedom, wherever it encounters real resistance? No! no! you have let the lion and the spotted leopard into the sheep-fold. They certainly will not die of hunger there, nor retire from disgust with satiety. They will remain there so long as renewed appetite shall find multiplied prey. Be not self-deceived. Whenever a property class of any kind is invited by society to oppress, it will continue to oppress. Whenever a slaveholding class finds the non-slaveholding classes yielding, it will continue its work of subjugation.

"You admit all this, and you ask how are these great evils, now so apparent, to be corrected—these great dangers, now so manifest, to be avoided. I answer, it is to be done, not as some of you have supposed, by heated debates sustained by rifles or revolvers at Washington, nor yet by sending armies with supplies and Sharpe's rifles into Kansas. I condemn no necessary exercise of the right of self-defence, anywhere. Public safety is necessary to the practice of the real duties of champions of Freedom. But this is a contest in which the race is not to the physically swift, nor the battle to those who have most muscular strength. Least of all is it to be won by retaliation and revenge. The victory will be to those who shall practise the highest moral courage, with simple fidelity to the principles of humanity and justice. Notwithstanding all the heroism of your champions in Washington and Kansas, the contest will be fearfully endangered, if the slaveholding class shall win the President and the Congress in this great national canvass. Even although every one of these champions should perish in his proper field, yet the Rights of Man will be saved, and the tide of oppression will be rolled back from our northern plains, if a President and a Congress shall be chosen who are true to freedom. The people and the people only are sovereign and irresistible, whether they will the ascendency of slavery or the triumph of liberty.

"Harsh as my words may have seemed, I do my kinsmen and brethren of the free States no such injustice as to deny that great allowances are to be made for the demoralization I have described. We inherited complicity with the slave-holding class, and with it prejudices of caste. We inherited confidence and affection toward our Southern brethren—and with these, our political organizations, and profound reverence for political authorities, all adverse to the needful discussion of slavery. Above all, we inherited a fear of the dissolution of the Union, which can only be unwholesome when it ceases equally to affect the conduct of all the great parties to that sacred compact. All these inheritances have created influences upon our political conduct, which are rather to be deplored than condemned. I trust that at last these influences are about to cease. I trust so, because, if we have inherited the demoralization of slavery, we have also attained the virtue required for emancipation. If we have inherited prejudices of caste, we have also risen to the knowledge that political safety is dependent on the rendering of equal and exact justice to all men. And if we have suffered our love for the Union to be abused so as to make us tolerate the evils that more than all others endanger it, we have discerned that great error at last. If we should see a citizen who had erected a noble edifice, sit down inactively in its hall, avoiding all duty and enterprise, lest he might provoke enemies to pull it down over his head, or one who had built a majestic vessel, moor it to the wharf, through fear that he might peradventure run it upon the rocks, we should condemn his fatuity and folly. We have learned at last that the American people labor not only under the responsibility of preserving this Union, but also under the responsibility of making it subserve the advancement of justice and humanity, and that neglect of this last responsibility involves the chief peril to which the Union is exposed.

"I shall waste little time on the newly-invented apologies for continued demoralization. The question now to be decided is, whether a slaveholding class exclusively shall govern America, or whether it shall only bear divided sway with non-slaveholding citizens. It concerns all persons equally, whether they are Protestants or Catholics, native-born or exotic citizens. And therefore it seems to me that this is no time for trials of strength between the native-born and the adopted freeman, or between any two branches of one common Christian brotherhood.

"As little shall I dwell on merely personal partialities or prejudices affecting the candidates for public trusts. Each fitly personates the cause he represents. Beyond a doubt, Mr. Buchanan is faithful to the slaveholding class, as Mr. Fillmore vacillates between it and its opponents. I know Mr. Fremont well; and when I say that I know that he combines extraordinary genius and unquestionable sincerity of purpose with unusual modesty, I am sure that you will admit that he is a true representative of the Cause of Freedom.

"Discarding sectionalism, and loving my country and all its parts, and bearing an affection even to the slaveholding class, none the less sincere because it repels me, I cordially adopt the motto which it too often hangs out to delude us. I know no North, no South, no East, and no West; for I know that he who would offer an acceptable sacrifice in the present crisis must conform himself to the divine instructions, that neither in this mountain, nor yet at Jerusalem, shall we worship the Father; but the hour cometh, and now is, when the true worshippers shall worship the Father in spirit and in truth.

"Last of all, I stop not to argue with those who decry agitation and extol conservatism, not knowing that conservatism is of two kinds—that one which, yielding to cowardly fear of present inconvenience or danger, covers even political leprosy with protecting folds ; and that other and better conservatism, that heals, in order that the body of the Commonwealth may be healthful and immortal.

"Fellow-citizens, I am aware that I have spoken with seriousness amounting to solemnity. Do not infer from thence that I am despondent or distrustful of present triumph and ultimate regeneration. It has required a strong pressure upon the main-spring of the public virtue to awaken its elasticity. Such pressure has reached the centre of the spring at last. They who have reckoned that its elasticity was lost, are now discovering their profound mistake. The people of the United States have dallied long with the cactus, and floated carelessly on the calm seas that always reflect summer skies, but they have not lost their preference for their own changeless *fleur de lis*, and they consult no other guidance, in their course over the waters, than that of their own bright, particular, and constant star, the harbinger of Liberty."

Mr. Seward's famous Rochester speech has been so often misquoted and misrepresented that we will quote from it a few passages:

"The slave system is one of constant danger, distrust, suspicion and watchfulness. It debases those whose toil alone can produce wealth and resources for defence, to the lowest degree of which human nature is capable, to guard against mutiny and insurrection, and thus wastes energies which otherwise might be employed in national development and aggrandizement.

"The free-labor system educates all alike, and, by opening all the fields of industrial employment, and all the departments of authority, to the unchecked and equal rivalry of all classes of men, at once secures universal contentment, and brings into the highest possible activity all the physical, moral and social energies of the State. In States where the slave system prevails, the masters, directly or indirectly, secure all political power, and constitute a ruling aristocracy. In the States where the free-labor system prevails, universal suffrage necessarily obtains, and the State inevitably becomes, sooner or later, a republic or democracy.

"Russia yet maintains slavery, and is a despotism. Most of the other European states have abolished slavery, and adopted the system of free labor. It was the antagonistic political tendencies of the two systems which the first Napoleon was contemplating when he predicted that Europe would ultimately be either all Cossack or all Republican. Never did human sagacity utter a more pregnant truth. The two systems are at once perceived to be incongruous, but they are more than incongruous, they are incompatible. They never have permanently existed together in one country, and they never can. It would be easy to demonstrate this impossibility, from the irreconcilable contrast between their great principles and characteristics. But the experience of mankind has conclusively established it. Slavery, as I have already intimated, existed in every state in Europe. Free labor has supplanted it everywhere except in Russia and Turkey. State necessities, developed in modern times, are now obliging even those two nations to encourage and employ free labor; and already, despotic as they are, we find them engaged in abolishing slavery. In the United States, slavery came into collision with free labor at the close of the last century, and fell before it in New England, New York, New Jersey, and Pennsylvania, but triumphed over it effectually, and excluded it for a period yet undetermined, from Virginia, the Carolinas, and Georgia. Indeed, so incompatible are the two systems, that every new State which is organized within our ever-extending domain makes its first political act a choice of the one and an exclusion of the other, even at the cost of civil war, if necessary. The slave States, without law, at the last national election, successfully forbade, within their own limits, even the casting of votes for a candidate for President of the United States supposed to be favorable to the establishment of the free-labor system in the new States.

"Hitherto, the two systems have existed in different States, but side by side within the American Union. This has happened because the Union is a confederation of States. But in another aspect, the United States constitute only one nation. Increase of population, which is filling the States out to their very borders, together with a new and extended net-work of railroads and other avenues, and an internal commerce which daily becomes more intimate, is rapidly bringing the States into a higher and more perfect social unity or consolidation. Thus these antagonistic systems are continually coming into closer contact, and collision results.

"Shall I tell you what this collision means? They who think that it is accidental, unnecessary, the work of interested or fanatical agitators, and therefore ephemeral, mistake the case altogether. It is an irrepressible conflict between opposing and enduring forces, and it means that the United States must and will, sooner or later, become either entirely a slaveholding nation, or entirely a free-labor nation. Either the cotton and rice fields of South Carolina and the sugar plantations of Louisiana will ultimately be tilled by free labor, and Charleston and New Orleans become marts for legitimate merchandise alone, or else the rye fields and wheat fields of Massachusetts and New York must again be surrendered by their farmers to slave culture and to the production of slaves, and Boston and New York become once more markets for trade in the bodies and souls of men. It is the failure to apprehend this great truth that induces so many unsuccessful attempts at final compromise between the slave and free States, and it is the existence of this great fact that renders all such pretended compromises, when made, vain and ephemeral. Startling as this saying may appear to you, fellow-citizens, it is by no means an original or even a modern one. Our forefathers knew it to be true, and unanimously acted upon it when they framed the Constitution of the United States. They regarded the existence of the servile system in so many of the States with sorrow and shame, which they openly confessed, and they looked upon the collision between them, which was then just revealing itself, and which we are now accustomed to deplore, with favor and hope. They knew that either the one or the other system must exclusively prevail.

"Unlike too many of those who in modern times invoke their authority, they had a choice between the two. They preferred the system of free labor, and they determined to organize the Government, and so to direct its activity, that that system should surely and certainly prevail. For this purpose, and no other, they based the whole structure of government broadly on the principle that all men are created equal, and therefore free—little dreaming that within the short period of one hundred years, their descendants would bear to be told by any orator, however popular, that the utterance of that principle was merely a rhetorical rhapsody; or by any judge, however venerated, that it was attended by mental reservations, which render it hypocritical and false. By the ordinance of 1787, they dedicated all the national domain not yet polluted by slavery to free labor immediately, thenceforth and forever, while by the new Constitution and laws they invited foreign free labor from all lands under the sun, and interdicted the importation of African slave labor, at all times, in all places, and under all circumstances whatsoever. It is true that they necessarily and wisely modified this policy of freedom by leaving it to the several States, affected as they were by differing circumstances, to abolish slavery in their own way, and at their own pleasure, instead of confiding that duty to Congress, and that they secured to the slave States, while yet retaining the system of slavery, a three-fifths representation of slaves in the Federal Government, until they should find themselves able to relinquish it with safety. But the very nature of these modifications fortifies my position that the fathers knew that the two systems could not endure within the Union, and expected that within a short period slavery would disappear forever. Moreover, in order that these modifications might not altogether defeat their grand design of a republic maintaining universal equality, they provided that two-thirds of the States might amend the Constitution.

"*It remains to say on this point only one word, to guard against misapprehension. If these States are to again become universally slaveholding, I do not pretend to say with what violations of the Constitution that end shall be accomplished. On the other hand, while I do confidently believe and hope that my country will yet become a land of universal freedom, I do not expect that it will be made so otherwise than through the action of the several States coöperating with the Federal Government, and all acting in strict conformity with their respective Constitutions.*"

In a speech in the Senate, last spring, March 2, 1859, Mr. Seward said—he was speaking of the "Expenses and Revenues"—

"We are for free trade to a practical extent, and we all are in favor of a judicious tariff. The exigency of this debate does not require me to survey the whole range of productive industry of the country, and to suggest a comparative system of imposts adjusted to them all. It would be labor lost to do so ; for, as I have already said, it is in the House of Representatives, and not here, that the act originating any revision of the tariff must be introduced, and perfected, at least in degree. But I can say, with entire freedom, that it would present no ground of objection, in my judgment, if such a bill should be so constructed as to favor and encourage the mining and manufacture of iron. I select and distinguish this great interest, because I think that the disasters which have overtaken the National Treasury and have crushed the prosperity of the country, have resulted from neglect and improvidence in regard to it. We have been engaged, as most other civilized states have been engaged, during the last fifteen or twenty years, in adopting the great invention of railroads, or, as the Frenchmen accurately describe them, iron roads, and bringing it into universal use. If we could only have understood ourselves in the beginning of this period, and adhered persistently throughout to just convictions then formed, we should have so discriminated in our revenue system as to have made this great enterprise work out an establishment of the iron manufacture in this country, so as to derive from it our chief supplies. But the country has not been willing to look steadily to that ultimate interest. It has asked always the cheapest iron that could be gotten, and, of course, has demanded that the imposts should be fixed at the lowest possible rates. So the protection afforded by the tariff of 1846 gave place to a lower protection in 1857 ; and it has not been without much difficulty that at times Congress has been stayed from remitting all duties on foreign manufactures of railroad iron. The Legislatures of the States, acting on the same erroneous principles, have authorized combinations and associations on doubtful principles to force forward the same precipitancy of action. Loans of the credit of States, of counties, cities, and even towns, have been authorized, to furnish capital to railroad corporations, and at the same time they have been continually allowed to borrow money, at usurious and ruinous rates of interest. Securities thus obtained, doubted and comparatively valueless at home, have been pledged to the iron manufacturers abroad, and their enterprise has been excessively stimulated, while that of our own manufacturers has been disheartened and suppressed. These improvement measures have at last produced their inevitable effect—an undue diversion of capital into railroad enterprises, a derangement of internal exchanges at home, and a collapse of the national credit abroad, and a suspension equally of domestic manufactures and of foreign commerce. Such are the legitimate results of the improvidence which caused roads to be built of foreign iron, over the coal and iron beds in our mountains. I hope, sir, that the House of Representatives will make the needed initial step in a return to a wise policy, and will send the miner once more with his torch into the deserted chambers where the coal and the ore are stored away by the hand of nature, and will adopt such a policy as will rekindle the slumbering fires in the forges and furnaces of Pennsylvania, New Jersey, Maryland, Tennessee and Missouri. It would be a benevolent work. I do not say that I would force the Government to assume it merely as a work of benevolence; but I do say, that since there is need of taxes to avoid debt, I would so levy the taxes as to secure incidentally that benevolent object."

To show that Mr. Seward indulged in no feelings of personal hostility toward any slaveholder, we quote from his remarks on the death of Senator Rusk of Texas, a man in his politics *utterly* opposed to Mr. Seward as we can suppose any southern politician, however ultra, to be.

Said Mr. Seward of his fellow-senator:

"On the last day of August, I was reëntering the port of Quebec, after a voyage of thirty days, in search of health, along the inhospitable coasts of Labrador. The sympathies of home and country, so long suppressed, were revived within me, and I was even meditating new labors and studies here, when the pilot, who came on board, handed me a newspaper which announced the death of the senator from Texas. My first emotions were those of sadness and sorrow over this bereavement of a personal friend. When these had had their time, I tried to divine why it was that he, among all the associates whom I honored, esteemed and loved here, was thus suddenly and prematurely withdrawn from the scene of our common labors ; he for whom I thought higher honors were preparing, and a fuller wreath was being woven ; he who seemed to me to stand a monument against which the waves of faction must break, if ever they should be stirred up from their lowest depths ; he, in short, with whom I thought I might do so much, and without whom I could do almost nothing, to magnify and honor the Republic. That question I could not solve—I cannot solve it now. It is only another occasion in which I am required to trust, where I am not permitted to know, the ways of the Great Disposer.

"Mr. President, the teeming thoughts of this solemn hour bring up once more before me the manly form and beaming countenance of my friend, though it is but for that formal parting which has, until now, been denied me. Farewell, noble patriot, heroic soldier, faithful statesman, generous friend ! loved by no means the least, although among the last of friends secured. I little thought that our whisperings about travels over earth's fairest lands and broadest seas were only the suggestions of our inward natures to prepare for the sad journey* that leads through the gate of death."

Feb. 25, 1859, the famous night session of the Senate on the Cuba Thirty Million Bill occurred. Mr. Seward had previously spoken against the measure,

* Mr. Rusk and Mr. Seward had planned a voyage around the world together.

and opposed the friends of the bill, but he was treated with courtesy till this night session, when Mr. Tombs made a fierce onslaught upon him. Let us recall the debate:

Mr. Dixon, of Connecticut, spoke for two hours, replying to the points of Mr. Benjamin's recent speech. Mr. Benjamin had urged, he said, that unless we acquire Cuba, Spain will emancipate the negroes. Mr. Dixon reasoned, that if negro freedom in Cuba would be injurious to the United States, in Jamaica it must be equally so; yet it is not used as an argument to buy Jamaica from Great Britain. Mr. Benjamin had reasoned that compulsory labor was necessary to develop tropical production; but Mr. Dixon thought that the sugar for the world could be grown by free labor; and if it could not, sugar was not a sufficient equivalent for the perpetuation of slavery. In the course of his remarks, Mr. Dixon had occasion to say that slavery degrades free labor.

Mr. Reid controverted this opinion, and said the doctrine was new in the South. He maintained that the white man was not degraded by labor, although he worked at the bench, or in a field, side by side with his slave.

Mr. Dixon refused to admit the correctness of this assertion as an exposition of the general southern feeling.

Mr. Bell traced the rise and progress of the filibuster spirit, until it culminated in the Ostend manifesto, and became reflected in this Cuban bill. Both were in a form offensive to Spain. No nation would be apt to receive kindly an offer made to purchase its territory when accompanied by a studied reminder of its fallen fortunes. His (Mr. Bell's) opinion was that the Ostend manifesto and the present proposal were framed on the perfect knowledge that Cuba could not be acquired, and that they were addressed to what is supposed to be the dominant traits in our national character. The committee's report is skillfully drawn up. It promises to extend the trade and commerce of the North, the peculiar industry of the South, and the agriculture of the West. It is framed to habituate the country to the cry of "war," but we are making no preparation for war. On the contrary, we are trying to get along without a revenue. For himself, he would favor our acquiring control of the island, either as a protectorate or independent power; but he likewise held that the time has not yet come when its possession was necessary, either to our development or security. We are not now in position to accept Cuba, if Spain should offer it as a gift. We cannot accept it until we have built up a navy of sufficient strength to maintain it. The first blow that would be struck in a war with a naval power would be to wrest it from us, and hold its harbors as a means of annoyance against us. The committee's promise that the acquisition of the island will give us the monopoly of sugar is equally fallacious. The increasing production of that article would soon create its production throughout the whole temperate zone. Neither is it true, as the committee says, that when a nation ceases growth, its decadence commences. History does not teach this doctrine of expansion, nor is there any parallelism between the growth of a nation and an individual man. Are our internal affairs so perfectly organized as to leave no range for our ambition? Has even the question of currency been placed on a satisfactory basis? Is our great internal domain reduced to such narrow limits as to afford no scope to our energies? Our territory is now greater than the whole area of the Roman Empire. All this we are bound to protect and defend; and to defend the accessible points of our extended frontier would require 100,000 men, with at least 250 war steamers, The chairman of the Naval Committee says our whole guns are 1,100. The French navy alone has 15,000 cannon afloat, with 500 ships, of which half are war steamers. We are not now prepared for such a war; and yet the President announced, on a recent occasion, that our policy henceforth is expansion

Mr. Kennedy, of Maryland, addressed the Senate, arguing that the acquisition of Cuba is subversive of the best interests of the South. Referring to the aspect of our domestic affairs, he considered that innovations had been ingrafted on the policy of this government, which inevitably betokens its dissolution. The doctrine of State Rights did well while we were a homogeneous people, bound together by common troubles; but that day has passed. The unbounded prosperity of this country, its fertile lands, and increasing wealth, have attracted to it people from every clime. There is no common interest to bind us together. The Constitution and the Supreme Court are derided, and the Constitution threatens to be but a rope of sand, unable to bind, from having no power to punish infractions of that Constitution. He had been derided as an old Federalist, and the men who so denounced him had now on the table two bills more dangerous, in consolidating the power in the hands of one man, than any that ever emanated from the old Federal party. They had also a bill to give away the public lands to the sweepings of European lazar-houses, to squat thereon, and, under an easy franchise, to control that government, before they know a word of our language, or have one idea toward a comprehension of our institutions. Yet, while offering this extraordinary bonus to the discontented spirits of the old world, they refuse to vote for and denounce the old soldiers' bill. How comes it, he asked, that there is such a diversity of opinion in the democratic party, marching under one banner, and professing common principles?

He proceeded to ask how it is possible for us to hold Cuba, with but fifty-seven ships in our navy to protect the fifty Cuban harbors? Our Paraguay armada consists of canal-boats, and side-wheel steamers. Have senators reflected on the baneful effect the acquisition of Cuba would have on slave property? He remembered the opening of Alabama. Virginia has scarcely yet recovered from the effect of that exodus of her labor to localities where it would be more remunerative. With the slave trade stopped, Cuba would be a perpetual drain, and would put planters into a more unequal contest by withdrawing the labor from their cotton fields into sugar production. It is estimated that five hundred thousand slaves will be abstracted from the southern States, and a thousand millions of capital, within five years. And if we drift into a war with England and France, we will have to maintain a contest with fifteen hundred ships on our extended coast line. These are considerations, for the American people, as they will change the whole course of our policy, and inaugurate a new era of standing armies and enormous fleets. The time is also inopportune for the acquisition of that island. In conclusion, he did not admit the right to bring in a foreign nation, with a foreign tongue and foreign teachings, and incapable of understanding our institutions. In his opinion, we were fast losing all those landmarks which characterized our early nationality, and were fast becoming a mere confederation of heterogeneous States. For these and other considerations, he was opposed to the acquisition of Cuba.

Mr. Wade here moved to adjourn. Lost by 17 to 28.

At eight o'clock in the evening the Senate was crowded—the galleries were one sea of faces. The Republicans wanted to adjourn the discussion to the next day—the Democrats were determined to force a vote on the bill that evening.

Mr. Doolittle, of Wisconsin, moved to postpone the Cuba and take up the homestead bill, and proceeded to speak on the latter.

Mr. Slidell called him to order.

Mr. Doolittle insisted on his motion.

Mr. Johnson, of Tennessee, although he had for fifteen years advocated the homestead bill, asked Mr. Doolittle to withdraw his motion.

Mr. Douglas, as a friend of the homestead bill, made the same request.

Mr. Clark, of Connecticut, as a friend of the homestead bill, moved the Senate adjourn. Lost, by 17 to 30.

Mr. Trumbull asked Mr. Hunter to pledge himself not to bring forward the appropriation bills, to prevent a vote on the homestead bill.

Mr. Hunter would give no such promise.

Mr. Trumbull appealed to Mr. Johnson to stand by and press the homestead bill.

Mr. Bigler asked Mr. Trumbull, for himself and the Republicans, to name the hour at which they would vote on both measures.

Mr. Trumbull, for himself, was ready now, but could not make any pledge for his friends.

Mr. Seward said that after nine hours' discussion on the Cuba bill, it was time to come back to the great question of the age. Two propositions now stand face to face; one is the question of land for the landless, and the other is a question of land for slaves.

Mr. Slidell here rose.

The Vice-President. Will the Senator from New York yield the floor to the Senator from Louisiana?

Mr. Seward. No, sir, I do not.

Mr. Slidell called Mr. Seward to order. He was discussing the comparative merits of the two bills.

The Vice-President decided that Mr. Seward was in order.

Mr. Seward went on with a few words, when Mr. Fitch appealed to the Chair to put the question of order to the Senate, with a view of stopping what threatened to be an interminable discussion.

The Vice-President refused to do so.

Mr. Seward went on, saying: "It is in the Thirty-fifth Congress that the homestead bill has been put aside." He then contrasted the merits of the two bills.

Mr. Toombs said, as to "land for the landless," it carried with it some demagogical power. He despised a demagogue, but despised still more those who are driven by demagogues. What are the other side afraid of? If they do not want to give $30,000,000 to carry out a great national policy, let them say so and not attempt to get rid of the issue by saying, "We want to give land to the landless."

Mr. Wade said the question was land to the landless, or niggers to the niggerless. He would antagonize these issues, and carry the appeal to the country. The whole object of the Democratic party was to go round the world hunting for niggers. They could no more sustain their party without niggers, than they could a steam engine without fuel.

Mr. Fessenden took Mr. Toombs to task, and asked if the language he had used was not in imitation of the great man at the other end of the Avenue (the President), who recently addressed an out-of-door crowd, saying none but cowards shirk this Cuban bill. He told the senator the Republicans did not tremble nor shrink. He referred to the trial of physical endurance at the last session, and hinted that they could endure as much again. He denied that the Republicans were obstructing legitimate business, but said they were opposed to this Cuban measure, by which nothing was intended but a party result.

Mr. Seward was not in the habit of impugning the courage of any man. He believed every senator had sufficient. He himself had enough for his own purposes. But other qualities are also necessary. There is moral courage. There is truthfulness to pledges. The President had power to carry out his pledges, and has he done so? Where is the Pacific Railroad bill? where his protection? where relief to the bankrupt? Lost, sunk, sacrificed, in his attempt to fasten slavery on the Spanish American States. No part of the President's policy has been carried out, but it is all sacrificed to a false and pretended issue. Out of nothing, nothing is expected to come. He (Mr. Seward) had never mistaken the President's policy. He never mistook it for a giant in arms, but for a windmill with sails. Mr. Seward concluded by an energetic declaration that he is to be found on the side of liberty, everywhere and always.

Mr. Toombs replied at some length, till Mr. Johnson, of Arkansas, again raised a question of order, to cut off debate.

At eleven o'clock there was a crowded audience; half the senators were in their seats, while the rest were reading and smoking in the ante-room.

Mr. Doolittle finally declined to withdraw his motion.

At midnight, Mr. Chandler attempted to reply to the remarks of Mr. Toombs respecting demagogues.

The Vice-President ruled that he was not in order.

Mr. Fessenden appealed from the ruling of the Chair.

Mr. Mason again moved to adjourn. Lost by 20 to 30.

The appeal of Mr. Fessenden was then laid on the table.

Mr. Clark then spoke; after which Mr. Doolittle's motion to take up the homestead bill was voted on, and lost, by yeas 17, nays 28.

At last, wearied out, and convinced that the Republicans were not to be intimidated or driven into a vote upon the bill without more discussion, Mr. Slidell, himself, moved an adjournment, at one o'clock at night, which was of course carried.

STEPHEN A. DOUGLAS.

Stephen Arnold Douglas was born in the town of Brandon, Vermont, on the 23d of April, 1813. His father, S. A. Douglas, was a doctor and native of Rensselaer County, New York. The father removed to Vermont in early life, and was educated at Middlebury College. He was a physician of some eminence. He died suddenly in 1813, leaving two children—a daughter, twenty months old, and a son (the subject of this sketch) only two months of age. The mother of Mr. Douglas, was the daughter of a large farmer in Brandon, Vermont. Upon the death of her husband, she went back to the old homestead which she inherited with a bachelor brother. The brother and sister lived for many years on this retired farm in one of the valleys of the Green Mountains, caring for the two children with economy, prudence and the most ardent affection. The farm-property increased in value, and the sister and mother had no doubt that she could leave her children a comfortable competence, enough to educate them and help them to an independence in after life. After fourteen years had elapsed, the uncle visited the State of New York, and very singularly took the idea into his head of marriage, and returned with a young and handsome wife, who, at the end of a year, presented him with a son. Stephen was at this time fifteen years old, and had received a good common-school education, and he began at once to prepare for college. His uncle was applied to, who by this time began to grow selfish, and desired to keep his property for *his own son*, and he very frankly informed the young man, that he did not possess property sufficient to warrant him in getting a collegiate education, and he advised him to stay at work upon the farm. The farm and all the property attached to it was held in his uncle's name, was legally his, and his mother only possessed a few worn-out acres, barely sufficient to support her and her daughter. Until the marriage of her brother, she had not dreamed of such a contingency and had relied upon their joint property for her children, who had been great favorites with the bachelor, who had frequently promised them all he had. In this change of circumstances, young Stephen did not long hesitate what to do, but apprenticed himself to a cabinet-maker in Middlebury. He remained here for some eight months, working hard, but, at the expiration of that time, he came to some misunderstanding with his employer, and left him. He came back to his native town and entered the cabinet-shop of one Deacon Knowlton, where he remained a year, making French bedsteads of hard, curled maple, which was so severe labor as to injure his health. He was now obliged to leave his employer, and, while waiting to regain his health, he became a student in the Brandon Academy. At the end of another year, he gave up all hopes of being able to prosecute the cabinet business, and determined on trying to get an education. His sister had married Julius N. Granger, and moved to Ontario County, New York. His mother, a little later, married her daughter's husband's father, Gehazi Granger, and Stephen accompanied her, joining the Canandaigua Academy, where he pursued the classical course till the spring of 1833. At the same time, he was also studying law in the village with the Messrs. Hubbell. He was at this time, though young, an ardent politician, and gave abundant evidence that politics would, in after-life, be his chosen field for action. In the spring of 1833, he turned his face westward, and entered the law-office of S. T. Andrews, then a member of Congress. He was here attacked with a bilious fever, and was ill an entire summer, which threw him out of his place and used up his small stock of funds. When he finally recovered, he was without place and money, and in a situation which would completely dishearten most young men. He started on westward, and seeing no good opening, and being reduced to great straits, engaged to teach a school in the village of Winchester, Illinois. When he came there, he had *but thirty-seven and a half cents in his pocket*, but by a fortunate occurrence he was enabled to earn a few dollars as clerk before his school opened. The first Monday in December, 1833, he opened his school of forty scholars, at a tuition of three dollars each. He studied law evenings, and, in the course of the following spring, opened a law-office in the place, having obtained a license upon examination from the Supreme Court judges. He sprang at once into the full tide of success, for in less than a year he was elected State's Attorney by the joint vote of the Legislature? He was but twenty-two years of age, yet, by the very nature of his office, he was pitted against the ablest and most acute lawyers in the State. Nothing but the most untiring industry held him up in this position. He endeavored to make up for his lack of experience by the closest study and application, and he very naturally exerted himself to the extent of all his abilities. The result was that he attained distinguished success. In December, 1836, he was elected to the Legislature of his State, and resigned the office of State's Attorney to sit in the Legislature. He was the youngest member of the House, yet he soon created for himself an excellent reputation as a legislator. The State was then going mad with speculation and wild-cat banking. Mr. Douglas opposed the banking institutions—their increase in any shape or manner—but was overborne by numbers. The majority were in favor of extending the then vicious system of banking, and so voted. The very same year, all the banks suspended specie payments, their paper depreciated to a frightful extent, and after a few years they were wound up. Mr. Douglas participated in the great struggle over internal improvements, giving his voice and vote in favor of any plan of public works which would stand the test of an examination. No public man could go through this ordeal without making enemies, for there were rival routes for canals, rival interests, and Mr. Douglas was too outspoken and independent not to take sides upon these local questions. Of course, he made temporary enemies. The railroad mania now began, and Mr. Douglas favored a plan which put the public works *completely* in the power of the State. The other plan was to join the State with individual stockholders, but really give the control of the works to the private stockholders. In all these local quarrels Mr. Douglas participated with the enthusiasm and energy which have always been characteristic of the man.

Soon after the adjournment of the Legislature, Mr. Douglas was appointed by the President of the United States, Register of the Land Office at Springfield, Illinois. He desired to return to the law, but the acceptance of the office would be to his pecuniary advantage, and he felt it to be his duty to accept.

In November 1837, he was nominated to Congress by a Convention of the Democratic party in his district. The time was peculiarly unfavorable to him, for the country was in a whirlpool of agitation and the Democratic party of Illinois on many questions of the day, sided with the Whigs, and were against Mr. Van Buren.

The election took place in August, 1838—thirty-six thousand votes were cast—and his Whig opponent was elected by a majority of *five votes!* At the ensuing Presidential election, the same district gave Harrison a majority of three thousand votes over Van Buren. Mr. Douglas devoted himself to the law till the Presidential campaign opened, when he gave himself zealously up to that. He stumped the State for seven months from one part to the other, making the acquaintance of almost the entire people. The State went democratic. In December, 1840, Mr. Douglas was elected Secretary of State, and in February, 1841, was elected by joint vote of the State Legislature a judge of the Supreme Court. He was now but twenty-eight years of age, and at first resolved to decline this fresh honor; but, upon a reconsideration, he accepted the appointment, though it was to his pecuniary hurt.

In 1843, Mr. Douglas's health became so impaired that he made a trip into the Indian country. During his absence he was nominated for Congress by his friends, and when he returned he resigned his judgship and went into the canvass with great spirit. Himself and competitor were soon prostrated with bilious fever, and they were unable to rise from their beds on election day. The result of the election was the triumph of Mr. Douglas by four hundred votes. At the next election he was reëlected by nineteen hundred majority, and on the third election by twenty-nine hundred majority. He did not take his seat in the House under the last election, for, before the time came for the Congress to meet, he had been chosen to the U. S. Senate for six years. election took place in 1847.

In April, 1847, M. Douglas was married to a Miss Martin, only daughter of Col. Robert Martin, of Rockingham County North Carolina. A few years since, Mr. Douglas lost his wife, and in the winter of 1856–7 married Miss Cutts of Washington, his present accomplished wife. By his first wife he had several children, and they inherited from their mother a large property in the South, consisting of land and slaves.

In 1838, Mr. Douglas took strong ground in Illinois against naturalization as a necessary pre-requisite to voting. He contended in the State courts—for the question was raised there—that though Congress has the exclusive right to prescribe uniform naturalization laws, yet that naturalization has necessarily no connection with the elective franchise, that being a privilege granted by the States. Mr. Douglas triumphed through a decision of the Supreme Court of Illinois.

In 1841, Mr. Douglas opposed the Bankrupt law of the time, which became so memorable. In the famous Oregon controversy and excitement he belonged to the "fifty-four forty or fight" party, and in his public speeches, as well as in private, took a very determined stand against the pretensions of Great Britain. Here is a paragraph from a speech of his in the House at this time:

"It therefore becomes us to put this nation in a state of defence; and when we are told that this will lead to war, all I have to say is this: preserve the honor and integrity of this country, but at the same time assert our right to the last inch, and then if war comes, let it come. We may regret the necessity which produced it, but when it does come, I would administer to our citizens Hannibal's oath of eternal enmity, and not terminate it until the question was all settled forever. I would blot out the lines on the map which now mark our national boundaries on this continent and make the area of liberty as broad as the continent itself."

To show the position of Mr. Douglas on the Oregon question, we will quote two paragraphs from one of his speeches:

"I choose to be frank and candid in this declaration of my sentiments on this question. For one, I never will be satisfied with the valley of the Columbia nor with 49°, nor with 54° 40′, nor will I be while Great Britain shall hold possession of one acre on the northwest coast of America. And I will never agree to any arrangement that shall recognize her right to one inch of soil upon the northwest coast; and for this simple reason. Great Britain never did own, she never had a valid title to one inch of that country. The question was only one of dispute between Russia, Spain and the United States. England never had a title to any part of the country. Our Government has always held that England had no title to it. In 1826, Mr. Clay, in his dispatches to Mr. Gallatin, said, 'it is not conceived that the British Government can make out even a colorable title to any part of the northwest coast!' . . . .

"The value of the Oregon Territory is not to be measured by the number of miles upon the coast, whether it shall terminate at 49°, or at 54° 40′, or reach to 61° and the Arctic Ocean. It does not depend on the character of the country, nor the quality of the soil. It is true that consideration is not virtually of attention; but the great point at issue—the great struggle between us and Great Britain—is for the freedom of the Pacific Ocean; for the trade of China and of Japan, of the East Indies, and for the maritime ascendency on all these waters. That is the great point at issue between the two countries, and the settlement of this Oregon question involves all these interests. And in order to maintain these interests, and secure all the benefits resulting from them, we must not only go to 54° 40′, but we have got to exclude Great Britain from the coast *in toto.*"

In the course of the debate in committee of the House upon resolutions giving notice to Great Britain of the abrogation of the treaty between this country and Great Britain, Mr. Ramsey moved to strike out all after the word resolved (in one of the resolutions) and insert, "That the Oregon question is no longer a subject of negotiation or compromise." We quote from the record:

"Tellers were ordered and *ten* members passed between them, amid shouts of laughter, cries of 54° 40′ forever, clapping of hands and stamping of feet, which the chairman was some time in suppressing; and the negative vote was then taken and stood 146. So the amendment was *rejected.*"

The names of the ten "fifty-four forties," were as follows:

ARCHIBALD BELL, of Arkansas.
ALEXANDER RAMSEY, of Pennsylvania.

WILLIAM SAWYER, of Ohio.
T. B. HOGE, of Illinois.
ROBERT SMITH, of Illinois.
STEPHEN A. DOUGLAS, of Illinois.
JOHN A. MCCLEELAND, "
JOHN WENTWORTH, "
CORNELIUS DARRAH, of Pennsylvania.
FELIX S. MCCONNEL, of Alabama.

It will be noticed, that then, as now, Mr. Douglas had the faculty of carrying his State delegation with him.

Mr. Douglas has, while in Congress, favored the appropriation by the general government of money for internal improvements upon the Jackson plan of strictly confining such appropriations to objects of national and general, not of State or local importance.

He has frequently voted for river and harbor bills—voted for the Independent Treasury bill, and has, in and out of Congress, utterly denied the power of Congress over the franchise in the States. Mr. Douglas was an early supporter of the Mexican war. "He opposed the incorporation of the Wilmot proviso into the two or three million bills. He believed the people's time had not come for any action on that subject. Slavery was now prohibited in Mexico. If any portion of that country should be annexed to the United States without any stipulation being made on that point, the existing laws would remain in force.

. . . . If the question was pressed for immediate decision, he could perceive no other mode of harmonizing conflicting sentiments, but by the adoption of the Missouri Compromise Line."

Mr. Douglas voted to bring up the Homestead bill which was before the last Congress and which passed the House, showing that he is in favor of that important measure.

We now come to the history of Mr. Douglas in connection with the Kansas-Nebraska bill.

The battle which he waged with his political opponents and won upon that bill is so fresh in the memory of all our readers that it will not be safe, or necessary, to go into a minute history of the struggle. In the winter of 1852–3, Mr. Douglas reported *a* Nebraska bill from the Territorial Committee of which he was chairman, which contained no repeal of the Missouri Compromise or enumeration of his peculiar Popular Sovereignty doctrines. In the great debate over the compromise measures in 1850, no one ever called in question the Missouri Compromise. In the winter of 1852–3, Senator Atchison, of Missouri, declared in his seat in the Senate that the Missouri prohibition could never be repealed.

The Kansas-Nebraska bill as reported from the Committee appeared first without any repeal of the Missouri restriction—on the 7th day of January it was first presented. On the 16th, Mr. Dixon, a

Whig senator from Kentucky, proposed an amendment to the bill reported from the committee which repealed the aforesaid compromise. This movement was at first opposed by leading Democrats and their organ the *Union*, but in a very few days Mr. Douglas, either because he saw the justice of the repeal of the restriction or thought it would advance his political interests, acquiesced in the amendment and made it a part of his bill. We make a few brief extracts from Mr. Douglas's argument in the Senate, Jan. 30, 1854, in support of his bill:

"Sir, I wish you to bear in mind, too, that this geographical line, established by the founders of the Republic between free territories and slave territories, extended as far westward as our territory then reached; the object being to avoid all agitation upon the slavery question by settling that question forever, as far as our territory extended, which was then to the Mississippi River.

"When, in 1803, we acquired from France the territory known as Louisiana, it became necessary to legislate for the protection of the inhabitants residing therein. It will be seen by looking into the bill establishing the territorial government in 1805 for the territory of New Orleans, embracing the same country now known as the State of Louisiana, that the ordinance of 1787 was expressly extended to that territory, excepting the sixth section, which prohibited slavery. Then that act implied that the Territory of New Orleans was to be a slaveholding territory, by making that exception in the law. But, sir, when they came to form what was then called the Territory of Louisiana, subsequently known as the Territory of Missouri, north of the thirty-third parallel, they used different language. They did not extend the ordinance of 1787 to it at all. They first provided that it should be governed by laws made by the governor and the judges, and when, in 1812, Congress gave to that territory, under the name of the Territory of Missouri, a territorial government, the people were allowed to do as they pleased upon the subject of slavery, subject only to the limitations of the Constitution of the United States. Now, what is the inference from that legislation? That slavery was, by implication, recognized south of the thirty-third parallel; and north of that, the people were left to exercise their own judgment and do as they pleased upon the subject, without any implication for or against the existence of the institution.

"This continued to be the condition of the country in the Missouri territory up to 1820, when the celebrated act which is now called the Missouri Compromise act was passed. Slavery did not exist in, nor was it excluded from the country now known as Nebraska. There was no code of laws upon the subject of slavery either way: First, for the reason that slavery had never been introduced into Louisiana and established by positive enactment. It had grown up there by a sort of common law, and been supported and protected. When a common law grows up, when an institution becomes established under a usage, it carries it so far as that usage actually goes, and no further. If it had been established by direct enactment, it might have carried it so far as the political jurisdiction extended; but, be that as it may, by the act of 1812, creating the territory of Missouri, that territory was allowed to legislate upon the subject of slavery as it saw proper, subject only to the limitations which I have stated; and the country not inhabited or thrown open to settlement was set apart as Indian country and rendered subject to Indian laws. Hence, the local legislation of the State of Missouri did not reach into that Indian country, but was excluded from it by the Indian code and Indian laws. The municipal regulations of Missouri could not go there until the Indian title had been extinguished and the country thrown open to settlement. Such being the case, the only legislation in existence in Nebraska territory at the time that the Missouri act passed, namely, the 6th of March, 1820, was a provision, in effect, that the people should be allowed to do as they pleased upon the subject of slavery.

"The territory of Missouri having been left in that legal condition, positive opposition was made to the bill to organize a state government, with a view to its admission into the Union; and a senator from my State, Mr. Jesse B. Thomas, introduced an amendment, known as the eighth section of the bill, in which it was provided that slavery should be prohibited north of 36° 30′ north latitude, in all that country which we had acquired from France. What was the object of the enactment of that eighth section? Was it not to go back to the original policy of prescribing boundaries to the limitation of free institutions, and of slave institutions, by a geographical line, in order to avoid all controversy in Congress upon the subject? Hence, they extended that geographical line through all the territory purchased from France, which was as far as our possessions then reached. It was not simply to settle the question on that piece of country, but it was to carry out a great principle, by extending that dividing line as far west as our territory went, and running it onward on each new acquisition of territory. True, the express enactment of the eighth section of the Missouri act, now called the Missouri Compromise act, only covered the territory acquired from France; but the principles of the act, the objects of its adoption, the reasons in its support, required that it should be extended indefinitely westward, so far as our territory might go, whenever new purchases should be made.

"Thus stood the question up to 1845, when the joint

resolution for the annexation of Texas passed. There was inserted in that a provision, suggested in the first instance and brought before the House of Representatives by myself, extending the Missouri Compromise line indefinitely westward through the territory of Texas. Why did I bring forward that proposition? Why did the Congress of the United States adopt it? Not because it was of the least practical importance, so far as the question of slavery within the limits of Texas was concerned; for no man ever dreamed that it had any practical effect there. Then, why was it brought forward? It was for the purpose of preserving the principle, in order that it might be extended still further westward, even to the Pacific Ocean, whenever we should the acquire country that far. I will here read that clause in the joint resolution for the annexation of Texas. It is the third article, second section, and is in these words:

"'New States, of convenient size, not exceeding four in number, in addition to said State of Texas, having sufficient population, may hereafter, by the consent of said State, be formed out of the territory thereof, which shall be entitled to admission under the provisions of the Federal Constitution. And such States as may be formed out of that portion of said territory, lying south of 36° 30′ north latitude, commonly known as the Missouri Compromise line, shall be admitted into the Union with or without slavery, as the people of each State asking admission may desire. And in such State or States as shall be formed out of said territory north of said Missouri Compromise line, slavery or involuntary servitude (except for crime) shall be prohibited."

"It will be seen that that contains a very remarkable provision, which is, that when States lying north of 36° 30′ apply for admission, slavery shall be prohibited in their constitutions. I presume no one pretends that Congress could have power thus to fetter a State applying for admission into this Union; but it was necessary to preserve the principle of the Missouri Compromise line, in order that it might afterward be extended, and it was supposed that while Congress had no power to impose any such limitation, yet, as that was a compact with the State of Texas, that State could consent for herself, that, when any portion of her own territory, subject to her own jurisdiction and control, applied for a constitution, it should be in a particular form ; but that provision would not be binding on the new State one day after it was admitted into the Union. The other provision was, that such States as should lie south of 36° 30′ min. should come into the Union with or without slavery, as each should decide, in its constitution. Then, by that act, the Missouri Compromise was extended indefinitely westward, so far as the State of Texas went, that is, to the Rio del Norte ; for our Government at the time recognized the Rio del Norte as its boundary. We recognized it, in many ways, and among them by even paying Texas for it, in order that it might be included in and form a portion of the territory of New Mexico.

"Then, sir, in 1848, we acquired from Mexico the country between the Rio del Norte and the Pacific Ocean. Immediately after that acquisition, the Senate, on my own motion, voted into a bill a provision to extend the Missouri Compromise indefinitely westward to the Pacific Ocean, in the same sense and with the same understanding with which it was originally adopted. That provision passed this body by a decided majority, I think by ten at least, and went to the House of Representatives, and was defeated there by northern votes.

"Now, sir, let us pause and consider for a moment. The first time that the principles of the Missouri Compromise were ever abandoned, the first time they were ever rejected by Congress, was by the defeat of that provision in the House of Representatives in 1848. By whom was that defeat effected? By northern votes with free soil proclivities. It was the defeat of that Missouri Compromise that reopened the slavery agitation with all its fury. It was the defeat of that Missouri Compromise that created the tremendous struggle of 1850. It was the defeat of that Missouri Compromise that created the necessity for making a new compromise in 1850. Had we been faithful to the principles of the Missouri Compromise in 1848, this question would not have arisen. Who was it that was faithless? I undertake to say it was the very men who now insist that the Missouri Compromise was a solemn compact, and should never be violated or departed from. Every man who is now assailing the principle of the bill under consideration, so far as I am advised, was opposed to the Missouri Compromise in 1848. The very men who now arraign me for a departure from the Missouri Compromise are the men who successfully violated it, repudiated it, and caused it to be superseded by the compromise measures of 1850. Sir, it is with rather bad grace that the men who proved false themselves should charge upon me and others, who were over faithful, the responsibilities and consequences of their own treachery.

"Then, sir, as I before remarked, the defeat of the Missouri Compromise in 1848 having created the necessity for the establishment of a new one in 1850, let us see what that Compromise was.

* * * * * * * * *

"Mr. President, I repeat that so far as the question of slavery is concerned, there is nothing in the bill under consideration which does not carry out the principle of the compromise measures of 1850, by leaving the people to do as they please, subject only to the provisions of the Constitution of the United States. If that principle is wrong, the bill is wrong. If that principle is right, the bill is right. It is unnecessary to quibble about phraseology or words; it is not the mere words, the mere phraseology, that our constituents wish to judge by. They wish to know the legal effect of our legislation.

"The legal effect of this bill, if it be passed as reported by the Committee on Territories, is neither to legislate slavery into these territories, nor out of them ; but to leave the people to do as they please, under the provisions and subject to the limitations of the Constitution of the United States. Why should not this principle prevail? Why should any man, North or South, object to it? I will especially address the argument to my own section of country, and ask why should any northern man object to this principle? If you will review the history of the slavery question in the United States, you will see that all the great results in behalf of free institutions which have been worked out, have been accomplished by the operation of this principle and by it alone.

"When these States were colonies of Great Britain, every one of them was a slaveholding province. When the Constitution of the United States was formed, twelve out of the thirteen were slaveholding States. Since that time six of those States have become free. How has this been effected? Was it by virtue of abolition agitation in Congress? Was it in obedience to the dictates of the Federal Government? Not at all ; but they have become free States under the silent but sure and irresistible working of that great principle of self-government, which teaches every people to do that which the interests of themselves and their posterity, morally and pecuniarily, may require.

"Under the operation of this principle, New Hampshire became free, while South Carolina continued to hold slaves ; Connecticut abolished slavery, while Georgia held on to it ; Rhode Island abandoned the institution, while Maryland preserved it ; New York, New Jersey, and Pennsylvania abolished slavery, while Virginia, North Carolina, and Kentucky, retained it. Did they do it at your bidding! Did they do it at the dictation of the Federal Government? Did they do it in obedience to any of your Wilmot Provisoes or Ordinances of '87? Not at all ; they did it by virtue of their rights as freemen under the Constitution of the United States, to establish and abolish such institutions as they thought their own good required.

"The leading feature of the Compromise of 1850 was Congressional non-intervention as to slavery in the territories; that the people of the territories and of all the States, were to be allowed to do as they pleased upon the subject of slavery, subject only to the provisions of the Constitution of the United States.

"That, sir, was the leading feature of the compromise measures of 1850. Those measures, therefore, abandoned the idea of a geographical line as a boundary between free States and slave States—abandoned it because compelled to do it from an inability to maintain it—and in lieu of that substituted a great principle of self-government, which would allow the people to do as they thought proper. Now the question is, when that new compromise, resting upon that great fundamental principle of freedom, was established, was it not an abandonment of the old one—the geographical line? Was it not a supersedure of the old one, within the very language of the substitute for the bill which is now under consideration? I say it did supersede it, because it applied its provisions as well to the north as to the south of 36° 30′. It established a principle which was equally applicable to the country north as well as south of the parallel of 36° 30′—a principle of universal application."

Mr. Douglas's bill passed both branches of Congress and became a law, after passing through a severe ordeal both in Congress and before the people. Its passage gave the popular branch of the next Congress into the control of Mr. Douglas's political enemies, for the bill in a majority of the free States was very unpopular.

On the first Monday in December, 1857, Mr. Douglas took his seat in the Senate with many anxious eyes upon him, for it had already been rumored that he would differ with the administration upon its conduct of Kansas affairs, and would take issue with the President in his forthcoming message. Rumor was right—the message was read—it did in effect recommend the indorsement of the Lecompton Constitution—and Mr. Douglas had the courage and boldness to stand up in defence of his peculiar doctrines of popular sovereignty, which he thought had been violated by the Lecompton Constitution. His great opening speech was delivered on the ninth of December, 1857. The President's message had been read the day previous and Mr. Douglas had indicated his purpose on the next day to speak upon it. Accordingly when the Senate assembled on Tuesday, the old Senate-hall was crowded to its utmost capacity and hundreds were unable to effect an entrance. The curiosity of the public to learn the position which the Illinois senator would take upon this important question was intense, and many of the members of the house were present. Mr. D. rose, apparently as cool as he ever was in his life, although, in the opinion of some of his Democratic friends, his decision, which after careful thought he had reached, to oppose the Lecompton Constitution, would ruin all his political prospects. He began by quoting the peculiar language of the President's message, and, perhaps in a vein of irony, contended that the President was opposed to this Lecompton Constitution, which, though under the circumstances he was for accepting, he did not like. It was evident that the President, in his absence at a foreign court, had fallen into an error in reference to the principle of the Nebraska bill. We now quote Mr. Douglas:

"Now, sir, what was the principle enunciated by the authors and supporters of that bill, when it was brought forward? Did we not come before the country and say that we repealed the Missouri restriction for the purpose of substituting and carrying out as a general rule the great principle of self-government, which left the people of each State and each Territory free to form and regulate their domestic institutions in their own way, subject only to the Constitution of the United States? In support of that proposition, it was argued here, and I have argued it wherever I have spoken in various States of the Union, at home and abroad, everywhere I have endeavored to prove that there was no reason why an exception should be made in regard to the slavery question. I have appealed to the people, if we did not all agree, men of all parties, that all other local and domestic questions should be submitted to the people. I said to them, 'We agree that the people shall decide for themselves what kind of a judiciary system they will have; we agree that the people shall decide what kind of a school system they will establish; we agree that the people shall determine for themselves what kind of a banking system they will have, or whether they will have any banks at all; we agree that the people may decide for themselves what shall be the elective franchise in their respective States; they shall decide for themselves what shall be the rule of taxation and the principles upon which their finance shall be regulated; we agree that they may decide for themselves the relations between husband and wife, parent and child, guardian and ward; and why should we not then allow them to decide for themselves the relations between master and servant? Why make an exception of the slavery question, by taking it out of that great rule of self-government which applies to all the other relations of life? The very first proposition in the Nebraska bill was to show that the Missouri restriction, prohibiting the people from deciding the slavery question for themselves, constituted an exception to a general rule, in violation of the principle of self-government; and hence that that exception should be repealed, and the slavery question, like all other questions, submitted to the people, to be decided for themselves.

"Sir, that was the principle on which the Nebraska bill was defended by its friends. Instead of making the slavery question an exception, it removed an odious exception which before existed. Its whole object was to abolish that odious exception, and make the rule general, universal in its application to all matters which were local and domestic, and not national or federal. For this reason was the language employed which the President has quoted; that the eighth section of the Missouri act, commonly called the Missouri Compromise, was repealed, because it was repugnant to the principle of non-intervention, established by the compromise measures of 1850, 'it being the true intent and meaning of this act, not to legislate slavery into any territory or State, nor to exclude it therefrom, but to leave the people thereof perfectly free to form and regulate their domestic institutions in their own way, subject only to the Constitution of the United States.' We repealed the Missouri restriction because that was confined to slavery. That was the only exception there was to the general principle of self-government. That exception was taken away for the avowed and express purpose of making the rule of self-government general and universal, so that the people should form and regulate all their domestic institutions in their own way.

"Sir, what would this boasted principle of popular sovereignty have been worth, if it applied only to the negro, and did not extend to the white man? Do you think we could have aroused the sympathies and the patriotism of this broad Republic, and have carried the Presidential election last year, in the face of a tremendous opposition, on the principle of extending the right of self-government to the negro question, but denying it as to all the relations affecting white men? No, sir. We aroused the patriotism of the country and carried the election in defence of that great principle, which allowed all white men to form and regulate their domestic institutions to suit themselves—institutions applicable to white men as well as to black men—institutions applicable to freemen as well as to slaves—institutions concerning all the relations of life, and not the mere paltry exception of the slavery question.

"Sir, I have spent too much strength and breath, and health, too, to establish this great principle in the popular heart, now to see it frittered away by bringing it down to an exception that applies to the negro, and does not extend to the benefit of the white man.

* * * * * * *

"So far as the act of the territorial Legislature of Kansas, calling this convention, was concerned, I have always been under the impression that it was fair and just in its provisions. I have always thought the people should have gone together, *en masse*, and voted for delegates, so that the voice expressed by the convention should have been the unquestioned and united voice of the people of Kansas. I have always thought that those who stayed away from that election stood in their own light, and should have gone and voted, and should have furnished their names to be put on the registered list, so as to be voters. I have always held that it was their own fault that they did not thus go and vote; but yet, if they chose, they had a right to stay away. They had a right to say that that convention, although not an unlawful assemblage, is not a legal convention to make a government, and hence we are under no obligation to go and express any opinion about it. They had a right to say, if they chose, 'We will stay away until we see the Constitution they shall frame, the petition they shall send to Congress; and when they submit it to us for ratification, we will vote for it if we like it, or vote it down if we do not like it.' I say they had a right to do either, though I thought, and think yet, as good citizens, they ought to have gone and voted; but that was their business, and not mine.

"Having thus shown that the convention at Lecompton had no power, no authority, to form and establish a government, but had power to draft a petition, and that petition, if it embodied the will of the people of Kansas, ought to be taken as such an exposition of their will, yet, if it did not embody their will, ought to be rejected. Having shown these facts, let me proceed and inquire what was the understanding of the people of Kansas when the delegates were elected? I understand, from the history of the transaction, that the people who voted for delegates to the Lecompton Convention, and those who refused to vote, both parties, understood the Territorial act to mean that they were to be elected only to frame a constitution, and submit it to the people for their ratification or rejection. I say that both parties in that territory, at the time of the election of delegates, so understood the object of the convention. Those who voted for delegates did so with the understanding that they had no power to make a government, but only to frame one for submission; and those who stayed away did so with the same understanding.

* * * * * *

"Now, let us stop to inquire how they redeemed the pledge to submit the constitution to the people. They first go on and make a constitution; then they make a schedule, in which they provide that the constitution, on the 21st of December, the present month, shall be submitted to all the *bonâ fide* inhabitants of the territory, on that day, for their free acceptance or rejection, in the following manner, to wit: Thus acknowledging that they were bound to submit it to the will of the people, conceding that they had no right to put it into operation without submitting it to the people, providing in the instrument that they should take effect from and after the date of its ratification, and not before; showing that the constitution derives its vitality, in their estimation, not from the authority of the convention, but from that vote of the people to which it was to be submitted for their acceptance or rejection. How is it to be submitted? It shall be submitted in this form: 'Constitution with Slavery, or Constitution with no Slavery.' All men must vote for the constitution, whether they like it or not, in order to be permitted to vote for or against slavery. Thus a constitution made by a convention that had authority to assemble and petition for a redress of grievances, but not to establish a government. A constitution made under a pledge of honor that it should be submitted to the people before it took effect; a constitution which provides on its face, that it shall have no validity, except what it derives from such submission, is submitted to the people at an election where all men are at liberty to come forward freely, without hindrance, and vote for it, but no man is permitted to record a vote against it.

"That would be as fair an election as some of the enemies of Napoleon attributed to him when he was elected first consul. He is said to have called out his troops, and had them reviewed by his officers with a speech, patriotic and fair in its professions, in which he said to them: 'Now, my soldiers, you are to go to the election, and vote freely just as you please. If you vote for Napoleon, all is well; vote against him, and you are to be instantly shot.' That was a fair election. This election is to be equally fair. All men in favor of the constitution may vote for it—all men against it shall not vote at all. Why not let them vote against it? I presume you have asked many a man this question. I have asked a very large number of the gentlemen who framed the constitution, quite a number of the delegates, and a still larger number of persons who are their friends, and I have received the same answer from every one of them. I never received any other answer, and I presume we never shall get any other answer. What is that? They say, if they allowed a negative vote, the constitution would have been voted down by an overwhelming majority, and hence the fellows shall not be allowed to vote at all.

* * * * * *

"Let me ask you, why force this constitution down the throats of the people of Kansas, in opposition to their wishes and in violation of our pledges. What great object is to be attained? *Cui bono?* What are you to gain by it! Will you sustain the party by violating its principles? Do you propose to keep the party united by forcing a division? Stand by the doctrine that leaves the people perfectly free to form and regulate their institutions for themselves, in their own way, and your party will be united and irresistible in power. Abandon that great principle, and the party is not worth saving, and cannot be saved after it shall be violated. I trust we are not to be rushed upon this question. Why shall it be done? Who is to be benefited? Is the South to be the gainer? Is the North to be the gainer? Neither the North nor the South has the right to gain a sectional advantage by trickery or fraud.

"But I am beseeched to wait until I hear from the election, on the 21st of December. I am told that perhaps that will put it all right, and will save the whole difficulty. How can it? Perhaps there may be a large vote. There may be a large vote returned. But I deny that it is possible to have a fair vote on the slavery clause; and I say that it is not possible to have any vote on the constitution. Why wait for the mockery of an election, when it is provided, unalterably, that the people cannot vote when the majority are disfranchised?

"But I am told on all sides, 'Oh, just wait; the pro-slavery clause will be voted down.' That does not obviate any of my objections; it does not diminish any of them. You have no more right to force a free-State constitution on Kansas than a slave-State constitution. If Kansas wants a slave-State constitution, she has a right to it; if she wants a free-State constitution she has a right to it. It is none of my business which way the slavery clause is decided. I care not whether it is voted down or voted up. Do you suppose, after the pledge of my honor that I would go for that principle, and leave the people to vote as they chose, that I would now degrade myself by voting one way if the slavery clause be voted down, and another way if it be voted up? I care not how that vote may stand. I take it for granted that it will be voted out. I think I have seen enough in the last three days to make it certain that it will be returned out, no matter how the vote may stand.

"Sir, I am opposed to that concern, because it looks to me like a system of trickery and jugglery to defeat the fair expression of the will of the people. There is no necessity for crowding this measure, so unfair, so unjust as it is in all its aspects, upon us. Why can we not now do what we proposed to do in the last Congress? We then voted through the Senate an enabling act, called 'the Toombs bill,' believed to be just and fair in all its provisions, pronounced to be almost perfect by the senator from New Hampshire (Mr. Hale), only he did not like the man, then President of the United States, who would have to make the appointments. Why can we not take that bill, and, out of compliment to the President, add to it a clause taken from the Minnesota act, which he thinks should be a general rule, requiring the constitution to be submitted to the people, and pass that? That unites the party. You all voted, with me, for that bill, at the last Congress. Why not stand by the same bill now? Ignore Lecompton, ignore Topeka; treat both those party movements as irregular and void; pass a fair bill—the one that we framed ourselves when we were acting as a unit; have a fair election, and you will have peace in the Democratic party, and peace throughout the country, in ninety days. The people want a fair vote. They never will be satisfied without it. They never should be satisfied without a fair vote on their constitution.

"If the Toombs bill does not suit my friends, take the Minnesota bill of the last session—the one so much commended by the President in his message as a model. Let us pass that as an enabling act, and allow the people of all parties to come together and have a fair vote, and I will go or it. Frame any other bill that secures a fair, honest vote, to men of all parties, and carries out the pledge that the people shall be left free to decide on their domestic institutions, for themselves, and I will go with you with pleasure, and with all the energy I may possess. But if this constitution is to be forced down our throats in violation of the fundamental principle of free government, under a mode of submission that is a mockery and insult, I will resist it to the last. I have no fear of any party associations being severed. I should regret any social or political estrangement, even temporarily; but if it must be, if I cannot act with you and preserve my faith and my honor; I will stand on the great principle of popular sovereignty, which declares the right of all people to be left perfectly free to form and regulate their domestic institutions in their own way. I will follow that principle wherever its logical consequences may take me, and

I will endeavor to defend it against assault from any and all quarters. No mortal man shall be responsible for my action but myself. By my action I will compromise no man."

This speech made a deep impression upon the country, but Mr. Douglas was unable to carry any considerable portion of his party in Congress with him. The history of the struggle is well known. The Republicans, a few Democrats, and a like number of Americans, united, were able to force the administration into an abandonment of the original Lecompton bill, and the English bill was substituted therefor. This bill was opposed by Mr. Douglas; but inasmuch as it gave the people of Kansas the privilege to reject the Lecompton Constitution, it passed by a small majority.

In the summer and autumn of 1858, Mr. Douglas went through a terrible ordeal in Illinois—a campaign, the issue of which was political life or death to him. He triumphed by a small majority—indeed the majority was the other way before the people—which shows that Mr. D. was wise in opposing the Lecompton measure, for if he had supported it, and thus trampled upon his own principle of Popular Sovereignty, he would have lost his election by thousands of votes.

We now come to still later issues—to the discussion between Mr. Douglas and his southern enemies, in the last session of the thirty-fifth Congress—the present year—upon Congressional intervention in favor of slavery. This great debate took place Feb. 23, 1859, in the Senate, and looked like a preconcerted attack upon Mr. Douglas by some of his southern opponents. We have not the space for the official report of the debate, and will endeavor faithfully to abridge it. The debate opened on an amendment by Senator Hale to the Appropriation bill before the Senate to repeal the restrictive clause of the Kansas Admission act. This amendment was offered the day previous, and the debate took an unexpected turn upon it.

Mr. Seward, of New York, said Congress had decided that Kansas should come in with the Lecompton Constitution, without reference to population; but, on the other hand, should not come in outside of the Lecompton Constitution unless she had 92,400 population. There was, therefore, a discrimination by the Congress of the United States, as against freedom, in favor of slavery. Oregon, because she was a Democratic State, was admitted without reference to population, and Kansas, because of her different politics, was excluded. He was glad of this occasion to renew his vote. He was glad, also, to hear that so many gentlemen on the other side will give Kansas a fair hearing. It indicates that the time is coming when any State applying for admission will be heard on its merits, apart from all other considerations. He thought it goes to show that if Texas should be divided, or free States, as he thought they would, be formed in Mexico, they will come in as free States.

Mr. Brown, of Mississippi, made a strong southern speech.

He held to the doctrine of State rights; denied the squatter sovereignty of territories; and threatened secession, with banners flying, if the South was deprived of her rights. His address was directed to northern Democrats. He placed his views frankly on record, and desired neither to cheat nor be cheated.

Mr. Douglas felt it incumbent on him, as a northern Democrat, to make a reply. He admired the frankness, candor, and directness with which Mr. Brown had approached the question. He (Douglas), too, would put his opinions on record in such a manner as will acquit him of a desire to cheat or be cheated. He agreed at the outset with Mr. Brown, and with the decision of the Supreme Court, that slaves are property, and that their owners have a right to carry them into the territories as any other property. Having the right of transit into the territory, the question arises, how far does the power of the territorial legislature extend to slave property? And the reply is, to the same extent, and no further, than to any other description of property. Mr. Brown has said that slave property needs more protection than any other description. If so, it is the misfortune of the owners of that kind of property. Mr. Douglas's remarks, from the frequent interruptions, assumed so much the form of question and reply, and running comments on the various issues started, that we can only notice the salient points of the main discussion, which extended throughout many hours, he sustaining the principal part. His general scope was, that he would leave all descriptions of property, slaves included, to the operation of the local law, and would not have Congress interfere in any way therewith. If the people of the territory want slavery there, they will foster and encourage it, and if they do not find it for their advantage, they will do otherwise. So it becomes a question of soil, climate, production, etc. He illustrated by saying, that if any discrimination is to be made in any description of property, the owner of stock, or liquors, or any other, might claim it likewise.

After some other illustrations, he went into discussion of the Kansas-Nebraska bill, which, he said, was passed by a distinct understanding between northern and southern Democrats, however differing on some points, to give to the territorial legislature the full power, with appeal to the Supreme Court, to test the constitutionality of any law, but not to Congress to repeal it. If the court decides such law to be constitutional, it must stand; if not, it must fall to the ground, without action of Congress. That doctrine of non-intervention by Congress with slavery in the States and territories, has been a fundamental principle of the Democratic platform, and every Democrat is pledged to it by the Cincinnati platform. Here Mr. Douglas, in reply to a question by Mr. Clay (who also made the remark that, according to Mr. Douglas's interpretation, squatter sovereignty is superior to the Constitution), said that the limit of territorial legislation is the organic act and the Constitution. In reply to Mr. Clay's question, "Can a slaveholder take his slave property into the territory?" he would reply, Yes; and hold it as other property. To the question, "Will Congress pass a law to protect other kinds of property in the territories?" he would answer, No; for the doctrine that Congress is to legislate on property and persons without representation, is the doctrine of the parliament of George III., that brought on the Revolutionary war. We said then it was a violation of the rights of power to assume to legislate for Englishmen without their consent. Now, was he (Mr. Douglas) to be called on to force this same odious doctrine on the people of the territories without their consent? He answered, No; let them govern themselves. If they make good laws, let them enjoy the blessings; if bad, let them suffer until they are repealed. Referring to the great battles fought and gained in 1854 and 1856, he said he would like to know how many votes Mr. Buchanan would have got in Pennsylvania or Ohio, if he had then understood the doctrine of popular sovereignty as he claims to do now.

Mr. Bigler asked how many votes Mr. Buchanan would have received in 1856, had the senator from Illinois and those who acted with him told the people that the Kansas act was not intended to extend to the territories the sacred right of self-government, but simply to give the people the right to petition for redress of grievances—a right not denied to any citizen, white or black?

Mr. Douglas said that there are no colored citizens, and he trusted in God there never would be. He did not recognize the black brothers.

Mr. Bigler knew that as well as the senator, and should have said inhabitants.

Mr. Douglas resumed. In 1856, he took the same ground as now, and Mr. Buchanan, when he accepted the nomination, took the same ground. His letter of acceptance to the Cincinnati Convention shows he then understood that the people of the territories should decide whether slavery should or should not exist within their limits. When gentlemen called for Congressional intervention, they step off the Democratic platform. He (Mr. Douglas) asserted that the Democratic creed was non-intervention by Congress, and the right of the people to govern themselves.

He would frankly tell gentlemen of the South, that no Democratic candidate can carry one State North but on the principles of the Cincinnati platform, as construed by Mr. Buchanan when he accepted his nomination, and which he (Mr. Douglas) stood here to-day to defend.

Mr. Davis replied to Mr. Douglas elaborately, denying that he (Douglas) rightly interpreted the obligations of the Democratic party.

Mr. Pugh said, Mr. Brown had asked if northern Democrats would vote for Congressional intervention to protect the people against local legislation. He would answer, Never. It is monstrous. It is against the plighted faith both of the South and North. Mr. Pugh discussed the question at length, and said he stood on the platform of his party with the interpretation which he explained.

Mr. Green was sorry that this subject of contention had been brought forward. It was to try and bring discord into the Democratic party, the only party able to override the Republican party. He hoped and believed there was no difference between the North and the South. A government is formed to protect persons and property; and when it ceases to do either, it ceases to perform its one great function. Mr. Hale's amendment had brought up the question, "What is property?" He (Green) maintained that, under the Constitution and by the decision of the Supreme Court, slaves are property; and he argued the subject in many aspects, concluding by calling on the Democratic party to stand united, and not permit a combination to make use of a mere figment to disorganize them. In the course of his remarks, he quoted from Mr. Douglas's Springfield speech, to show that he had therein proposed Congressional intervention in Utah. He could not see the consistency of the senator's course, then and now.

Mr. Douglas denied that he had proposed Congressional intervention to regulate the internal affairs of Utah. The intervention he proposed was alone on the ground of rebellion—not on account of their domestic affairs, but as aliens and rebels.

Mr. Green, in speaking of how territorial legislation could destroy the rights of slave property, said he had before him a copy of the bill passed by the Kansas Legislature to abolish slavery.

Mr. Douglas remarked that several speeches had been made very pointedly at him, making him out no better than an Abolitionist, for leaving the territories to carry out their own affairs. It does well to attack one man for his opinion; but when was the most aggravated act ever committed, that he did not say it was committed, in manumitting your slaves and confiscating your property? The gentleman who spoke thus, says: "It is not yet time." There is no better time than the present, to introduce a bill to repeal that act of the Kansas Legislature. Senators say that he (Douglas) may go out. No; he stands on the platform, and it is for those who jump off, to go out.

The chair called the Senate to order, threatening to clear the galleries, unless it was maintained.

Mr. Green said he had received information of the bill by telegraph; but could not legislate on such information.

Mr. Douglas would take it for granted that Mr. Green meant that he received authentic information, and would introduce a bill to repeal the act. The South, he said, had reluctantly acquiesced in the movement with the Democrats of the North to settle the question. He went at some length into a discussion and approval of the decision of the Supreme Court in the case of Dred Scott. He did not agree with Senator Douglas's views as to the power of the people of a territory, and did not believe that the Nebraska-Kansas bill gave them independent power. The senator from Virginia then gave his ideas as to the people of the territories, and the people of the States. The right of property is recognized in the former, but the inhabitants of a territory are unknown to the Constitution. Congress cannot divest itself of its power over the property of the territories, but it can grant them nothing. South of the Potomac River, to the confines of Mexico, there is not one dissentient voice. The South would be recreant to itself, if it would give one vote for its rights to be taken from the Constitution, and remitted to the pleasure of the people temporarily in the territories.

Mr. Davis took an animated part in the debate against Mr. Douglas, who in the Kansas-Nebraska act, had made a great error, and drawn the Senate into a great error.

Mr. Douglas resumed, saying it won't do to read him out, because they had fallen from the faith. There is no middle ground. It is either intervention or non-intervention.

Mr. Gwin said, if the senator from Illinois had given the same interpretation to the Kansas-Nebraska bill when it was before the Senate, he (Gwin) would not have voted for it, and believed those around him would not. When the senator proposed to speak for the Democracy of the free States, he had no right to speak for California, which thought otherwise.

Mr. Broderick contradicted Mr. Gwin's statement of the views of California. He considered the views of his State were those expressed by Mr. Douglas.

Mr. Gwin replied that he was sent here to do his duty in representing the Democracy of California, and he knew they indorse the action of the Administration, and do not at all indorse the interpretation given by the senator from Illinois.

Mr. Douglas (to Mr. Gwin.) I do say the records show a very general concurrence in the views I then expressed.

Mr. Iverson raised the question of order, that Mr. Douglas had spoken many times. He and Mr. Davis had occupied the floor four or five hours. The point of order was sustained.

Mr. Hunter said it was with reluctance that he occupied the time at the late period of the evening, but the turn the debate had taken rendered an explanation necessary, in justice to himself. He differed with the senator from Illinois, both in the history of the Kansas-Nebraska act, and what was intended by it. When the proposition was made to pass that, he maintained, as he has always done since he has had a place on that floor, that the South had a right to protection for their slave property in the territories.

Mr. Hunter read from his speech of that date, showing the views he then expressed. The case stood thus: southern men on one side maintained they had right, under the Constitution, to protection to their slave property; northern men thought the contrary, and there was no chance of agreement between them, as the act was very carefully framed, neither affirming nor disaffirming the power of the

the territory to abolish slavery, but reserving the question of right, and agreeing to refer to the judiciary any points arising out of it. It was in itself a compromise, in which neither party conceded their opinions or their rights. They were but placed in abeyance until a case affecting them might arise. No southern man with whom he acted ever considered he was conferring on the Territorial Legislature the absolute right to deal with this subject. They agreed to this settlement as a consequence, acting together upon points wherein they agreed, and expressing no opinion upon points where the differences were irreconcilable. By this they secured the repeal of the Missouri Compromise, upon which the Democrats were agreed, by confining the act to the general purpose to be accomplished. Justice to himself and the distinguished senator from South Carolina, now no more, with whom he had acted and consulted on the matter, required the explanation. Mr. Hunter then drew the attention of the Senate to the time consumed in the debate, and urged a vote upon the amendment.

Mr. Stuart, after some general remarks on the subject under discussion, asked, why should the Democratic party be racked and torn by the thought of the contingences which may not happen? If the Democratic party in a body, if its able and efficient members throughout the country, stand faithfully together, their flag will remain in the ascendant, and the party will rise out of all the difficulties which now beset it.

Mr. Bigler was opposed to Congress extending slavery in the territories, and against Congressional intervention with slavery, and would stand by the Baltimore and Cincinnati platforms of the Democratic party. He believed the best interests of the country were in the hope of the Democracy.

Mr. Douglas is a powerful debater, quick, ready at repartee, strong in his logic, and possessing that animal courage which is so necessary to the successful debater. Few men equal him in senatorial debate for rough power. There are many who surpass him in silvery eloquence, who excel him in winning, courteous debate, but no one in the present Senate who has quite his *force* and overwhelming courage. In the debate which we have abbreviated, Mr. Douglas was for hours—from noon till nine o'clock in the evening—obliged to defend himself against a half-dozen able and eloquent senators. His manner, his voice, were at times like that of a wounded lion—deep, strong and melancholy; but he fought to the last without a moment's thought of quailing.

Mr. Douglas has no sympathy with the anti-slavery sentiment of the free States, but plants himself upon his principle, and puts slavery and freedom upon the same footing. If the people want slavery, let them have it. If they want freedom—no interference in favor of slavery. This we understand to be his position, though some of his southern friends claim that he admits that the Supreme Court is bound to give slavery an existence *in all the territories.* In his New Orleans speech of last winter, Mr. Douglas is reported to have said:

"Whenever a territory has a climate, soil and production, making it the interest of the inhabitants to encourage slave property, they will pass a slave code, and give it encouragement. Whenever the climate, soil and production preclude the possibility of slavery being profitable, they will not permit it. You come right back to the principle of dollars and cents. I do not care where the migration in the southern country comes from; if old Joshua R. Giddings should raise a colony in Ohio, and settle down in Louisiana, he would be the strongest advocate for slavery in the whole South; he would find, when he got there, his opinion would be very much modified; he would find on those sugar plantations that it was not a question between the white man and the negro, but between the negro and the crocodile.

"He would say that, between the negro and the crocodile, he took the side of the negro. But, between the negro and the white man, he would go for the white man. The Almighty has drawn the line on this continent, on one side of which the soil must be cultivated by slave labor; on the other, by white labor. That line did not run on thirty-six degrees and thirty minutes, for thirty-six degrees and thirty minutes runs over mountains and through valleys. But this slave line meanders in the sugar-fields and plantations of the South—[the remainder of the sentence was lost by the confusion around the reporter.] And the people living in their different localities and in the territories must determine for themselves whether their 'middle bed' is best adapted to slavery or free labor.

"Hence, under the Constitution, there is no power to prevent a southern man going there with his slaves, more than a northern man."

Mr. Douglas is a man of very short stature, but of large body, and a frame and constitution capable of great endurance. He lives in Washington half the year, where he has a handsome residence, and the other half in Illinois among his constituents, where he has a country mansion. The mother of Mr. Douglas, who was so faithful to him and whom he has never ceased to love and reverence, still lives, and has witnessed his rise from the cabinet-maker's shop to the senatorial chair.

SALMON P. CHASE.

Salmon Porland Chase was born in Cornish, New Hampshire, Jan. 13th, 1808. He was seven years old when his father removed to the town of Keene, where he attended the village school. In 1817 his father died, and two years later the boy, then only twelve years old, went to Worthington, Ohio. His uncle, Philander Chase, was then Bishop of Ohio, and he superintended the education of his nephew. Shortly after this, he entered Cincinnati College, of which institution his uncle became president. He soon was promoted to the sophomore class. After a year's residence in Cincinnati, he returned to New Hampshire and his mother's house; and, in 1824, entered the junior class of Dartmouth College. He graduated in 1826. The following winter Mr. Chase went to the city of Washington, and opened a classical school for boys. Among his pupils were the sons of Henry Clay, William Niel, and other distinguished men. Many of the citizens of Washington at this day well remember Mr. Chase's efforts as a teacher among them, and at that time learned to esteem and respect the man who has since risen to so high a position as a politician and statesman. He closed his school in 1829, and soon was admitted to the bar, having studied law under Mr. Niel while teaching his school, manifesting by his industry and courage that he was possessed of the qualities which must certainly in the end bring him position and reputation.

In 1830, Mr. Chase left Washington for Cincinnati, where he has always since resided, save when serving his State in an official capacity, and pursued his profession. He was poor, unknown, and before he could hope to attract the attention of the public, must earn his bread and endure months, if not years, of serious toil and drudgery. During these early years in his professional career, he prepared an edition of Statutes of Ohio, and a preliminary sketch of the history the State. The work made three large volumes, and at once became an authority in the courts. The authorship of this volume was a happy idea, for it not only brought him a moderate pecuniary reward directly, but it also gave him the ear of the people, and practice at once flowed in upon him.

In 1834, Mr. Chase became solicitor of the Bank of the United States in Cincinnati, and other corporations. In 1837, he first gave public utterance to his views upon the slavery question in its legal aspects. The article in Appleton's Encylopædia upon Mr. Chase, which on many points is our authority in this sketch, gives the subjoined history of Mr. Chase's early legal arguments in reference to slavery:

"In 1837, Mr. Chase acted as counsel for a colored woman claimed as a fugitive slave and in an elaborate argument, afterward published, controverted the authority of Congress to impose any duties or confer any powers in fugitive slave cases on state magistrates, a position in which he has since been sustained by the U. S. Supreme Court; and maintained that the law of 1793, relative to fugitives from service, was void, because unwarranted by the Constitution of the United States. The same year, in an argument before the Supreme Court of Ohio, in defence of James G. Birney, prosecuted under a State law for harboring a negro slave, Mr. Chase asserted the doctrine that slavery is local, and independent on state law for existence and continuance, and insisted that the person alleged to have been harbored, having been brought within the territorial limits of Ohio by the individual claiming her as master, was thenceforth, in fact and by right, free. In 1838, in a newspaper review of a report of the judiciary committee of the senate of Ohio against the granting of trial by jury to alleged slaves, Mr. Chase took the same ground as in his legal arguments. In 1846, he was associated with the Hon. W. H. Seward as defendant's counsel in the case of Van Zandt, before the Supreme Court of the United States. The case excited much interest, and in a speech which attracted marked attention, Mr. Chase argued more elaborately the principles which he advanced in former cases, maintaining that under the ordinance of 1787 no fugitives from service could be reclaimed from Ohio, unless there had been an escape from one of the original States; that it was the clear understanding of the framers of the Constitution, and of the people who adopted it, that slavery was to be left exclusively to the disposal of the several States, without sanction or support from the National Government; and that the clause of the Constitution relative to persons held to service was one of compact between the States, and conferred no power of legislation on Congress, having been transferred from the ordinance of 1787, in which it conferred no power on the Confederation, and was never understood to confer any. He was subsequently engaged for the defence in the case of Driskell *vs.* Parish, before the U. S. Circuit Court at Columbus, and re-argued the same positions."

Mr. Chase's *political* history is thus summed up in the same article:

"Mr. Chase's sentiments of hostility to the nationalization of slavery were expressed by his position in the political movements of the country, as well as his efforts at the bar. Prior to 1841 he had taken little part in politics. He had voted sometimes with the Democrats, but more commonly with the Whigs, who, in the North, seemed to him more favorable to anti-slavery views than their opponents. He supported Gen. Harrison in 1840, but the tone of his inaugural address, and still more the course of the Tyler administration, convinced him that no effective resistance to the encroachments of slavery was to be expected from any party with a slaveholding and pro-slavery wing, modifying if not controlling its action; and in 1841 he united in a call for a convention of the opponents of slavery and slavery extension, which assembled in Columbus in December of that year. This convention organized the liberty party of Ohio, nominated a candidate for governor, and issued an address to the people defining its principles and purposes.—This address, written and reported by Mr. Chase, and unanimously adopted by the convention, deserves attention as one of the earliest expositions of the political movements against slavery. In 1843, a national liberty convention assembled at Buffalo. Mr. Chase was an active member of the committee on resolutions, to which was referred, under a rule of the convention, a resolution proposing 'to regard and treat the third clause of the Constitution, whenever applied to the case of a fugitive slave, as utterly null and void, and consequently as forming no part of the Constitution of the United States, whenever we are called upon or sworn to support it.' Mr. Chase opposed the resolution, and the committee refused to report it. It was, however, afterward moved in the convention by its author, and adopted. Having been charged in the U. S. Senate with the authorship and advocacy of this resolution, by Mr. Butler of South Carolina, who denounced the doctrine of mental reservation apparently sanctioned by it, Mr. Chase replied: 'I have only to say I never proposed the resolution; I never would propose or vote for such a resolution. I hold no doctrine of mental reservation. Every man, in my judgment, should speak just as he thinks, keeping nothing back, here or elsewhere.' In 1843 it became Mr. Chase's duty to prepare an address on behalf of the friends of liberty, Ireland, and repeal in Cincinnati, to the loyal national repeal association in Ireland, in reply to a letter from Daniel O'Connell.

"In this address Mr. Chase reviewed the relations of the federal government to slavery at the period of its organization, set forth its original anti-slavery policy, and the subsequent growth of the political power of slavery, vindicated the action of the liberal party, and repelled the aspersions cast by a repeal association in Cincinnati upon anti-slavery men. In 1845 Mr. Chase projected a southern and western liberty convention, designed to embrace 'all who, believing that whatever is worth preserving in republicanism can be maintained only by uncompromising war against the usurpations of the slave power, and are therefore resolved to use all constitutional and honorable means to effect the extinction of slavery in their respective States, and its reduction to its constitutional limits in the United States.' The convention was held in Cincinnati in June, 1845, and was attended by 4,000 persons; delegates were present to the number of 2,000. Mr. Chase, as chairman of the committee, prepared the address, giving a history of slavery in the United States, showing the position of the Whig and Democratic parties, and arguing the necessity of a political organization unequivocally committed to the denationalization of slavery and the overthrow of the slave power, and exhibiting what he regarded as the necessary hostility of the slaveholding interest to democracy and all liberal measures. This address was widely circulated.

"In 1847, Mr. Chase was a member of the Second National Liberty Convention, and opposed the making of any national nomination at that time, urging that a more general movement against slavery extension and denomination, was likely to grow out of the agitation of the Wilmot Proviso, and the action of Congress and political parties in reference to slavery. In 1848, anticipating that the conventions of the

Whig and Democratic parties would probably refuse to take grounds against the extensions of slavery, he prepared a call for a free territory state convention at Columbus, which was signed by more than 3,000 voters of all political parties. The convention thus called was largely attended, and invited a national convention to meet at Buffalo in August. The influence of Mr. Chase was conspicuous in the state convention, and no less so in the national convention, which assembled upon its invitation, and nominated Mr. Van Buren for President. An immense mass meeting was held at Buffalo at the same time. Mr. Chase was president of the national convention, and also a member of its committee on resolutions. The platform was substantially his work. On February 22d, 1849, Mr. Chase was chosen a senator of the United States from Ohio, receiving the entire vote of the Democratic members of the Legislature, and of those freesoil members who favored Democratic views. The Democratic party of Ohio, by the resotions of its state convention, had already declared slavery an evil; and practically, through its press and the declarations of its leading men, had committed itself to the denationalization of slavery. Mr. Chase, therefore, coinciding with the Democrats in their general views of the state policy, supported their state nominees, distinctly announcing his intention, in the event of the party's desertion of its anti-slavery position, in state or national conventions, to end at once his connection with it. When the nomination of Mr. Pierce by the Baltimore convention of 1852, with a platform approving the compromise acts of 1850, and denouncing the further discussion of the slavery question, was sanctioned by the Democratic party in Ohio, Mr. Chase, true to his word, withdrew from it, and addressed to the Hon. B. F. Butler, of New York, his associate in the Buffalo convention, a letter in vindication of an independent Democratic party. He prepared a platform, which was substantially adopted by the convention of the independent Democracy at Pittsburg in 1852. Having thus gone into a minority rather than compromise his principles, Mr. Chase gave a cordial and energetic support to the nominees and measures of the independent Democracy, until the Nebraska bill gave rise to a new and powerful party, based substantially upon the ideas he had so long maintained. As a senator of the United States, Mr. Chase delivered on March 26 and 27, 1850, a speech against Mr. Clay's compromise bill, reviewing thoroughly all the questions presented in it. He moved an amendment providing against the introduction of slavery in the territories to which the bill applied, but it failed by a vote of 25 to 30. He proposed also, though without success, an amendment to the fugitive slave bill, securing trial by jury to alleged slaves, and another conforming its provisions to the terms of the Constitution, by excluding from its operation persons escaping from State or territories, and *vice versâ*. In 1854, when the bill for the repeal of the Missouri Compromise, commonly called the Nebraska Kansas bill, was introduced, he drafted an appeal to the people against the measure, which was signed by the senators and representatives in Congress, concurring in his political opinions; and in a speech on February 3, attempted the first elaborate exposure of the features of that bill, as viewed by its opponents. In the general opposition to the Nebraska bill he took a leading part, and the rejection of three of his proposed amendments, was thought to be of such significance as bearing on the slavery question, that it may be well to state them. The first proposed to add after the words, 'subject only to the Constitution of the United States,' in section 14, the following clause: 'Under which the people of the territory, through their appropriate representatives, may, if they see fit, prohibit the existence of slavery therein.' This was rejected, yeas 10, nays 36. The second proposed to give practical effect to the principle of popular sovereignty by providing for the election by the people of the territory of their own governor, judges, and secretary, instead of leaving, as in the bill, their appointment to the Federal Executive. This was defeated, yeas 10, nays 30. He then proposed an amendment of the boundary, so as to have but one territory, named Nebraska, instead of two entitled respectively Nebraska and Kansas. This was rejected, yeas 8, nays 34. His opposition to the bill was ended by a final and earnest protest against it on the night of its passage. While thus vigilant in maintaining his principles on the slavery question, Mr. Chase was constant in the discharge of the general duties of his position. To divorce the Federal Government from all connection with slavery; to confine its action strictly within Constitutional limits; to uphold the rights of individuals and of States; to foster with equal care all the great interests of the country, and to secure an economical administration of the national finances, were the general aims, which he endeavored, both by his votes and his speeches, to promote. On the interests of the West, he always kept a watchful eye, claiming that the Federal treasury should defray the expenses of providing for the safety of navigation on our great inland seas, as well as on the Atlantic and Pacific coasts, and advocating liberal aid by the Federal Government to the construction of a railroad to the Pacific by the best, shortest, and cheapest route.

"He was an earnest supporter of the policy of the free homestead movement, in behalf of which he expressed his views during the first session of his term, on presenting a petition for granting the public lands, in limited quantities, to actual settlers not possessed of other land. He was also an early advocate of cheap postage and an unwearied opponent of extravagant appropriations. In July, 1855, Mr. Chase was nominated by the opponents of the Nebraska bill and the Pierce administration for governor of Ohio, and was elected. His inaugural address, delivered in 1856, recommended economy in the administration of public affairs, single districts for legislative representation, annual instead of biennial sessions of the legislature, and ample provision for the educational interests of the State. His state policy and senatorial course were now so much approved that at the national convention of the Republican party, held the same year, a majority of the Ohio delegation and many delegates from other States, desired his nomination for the presidency; but his name was, at his request, withdrawn. His first annual message to the Ohio legislature, in 1857, after reviewing the material resources, and the financial and educational condition of the State, together with its federal relations, recommended a bureau of statistics, which was accordingly established.

"During the same year, a deficit of over $500,000 being discovered in the State treasury, a few days before the semi-annual interest of the State debt became due, the decided action of Gov. Chase compelled the resignation of the State treasurer, who had concealed its existence, secured a thorough investigation, and, through a prompt and judicious arrangement, protected the credit of the State and averted a large pecuniary loss. At the close of his first term, Gov. Chase desired to retire from office, but the Republicans insisted on his renomination, which was made by acclamation. After an active canvass, the continued confidence of the people in his administration was manifested by his reëlection by the largest vote ever given for a governor in Ohio. In his annual message, in 1858, after submitting an elaborate exposition of the financial condition and resources of Ohio, he recommended semi-annual taxation, more stringent provisions for the security of the treasury, and a special attention to the State benevolent institutions, including the reform school, in which he had always manifested a deep interest. These suggestions met the approbation of the legislature, and laws were passed accordingly."

The sketch we have quoted, gives an *exact* and impartial, though brief, history of the political acts of Mr. Chase, but it is bloodless, without enthusiasm, and *to the friends* of the distinguished subject of the sketch, will seem cold, giving no adequate idea of the ability and greatness of the man; but the sketch is perfectly impartial, and accurate in every particular.

Mr. Chase, while in the Senate of the United States, bore a very high reputation as a debater and as an orator. He never descended to notice personal attacks unless his political history was called in question, and remained cool and unruffled through scenes of great excitement and under a storm of personalities. His manner is dignified and his eloquence massive. Few men can deliver a speech, which for force, solid arguments, and high-toned eloquence, will equal the best of his. He is not an impetuous orator, or man, but is always collected, calm, and self-poised. Nevertheless, he has warm and enthusiastic friends, and those who know him best esteem him most.

In his personal appearance, Mr. Chase is somewhat imposing, for he is tall, of large proportions, with a large head and face, a fine port, dignified bearing, and an eye of quick intelligence. Through his entire career, whether at the bar, in Congress, or in the gubernatorial chair, Mr. Chase has never for an instant compromised the integrity or dignity of his character.

One of the finest of his senatorial speeches was made Feb. 3, 1854, in reply to a severe attack of Mr. Douglas upon himself and two or three other gentlemen, who had issued an address to the people upon the Kansas-Nebraska act. We can only quote the closing portions of this great speech:

"Mr. President, three great eras have marked the history of this country, in respect of slavery. The first may be characterized as the era of enfranchisement. It commenced with the earliest struggle for national independence. The spirit which inspired it animated the hearts and prompted the efforts of Washington, of Jefferson, of Patrick Henry, of Wythe, of Adams, of Jay, of Hamilton, of Morris—in short, of all the great men of our early history. All these hoped, all these labored for, all these believed in the final deliverance of the country from the curse of slavery. That spirit burned in the Declaration of Independence, and inspired the provisions of the Constitution, and of the Ordinance of 1787. Under its influence, when in full vigor, State after State provided for the emancipation of the slaves within their limits, prior to the adoption of the Constitution. Under its feebler influence at a later perior, and during the administration of Mr. Jefferson, the importation of slaves was prohibited into Mississippi and Louisiana, in the faint hope that these territories might finally become free States. Gradually that spirit ceased to influence our public councils, and lost its control over the American heart and the American policy. Another era succeeded, but by such imperceptible gradations that the lines which separate the two cannot be traced with absolute precision. The facts of the two eras meet and mingle as the currents of confluent streams mix so imperceptibly that the observer cannot fix the spot where the meeting waters blend.

"This second era was the era of Conservatism. Its great maxim was to preserve the existing condition. Men said, let things remain as they are ; let slavery stay where it is ; exclude it where it is not ; refrain from disturbing the public quiet by agitation ; adjust all differences that arise, not by the application of principles, but by compromises.

"It was during this period that the senator tells us that slavery was maintained in Illinois, both while a territory and after it became a State, in despite of the provisions of the ordinance. It is true, sir, that the slaves held in the Illinois country, under the French law, were not regarded as absolutely emancipated by the provisions of the ordinance. But full effect was given to the ordinance in excluding the introduction of slaves, and thus the territory was preserved from eventually becoming a slave State. The few slaveholders in the territory of Indiana, which then included Illinois, succeeded in obtaining such an ascendency in its affairs, that repeated applications were made, not merely by conventions of delegates, but by the Territorial Legislature itself, for a suspension of a clause in the ordinance prohibiting slavery. These applications were reported upon by John Randolph, of Virginia, in the House, and by Mr. Franklin, in the Senate. Both the reports were against suspension. The grounds stated by Randolph are specially worthy of being considered now. They are thus stated in the report :

" 'That the committee deem it highly dangerous and inexpedient to impair a provision wisely calculated to promote the happiness and prosperity of the northwestern country, and to give strength and security to that extensive frontier. In the salutary operation of this sagacious and benevolent restraint, it is believed that the inhabitants of Indiana will, at no very distant day, find ample remuneration for a temporary privation of labor and of emigration.'

" Sir, these reports, made in 1803 and 1807, and the action of Congress upon them, in conformity with their recommendation, saved Illinois, and perhaps Indiana, from becoming slave States. When the people of Illinois formed their State constitution, they incorporated into it a section providing that neither slavery nor involuntary servitude shall be hereafter introduced into this State. The constitution made provision for the continued service of the few persons who were originally held as slaves, and then bound to service under the Territorial laws, and for the freedom of their children, and thus secured the final extinction of slavery. The senator thinks that this result is not attributable to the ordinance. I differ from him. But for the ordinance I have no doubt slavery would have been introduced into Indiana, Illinois, and Ohio.

It is something to the credit of the era of conservatism, uniting its influences with those of the expiring era of enfranchisement, that it maintained the Ordinance of 1787 in the northwest.

"The era of conservatism passed, also, by imperceptible gradations, into the era of slavery propagandism. Under the influences of this new spirit, we opened the whole territory acquired from Mexico, except California, to the ingress of slavery. Every foot of it was covered by a Mexican prohibition; and yet, by the legislation of 1850, we consented to expose it to the introduction of slaves. Some, I believe, have actually been carried into Utah and into New Mexico. They may be few, perhaps, but a few are enough to affect materially the probable character of their future governments.

"Sir, I believe we are on the verge of another era. The introduction of this question here, and its discussion, will greatly hasten its advent. That era will be the era of reaction. We, who insist upon the denationalization of slavery, and upon the absolute divorce of the General Government from all connection with it, will stand with the men who favored the compromise acts, and who yet wish to adhere to them, in their letter and in their spirit, against the repeal of the Missouri prohibition. You may pass it here, you may send it to the other House, it may become law; but its effect will be to satisfy all thinking men that no compromise with slavery will endure, except so long as they serve the interests of slavery; and that there is no safe and honorable ground to stand upon, except that of restricting slavery within State limits, and excluding it absolutely from the whole sphere of federal jurisdiction. The old questions between political parties are at rest. No great question so thoroughly possesses the public mind as this of slavery. This discussion will hasten the inevitable reorganization of parties upon the new issues which our circumstances suggest. It will light up a fire in the country which may, perhaps, consume those who kindle it.

"I cannot believe that the people of this country have so far lost sight of the maxims and principles of the Revolution, or are so insensible to the obligations which those maxims and principles impose, as to acquiesce in the violation of this compact. Sir, the Senator from Illinois tells us that he proposes a final settlement of all territorial questions in respect to slavery, by the application of the principle of popular sovereignty. What kind of popular sovereignty is that which allows one portion of the people to enslave another portion? Is that the doctrine of equal rights? Is that exact justice? Is that the teaching of enlightened, liberal, progressive Democracy? No, sir; no! There can be no real Democracy which does not fully maintain the rights of man, as man. Living, practical, earnest Democracy imperatively requires us, while carefully abstaining from unconstitutional interference with the internal regulations of any State upon the subject of slavery, or any other subject, to insist upon the practical application of its great principles in all the legislation of Congress.

"I repeat, sir, that we who maintain these principles will stand shoulder to shoulder with the men who, differing from us upon other questions, will yet unite with us in opposition to the violation of plighted faith contemplated by this bill. There are men, and not a few, who are willing to adhere to the compromise of 1850. If the Missouri prohibition, which that compromise incorporates and preserves among its own provisions, shall be repealed, abrogated, broken up, thousands will say: Away with all compromises; they are not worth the paper on which they are printed; we will return to the old principles of the Constitution. We will assert the ancient doctrine, that no person shall be deprived of life, liberty or property, by the legislation of Congress, without due process of law. Carrying out that principle into its practical applications, we will not cease our efforts until slavery shall cease to exist wherever it can be reached by the constitutional action of the government.

"Sir, I have faith in progress. I have faith in Democracy. The planting and growth of this nation, upon this western continent, was not an accident. The establishment of the American Government, upon the sublime principles of the Declaration of Independence, and the organization of the Union of these States, under our existing Constitution, was the work of great men, inspired by great ideas, guided by Divine Providence. These men, the fathers of the Republic, have bequeathed to us the great duty of so administering the government which they organized, as to protect the rights, to guard the interests, and promote the well-being, of all persons within its jurisdiction, and thus present to the nations of the earth a noble example of wise and just self-government. Sir, I have faith enough to believe that we shall yet fulfill this high duty. Let me borrow the inspiration of Milton, while I declare my belief, that we have yet a country 'not degenerated, nor drooping to a fatal decay, but destined, by casting off the old and wrinkled skin of corruption, to outlive these pangs, and wax young again, and, entering the glorious ways of truth and prosperous virtue, become great and honorable in these latter ages. Methinks I see in my mind a great and puissant nation rousing herself like a strong man after sleep, and shaking her invincible locks. Methinks I see her as an eagle mewing her mighty youth, and kindling her undazzled eyes at the full mid-day beam; purging and unscaling her long-abused sight at the fountain itself of heavenly radiance; while the whole noise of timorous and flocking birds, with those also that love the twilight, flutter about, amazed at what she means, and in their envious gabble would prognosticate a year of sects and schisms.'

"Sir, we may fulfill this sublime destiny, if we will but faithfully adhere to the great maxims of the Revolution; honestly carrying into their legitimate practical applications the high principles of democracy; and preserve inviolate plighted faith and solemn compacts. Let us do this, putting our trust in the God of our fathers, and there is no dream of national prosperity, power, and glory, which ancient or modern builders of ideal commonwealths ever conceived, which we may not hope to realize. But if we turn aside from these ways of honor, to walk in the by-paths of temporary expedients, compromising with wrong, abetting oppression, and repudiating faith, the wisdom and devotion and labors of our fathers will have been all—all in vain.

"Sir, I trust that the result of this discussion will show that the American Senate will sanction no breach of compact. Let us strike from the bill the statement which historical facts and our personal recollections disprove, and then reject every proposition which looks toward a violation of the plighted faith and solemn compact which our fathers made, and which we, their sons, are bound, by every tie of obligation, sacredly to maintain."

Mr. Chase's opinions respecting the independence of the State courts can be gathered from his message to the Ohio Legislature, Jan. 4, 1858. We quote:

"A disposition has been manifested, within the last few years, by some of the officials of the Federal Government, exercising their functions within the limits of Ohio, to disregard the authority, and to encroach upon the rights of the State, to an extent and in a manner which demands your notice.

"In February, 1856, several colored persons were seized in Hamilton County as fugitive slaves. One of these persons, Margaret Garner, in the frenzy of the moment, impelled, as it seems, by the dread of seeing her children dragged, with herself, back to slavery, attempted to slay them on the spot, and actually succeeded in killing one. For this act, she and her companions were indicted by the grand jury for the crime of murder, and were taken into custody upon a writ. regularly issued from the Court of Common Pleas.

"While thus imprisoned under the legal process of a State court, for the highest crime known to our code, a writ of habeas corpus was issued by a judge of the District Court of the United States, requiring their production before him. The writ was obeyed by the sheriff, and, contrary to all expectations, and in disregard, as I must think, of principle and authority, the prisoners were taken from his custody by order of the judge, and, without allowing any opportunity for the interposition of the State authorities, delivered over to the Marshal of the United States, by whom they were immediately transported beyond our limits. The alleged ground for this action and order was that the indicted parties had been seized as fugitive slaves upon a Federal Commissioner's warrant, before the indictment and arrest, and that the right to their custody, thus acquired, was superior to that of the sheriff, under the process of the State. This doctrine must necessarily give practical impunity to murder whenever the murderer may be seized by a federal official as a fugitive from service before arrest for the crime under State authority. Imputing no wrong intention to the judge, I am constrained to add that his proceeding seems to me an abuse, rather than an exercise, of judicial power.

"A similar case occurred more recently in the county of Champaign. Several deputies of the federal marshal having arrested certain citizens of this State for some alleged offence against the Fugitive Slave act, a writ of habeas corpus was issued by the probate judge of that county, requiring the arrested parties to be brought before him for inquiry into the grounds of detention. The sheriff of Clark County, while attempting to execute this writ, was assaulted by these petty officials and seriously injured, while his deputy was fired upon, though happily without effect. A warrant was issued by a justice of the peace for the apprehension of the perpetrators of these offences. This warrant was duly executed and the prisoners committed to jail under the custody of the sheriff of Clark County. A writ of habeas corpus was then issued by the same district judge who had interposed in the case of Margaret Garner, requiring the sheriff of Clark County to produce his prisoners before him at the city of Cincinnati. This writ was also obeyed, and the prisoners were discharged from custody by the order of the judge, on the ground that being federal officers, and charged with the execution of a federal writ, they had a right to overcome, by any necessary violence, all attempts made under the process of a State court, to detain them or their prisoners, even for inquiry into the legality of the custody in which those prisoners were held.

"This principle cannot be sound. It subverts effectually the sovereignty of the State. It asserts the right of any district judge of the United States to arrest the execution of State process, and to nullify the functions of State courts and juries, whenever in his opinion a person charged with crime under State authority has acted in the matter forming the basis of the charge, in pursuance of any federal law or warrant. No act of Congress, in my judgment, sanctions this principle. Such an act, indeed, would be clearly unconstitutional, because in plain violation of the express provision which requires that the trial of all crimes shall be by jury.

"It is deeply to be regretted that collisions of this kind should occur. The authorities of Ohio have never failed in due consideration for the constitutional rights of federal courts, nor will they thus fail. But they cannot admit, without dishonor, that State process is entitled to less respect than federal, nor can they ever concede to federal writs or federal officials a deference which is not conceded to those of the State.

"The true course is one of mutual respect and mutual deference. Whenever, in any inquiry upon habeas corpus, by any court, State or federal, it may be ascertained that the applicant for the writ is detained under valid process in pursuance of a constitutional law, he should be remanded at once to the custody from which he may have been taken for trial in due course. No investigation should take place into the guilt or innocence of the party charged, or, what is substantially the same thing, whether the facts were justified by the authority under which the applicant was acting at the time. Inquiries of this character are for juries upon a regular trial and in open court; not for a judge at chambers. If made upon one side upon habeas corpus, they must also be made upon the other. If federal courts are to protect federal officials from prosecution by State courts for alleged violations of State law, State courts in their turn must protect State officers from prosecution in federal courts, under similar circumstances. Hence, dangerous conflicts must arise, and imminent peril both to liberty and union.

"If such conflicts must come, to the extent of the power vested in me, I shall maintain the honor of the State, and support the authority of her courts."

We have scarcely given the reader a sample of Mr. Chase's style of speech, or opinions on the slavery question, and it is quite possible we have not given the most eloquent extracts which may be found in his public speeches and messages, but we have quoted enough to show every intelligent reader who Mr. Chase is and what his opinions are.

EDWARD BATES.

We shall only give an outline sketch of Edward Bates, of Missouri, for though a man whose name is prominently before the public, yet he has seen little of that congressional life which gives a man a political record.

Mr. Bates was born in Goochland County, Virginia, on the 4th of September, 1793, being the seventh son and twelfth child of Thomas F. Bates. His ancestors came from the west of England to the Jamestown settlement as early as 1625, and they were plain people of the middle rank of English life. They were Quakers, and remained so for more than a century—some of the descendants to this day. The ancestors of Mr. Bates, however, forfeited membership in the Society of Friends—or we should say, rather, Mr. Bates' *father*, Thomas F. Bates, lost his membership with the Society for bearing arms in the war of the Revolution. A noble cause to die for, and certainly to lose ecclesiastical relations for! He was at the siege of York; and his children from that day were no more Quakers.

The scholastic education of Mr. Bates was not

perhaps first-class. He entered no college and passed through with no "course," but was, nevertheless, well taught in the elements, at home, by his father and a kinsman, Benj. Bates, of Hanover; at school, for several years, at Charlotte Hall Academy, Maryland; and a most excellent school it was.

The choice of the young man for a profession was the navy, and in the winter of 1811–12, a midshipman's warrant was offered him; but in deference to the wishes of his mother, he declined it and gave up his choice. This fact gives a key to the man's character. He has always been willing to do his duty, however great the personal sacrifice. In 1813, he served as a volunteer at Norfolk, Va., in a militia regiment. In 1814, he emigrated to St. Louis, under the kind care of his elder brother, Frederick Bates, then Secretary of Missouri Territory, and afterward Governor of the State. He entered the law office of Rufus Easton, an eminent lawyer, who was in his time a delegate from the territory in Congress. In 1816, he was duly licensed to practise law, and succeeded so well that in 1819 he was appointed Circuit Attorney. In 1820, he was one of the eight men who represented St. Louis County in the convention which formed the State Constitution for Missouri. Later, he was the Attorney-General of the State; and later yet, was elected for several times to both houses of the Missouri General Assembly. In 1824, President Monroe appointed him U. S. Attorney-General for the Missouri District. In 1826, he was elected to Congress, where he served honorably for two years. In 1828, he ran again, but was beaten by the storm of Jackson politics. This result of the congressional campaign seemed to disgust him with public political life, and he quietly withdrew to private life. He has since steadily practised law to support a large family—with one exception. In 1853, he was elected Judge of the St. Louis Land Court. After performing the duties of the office for about three years, he resigned it and went back to the practice of the law.

In 1847, to go back a little, Mr. Bates presided over the Internal Improvement Convention at Chicago. In 1850, Mr. Fillmore appointed him Secretary of War, but he declined the office. In 1856, he presided at the Whig Convention in Baltimore; in 1858, received from Harvard University the honorary degree of Doctor of Laws. We omitted to mention that, in 1823, Mr. Bates married Julia D. Coulter, a native of South Carolina, by whom he has had seventeen children, eight of whom survive.

Before we give a few of Mr. Bates' political opin ions, one fact should be stated. He, a southern man, went to Missouri and became a slaveholder, by inheritance and otherwise; yet, a few years since, set his slaves free, and is understood to be unequivocally in favor of emancipation in the State of Missouri.

Now for Mr. Bates' political opinions—and we shall quote from his late letter. He says, speaking of slavery:

"As to the negro question, I have always thought, and often declared, in speech and in print, that it is a pestilent question, the agitation of which has never done good to any party, section, or class, and never can do good, unless it be accounted good to stir up the angry passions of men, and exasperate the unreasoning jealousies of sections, and by these bad means foist some unfit men into office, and keep some fit men out. It is a sensitive question, into whose dangerous vortex it is quite possible for good men to be drawn unawares. But when I see a man, at the South or the North, of mature age and some experience, persist in urging the question, after the successful experience of the last few years, I can attribute his conduct to no higher motive than personal ambition or sectional prejudice."

This is all Mr. Bates says on the slavery question. He then goes on to speak in favor of internal improvements to advance the interests and protect the rights and industry of the country.

"Protection, if not the sole, is the chief end of government. It is for the governing power to judge, in every instance, what kind and what degree of protection is needful—whether a navy to guard our commerce all around the world, or an army to defend the country against armed invasion from without, or domestic insurrection from within; or a tariff to protect our home industry against the dangerous obtrusion of foreign labor and capital.

As to our foreign policy generally, he says he is

willing to leave it where Washington placed it, on the sage maxim, "Peace with all nations; entangling alliances with none." The greedy appetite for foreign acquisition which makes us covet our neighbor's lands, and devise cunning schemes to get them, has little of his sympathy. He argues this point briefly, but forcibly, opposing the acquisition of Cuba, and the other islands and Central American countries which would then be demanded. As to buying them, we had better wait till we cease borrowing money to pay current expenses; and before conquering, pause and estimate the cost of rushing into war with all maritime Europe, and half of America. Cuba has much more to fear from us than we have to fear from Cuba. Mr. Bates continues:

"But suppose we could get, honestly and peaceably, the whole country, continental and insular, from the Rio Grande to the Orinoco, and from Trinidad to Cuba, and thus establish our *mare clausum,* and shut the gate of the world across the Isthmus, can we govern them wisely and well? For the last few years, in the attempt to govern our home territories of Kansas and Utah, we have not very well maintained the dignity and justice of the nation, nor secured the peace and prosperity of the subject people. . . .

"For my part, I should grieve to have my country become, like Rome, a conquering and dominant nation; for I think there are few or no examples in history, of governments whose chief objects were glory and power, which did ever secure the happiness and prosperity of their own people. Such governments may grow great and famous, and advance a few of their citizens to wealth and nobility, but the price of their grandeur is the personal independence and individual freedom of their people. Still less am I inclined to see absorbed into our system, "on an equal footing with the original States," the various and mixed races (amounting to I know not how many millions) which inhabit the continent and isthmus south of our present border. I am not willing to inoculate our body politic with the virus of their diseases, political and social—diseases which, with them, are chronic and hereditary, and with us could hardly fail to produce corruption in the mind and weakness in the members."

The letter concludes as follows:

"It seems to me that an efficient, home-loving government, moderate and economical in its administration, peaceful in its objects, and just to all nations, need have no fear of invasion at home, or serious aggressions abroad. The nations of Europe have to stand continually in defence of their existence, but the conquest of our country by a foreign power is simply impossible, and no nation is so absurd as to entertain the thought. We may conquer ourselves by local strifes and sectional animosities, and when, by our folly and wickedness, we have accomplished that great calamity, there will be none to pity us for the consequences of so great a crime.

"If our government would devote all its energies to the promotion of peace and friendship with all foreign countries; the advancement of commerce; the increase of agriculture; the growth and stability of manufactures, and the cheapening, quickening, and securing the internal trade and travel of our country; in short, if it would devote itself in earnest to the establishment of a wise and steady policy of internal government, I think we should witness a growth and consolidation of wealth and comfort, and power for good, which cannot be reasonably hoped for from a fluctuating policy, always watching for the turns of good fortune, or from a grasping ambition to seize new territories, which are hard to get and harder to govern.

"The present position of the administration is a sorrowful commentary upon the broad democracy of its professions. In theory, the people have the right and ability to do anything—in practice, we are verging rapidly to the one man power.

"The President, the ostensible head of the national Democrats, is eagerly striving to concentrate power in his own hands, and thus exclude both the people and their representatives from the actual affairs of government. Having emptied the treasury, which he found full, and living precariously upon the borrowed money, he now demands of Congress to intrust to his unchecked discretion the war power, the purse, and the sword.

"First, he asks Congress to authorize him, by statute, to use the army to take *military* possession of northern Mexico, and hold it under his *protectorate*, and as a security for debts due to our citizens. *Civil* possession would not answer, for that exposes him, as in the case of Kansas, to be annoyed by a factious Congress, and a rebellious territorial legislature.

"Second, not content with this, he demands discretionary power to use the army and navy in the South also, in blockading the coast and marching his troops into the interior of Mexico and New Granada, to protect our citizens against all evil doers along the transit route of Tehuantepec and Panama, and he and his supporters claim this enormous power upon the ground that, in this particular at least, he ought to be the equal of the greatest monarch of Europe. They forget that our fathers limited the power of the President by design, and for the reason that they had found out, by sad experience, that the monarchs of Europe were too strong for freedom.

"Third, in strict pursuance of his doctrine, first publicly announced from Ostend, he demands of Congress to hand over to him thirty millions of dollars, to be used at his discretion, to facilitate his acquisition of Cuba. Facilitate—how? Perhaps it would be imprudent to tell.

Add to all this the fact (as yet unexplained) that one of the largest naval armaments which sailed from our coasts is now operating in South America, ostensibly against a poor little republic far up the Plata River, to settle some little quarrel between the two Presidents. If Congress had been polite enough to grant the President's demand of the sword and the purse against Mexico, Central America and Cuba, this navy, its duty done at the South, might be made, on its way home, to arrive in the Gulf very opportunely, to aid the 'Commander-in-Chief' in the acquisition of some very valuable territory.

"I allude to these facts with no malice against Mr. Buchanan, but as evidences of the dangerous change which is now obviously sought to be made in the practical working of the Government—the concentration of power in the hands of the President—and the dangerous policy, now almost established, of looking abroad for temporary glory and aggrandizement, instead of looking at home for all the purposes of good government—peaceable, moderate, economical—protecting all interests, and by a fixed policy calling into safe exercise all the talents and industry of our people, and thus steadily advancing our country in everything which can make a nation great, happy, and permanent.

"The rapid increase of the public expenditures (and that, too, under the management of statesmen professing to be peculiarly economical) is an alarming sign of corruption and decay.

"The increase bears no fair proportion to the growth and expansion of the country, but looks rather like wanton waste and criminal negligence. The ordinary objects are not materially augmented—the army and navy remained on a low peace establishment—the military defences are little, if at all enlarged—the improvement of harbors, lakes and rivers is abandoned, and the Pacific railway is not only not begun, but its very location is scrambled for by hungry sections, which succeed in nothing but mutual defeat. In short, the money, to an enormous amount (I am told at the rate of from eighty to one hundred millions a year), is gone, and we have little or nothing to show for it.

"In profound peace with foreign nations, and surrounded by the proofs of national growth and individual prosperity, the treasury, by less than two years of mismanagement, is made bankrupt, and the government itself is living from hand to mouth on bills of credit and borrowed money! This humiliating state of things could hardly happen, if the men in power were both honest and wise. The democratic economists in Congress confess that they have recklessly wasted the public revenue; they confess it by refusing to raise the tariff to meet the present exigency, and by insisting that they can replenish the exhausted treasury and support the government, in credit and efficiency, by simply striking off their former extravagances.

"An illustrious predecessor of the President is reported to have declared 'that those who live on borrowed money ought to break.' I do not concur in that harsh saying; yet I am clearly of the opinion that the government, in common prudence (to say nothing of pride and dignity), ought to reserve its credit for great transactions and unforeseen emergencies. In common times of peace, it ought always to have an established revenue, equal, at least, to its current expenses. And that revenue ought to be so levied as to foster and protect the industry of the country, employed in our most necessary and important manufactures."

DANIEL S. DICKINSON.

DANIEL STEVENS DICKINSON was born at Goshen, Litchfield County, Conn., Sept. 11, 1800.

His father, Daniel T. Dickinson, was a farmer, an intelligent, upright man, who through life was devoted to his calling as the most honorable and useful, and left an unsullied name.

In 1806, the family removed to what is now Guilford, Chenango County, New York, where Daniel S. Dickinson spent his boyhood, mostly on the farm, in the usual occupations of a farmer's boy.

His education, as far as public advantages were concerned, was limited to the common schools of the country; but with a spirit of self-reliance, untiring industry and an ardent desire for knowledge and advancement, he availed himself of such private facilities as he could command or devise, and persevering in a plan of self-education systematically, with a fine literary taste and extensive reading and study, he early became a thorough English scholar, well versed in the classics and familiar with general literature.

Between 1816 and 1820, he learned, and worked

as apprentice and journeyman at, a mechanic's trade. In 1820, he commenced teaching and was successfully engaged in it considerably up to 1825, both in the common and in academical or select schools.

About 1820, he learned, without a teacher, the art of land surveying, in which he became expert, and practised somewhat extensively until 1828. During a portion of the time, while teaching and surveying, he was also engaged in the study of the law. He married, in 1822, Lydia Knapp, daughter of the late Colby Knapp, M.D., an early settler of Guilford, a prominent member of the medical profession, and extensively identified with the early history of the town and county. They have had four children, only two of whom, the youngest—daughters—are living. In 1828, he was admitted to the practice of the law, and opened an office at Guilford, where he remained in practice until 1831.

In December, 1831, he removed to Binghamton, the county seat of Broome County, New York, where he has ever since resided. He immediately entered upon an extensive legal practice, and soon took rank among the ablest lawyers of the State. He was made the first President of Binghamton, on its municipal organization in 1834. Was a member of the Baltimore Convention which nominated Van Buren and Johnson, in 1835. Was elected to the State Senate in the fall of 1836; took his seat 1st January, 1837, and served for four years as a senator and member of the Court for the Correction of Errors, in both of which capacities, as a debater, legislator and jurist, he maintained a prominent rank. His review in the Senate of the message of Governor Seward established him at once as a leader of his party, and is still referred to among politicians as exhibiting both the tact and power which afterward so strongly marked his public career. His opinions delivered in the Court of Errors are models of conciseness and force, and temper in just proportion the technicalities of law with the deductions of sound reason and strong common sense.

His term in the State Senate expired Dec. 31, 1840. At the election in 1840, he was a candidate for the office of Lieut. Governor, at the time Mr. Van Buren ran the second time for President, and was defeated, though he received 5,000 more votes than Mr. Van Buren.

In 1842, finding that his name was being used again in connection with the office of Lieut. Governor, he declined the nomination in advance of the meeting of the convention, but was nevertheless nominated unanimously and by acclamation, and compelled by circumstances to accept, and was elected by 25,000 majority. The office of Lieut. Governor made him President of the Senate, Presiding Judge of the Court for the Correction of Errors, member of the Canal Board, Regent of the University, etc., etc. His term of office expired Dec. 31, 1844, and he declined a reëlection. It was held during a somewhat stormy period in the history of the State, but was so discharged as to add to his reputation with the people and his standing with the Democratic party. As the presiding officer of the Senate, in particular, he showed a decision, firmness and dignity of character which elicited the admiration and approval of opponents as well as friends.

At the election in 1844, he opened the Presidential campaign in New York on the annexation of Texas, which he warmly advocated against the opinion of many leading Democrats. He spent the whole campaign upon the stump; was one of the Democratic *State* electors, and united in casting the vote of the State for Polk and Dallas. About the 1st of December, 1844, he was appointed by Governor Bouck United State senator in place of N. P. Tallmadge, resigned, and immediately proceeded to Washington and took his seat as such. Governor Tallmadge's term expired on the 4th of March, 1845. On the meeting of the Legislature in January, 1845, he was elected for the unexpired term of Governor Tallmadge, and subsequently for the regular term of six years, from 4th March, 1845; during which term he remained in the Senate, closing his public service 4th

March, 1851. For a number of years he was Chairman of the Committee of Finance in the Senate, but declined it, and all committee service, the last short session of the term.

He was a member of the committee to bear the remains of Mr. Calhoun to his native State, and discharged the duty with the almost filial regard he felt for the great man who had been called away from the field of his public labors. This is the only time he ever visited the South; but, though necessarily a hasty trip, he received many tokens of public and private appreciation.

In 1847, he introduced into the Senate, and advocated in an able speech, his celebrated resolution on the acquisition and annexation of territory, and asserting, in opposition to the doctrines of the Wilmot Proviso, the principles of "popular sovereignty," which formed the basis of the adjustment of 1850, and has since been so fully approved by the people.

He opposed the Oregon Treaty, which surrendered several degrees of American territory to Great Britain.

He opposed the Clayton-Bulwer Treaty, which he conceived to be a cheat, and has been a constant source of embarrassment and misunderstanding between the two governments.

During the session of 1850, he was given a public dinner by the Democrats of the counties of New

York, Kings, Queens, Richmond and Westchester, at the city of New York. The invitation was tendered by the leading Democrats of the five counties. They said in it that the occasion was sought for the purpose of "giving full utterance to the sentiments of respect and confidence with which his distinguished political services to our common country had inspired them," and closed as follows: "In the trying crisis through which our country, and we may add the cause of the world's freedom, and of Republicanism, is now passing, the State of New York is most fortunate in being represented in the Senate of the Union, by one whose patriotism soars above the level of time-serving purposes, and whose eminent talents and moral worth command respect both in the State he represents, and in the councils of the nation."

On his visit to New York, in compliance with this invitation, besides the splendid public *fête*, at which Charles O'Connor presided, he was waited upon by the various Democratic committees with resolutions and congratulatory addresses approving his course; was made the guest of the Common Council, although it was then politically Whig, who unanimously presented him the "freedom of the city," and passed resolutions thanking him for his public services in behalf of the city and State.

He was a member of the Committee of Thirteen in the Senate, of which Mr. Clay was chairman, which perfected the compromise measures of 1850, and took a leading part in their advocacy and adoption: a policy which, though often disturbed by demagogues of both parties since, has signally borne the test of the public judgment. At the close of the session at which those measures were adopted, he received from Mr. Webster the beautiful letter in reference to his course, which we append.

MR. WEBSTER TO MR. DICKINSON.

WASHINGTON, *Sept.* 27, 1850.

MY DEAR SIR: Our companionship in the Senate is dissolved. After this long and important session, you are about to return to your home, and I shall try to find leisure to visit mine. I hope we may meet each other again two months hence for the discharge of our duties in our respective stations in the government. But life is uncertain, and I have not felt willing to take leave of you without placing in your hands a note containing a few words which I wish to say to you.

In the earlier part of our acquaintance, my dear sir, occurrences took place which I remember with constantly increasing pain, because the more I have known of you the greater has been my respect for your talents. But it is your noble, able, manly and patriotic conduct in support of the great measures of this session which has entirely won my heart, and secured my highest regard. I hope you may live long to serve your country; but I do not think you are ever likely to see a crisis in which you may be able to do so much either for your own distinction or for the public good. You have stood where others have fallen; you have advanced with firm and manly step where others have wavered, faltered and fallen back, and, for one, I desire to thank you, and to commend your conduct out of the fullness of an honest heart.

This letter needs no reply; it is, I am aware, of very little value, but I have thought you might be willing to receive it, and perhaps to leave it where it would be seen by those who may come after you.

I pray you, when you reach your own threshold, to remember me most kindly to your wife and daughter, and I remain, dear sir, with the truest esteem, your friend and obedient servant,

DAN'L WEBSTER.

MR. DICKINSON TO MR. WEBSTER.

BINGHAMTON, *Oct.* 5, 1850.

MY DEAR SIR: I perused and re-perused the beautiful note which you placed in my hands as I was about leaving Washington, with deeper emotion than I have ever experienced, except under some domestic vicissitude. Since I learned the noble and generous qualities of your nature, the unfortunate occurrence in our early acquaintance, to which you refer, has caused me many moments of painful regret, and your confiding communication has furnished a powerful illustration of the truth that "to err is human, to forgive divine." Numerous and valued are the testimonials of confidence and regard which a somewhat extended acquaintance and lengthened public service have gathered around me, but among them all there is none to which my heart clings so fondly as this.

I have presented it to my family and friends as the proudest passage in the history of an eventful life, and shall transmit it to my posterity as a sacred and cherished memento of friendship. I thank Heaven that it has fallen to my lot to be associated with yourself and others in resisting the mad current of disunion which threatened to overwhelm us; and the recollection that my course upon a question so momentous has received the approbation of the most distinguished American statesman, has more than satisfied my ambition. Believe me, my dear sir, that of all the patriots that came forward in the evil day of their country, there was no voice so potential as your own. Others could buffet the dark and angry waves, but it was your strong arm that could roll them back from the holy citadel.

May that beneficent Being who holds the destiny of men and nations, long spare you to the public service, and may your vision never rest upon the disjointed fragments of a convulsed and ruined confederacy.

I pray you to accept and to present to Mrs. Webster the kind remembrance of myself and family, and believe me sincerely yours,

D. S. Dickinson.

He (Mr. Dickinson) was a member of the Baltimore Convention of 1848. In 1852, he was again a member. The convention failed to nominate on the first day of its sitting. The second day, on assembling in the morning, the Virginia delegation presented his name for the Presidency. Having been the friend and supporter of Gen. Cass for the nomination, whose name in the balloting then stood at about 100, he thought that in honor he could not become a candidate, and arose in the convention and declined the use of his name in a speech which did honor to his patriotism and self-sacrifice, and was received with the warmest applause, though many of his friends and the sound democracy of the country regretted his decision. Virginia subsequently brought forward, in the same manner, the name of Gen. Pierce, and he was nominated and elected.

In 1853, he was appointed to the valuable office of Collector of the Port of New York, which he declined. In 1858, the honorary degree of Doctor of

Laws was conferred on him by the Faculty of Hamilton College, New York. Since the expiration of his senatorial term, he has been entirely devoted to professional and rural occupations, and is at present conducting a large professional business. He has not mingled extensively in political affairs since, but was upon the stump in the presidential campaigns of 1852 and 1856, in his own and some of the other States.

Mr. Dickinson possesses a strong constitution, and firm and uniform health. His habits are those of exact regularity and active industry. He is capable of great concentration of effort, and of endurance, and performs every day of his life, either at the courts, in his office, upon his grounds, or keeping up his extensive correspondence, a vast amount of labor.

He is devoted to his family and friends, is domestic in his tastes, and his most cherished hours are those spent in the confidence and quietude of home.

Cheerful, genial and hospitable in his disposition and intercourse, he is exceedingly popular in social life; his ready wit and fund of anecdote, with his varied and more solid powers of conversation, always make him welcome, and render him in society the centre of many a delighted circle.

He writes with facility, and in a style pointed and vigorous.

His speeches are characterized always by plain

and direct purpose, sound argument and happy illustration, and often by sparkling repartee and passages of stirring eloquence. Some of his most effective efforts have been made without previous preparation. In public life his distinguishing characteristics have been fidelity to friends and party, and the courage and intrepidity with which, regardless of considerations personal to himself, his opinions have been maintained.

In public or in private life, the integrity and purity of his character have never been questioned.

To show how Mr. Dickinson is regarded by his political friends, we quote a few paragraphs from a sketch of the man in a New York journal friendly to him:

"Mr. Dickinson is, in the true and democratic sense of the term, a *national* man. And while there have been, and still are, a few, both North and South, who have believed, and do believe, that emergencies may arise in the affairs of our country, when it would be better to 'let the Union slide,' his course will show that in his belief, under no possible or conceivable circumstances, could a greater misfortune happen to our conntry and the cause of humanity itself, than a rupture or dismemberment of the American Union. This conviction has animated and controlled all his conduct as a man and a public servant. In the elements of his character, there is no neutrality or non-committal; his leading peculiarities are point and positiveness—there is nothing negative about the man, his convictions are all absolute, and they are always vitalized into practical efficiency. Hence no man has warmer or more attached personal friends, and none more bitter political opponents, than he. The Van Buren men of New York, who defeated Gen. Cass, in 1848, by their treachery to the democratic party, have acted as though they thought his very political existence was a standing rebuke and shame for their treasonable desertion ; and hence they have spared no pains or efforts to vilify his character by the grossest misrepresentations. Yet notwithstanding these efforts of a false and disappointed faction, the people of the country feel, that there is no man to whom its true friends are more indebted than to him, for his fearless course in stemming the torrent of fanaticism and disunion. When the Abolitionists raised the '*Black Flag*' of treason in the North, and the decree went forth from the immediate friends and abettors of the Van Burens, that every man in the State of New York who did not join with them in their insane attempts to tear down the constitution of the country, and trample its sanctions and compromises in the dust, in order to invade the constitutionally guaranteed rights of the South, should be tabooed and turned over to the mercies of the political guillotine, Mr. D. threw himself into the van of the opposition and dared to beard the lion in his den ; and proclaimed in stern and patriotic tones of defiance, that for himself, 'he knew no North, no South, no East and no West—nothing but his country.'"

One of the editors of the "Dublin Nation," while travelling in this country, gave the subjoined sketch of Mr. Dickinson, as he found him in an American court:

"I learned that a court of assize was sitting just then in the town ; I was quite glad of an opportunity of seeing for myself a sight supposed to be such a compound of the farce and the row, 'an American court of justice in the rural districts.' I found out the courthouse ; a dilapidated old building, crowning the rising ground at one end of the principal street. I entered the hall. On one side a rickety door, with a half moon grating near the top, marked the apartment (about twelve feet by fifteen), which served as the district jail. It was strong enough, probably, to be any barrier to the liberty of a lame ewe ; yet it was large enough and strong enough for the requirements of the locality ! I ascended the stairs, and, pushing open a door on the first landing, I found myself in 'court.' Accuse me not, oh hilarious reader, if I herein depart from all precedent and prefer not fun to fact ; if I declare that I saw no revolvers, no bowie knives, heard neither cursing nor squabbling ; possibly these are to be seen, and I may see them ere I return to Ireland—but here, at least, I declare, that I saw gravity and dignity on the bench and at the bar ; order and decorum in the audience. The latter I attribute to the circumstance that there were no policemen to disturb the quiet of the place, by perpetually bawling out 'silence !'—an intolerable nuisance which *we* have to endure. The room was about thirty feet square and fifteen in height. At the end opposite the entrance was the bench ; in the middle of the apartment an oval shaped space was railed off on the floor ; one end reaching to the desk (immediately under the bench), at which sat the county clerk and the sheriff. The oval space was alloted to the professors of the law. On each side, rising gradually to the rear, were rows of seats, or rather pews, for the auditors. The jury sat in one of these 'pews,' immediately on the left of the judge. Two large stoves, whose flue-pipes cut sundry capers in the air—with the laudable intention of giving us all the benefit possible of the heat they contained—kept the place comfortably warm. Occasionally the high sheriff would walk quietly down to one of the stoves, open the door, poke up the fire, and put in a fresh log. Accustomed from childhood to associate so largely the judicial functions with a horse-hair wig, and a black silk gown—indeed, rather inclined to think that these constituted the judge, and that without them there could be no law in the land, it seemed hard to believe that the gentleman on the bench before me, in civilian costume, could be a real genuine judge and no mistake. . . . . . .

"Yet I do not know that I ever saw in the same official position more dignified demeanor. I never saw a judge listened to with more deference, and treated with more respect than in this instance, in this same village court, in the 'wilds' of western New York, though Judge Balcom wears his own hair—black as Morven's—and came to court without the blowing of even so much as a penny whistle.

* * * * * * * * *

"Seated within the railed space—his arms folded on his breast, his face raised upward in attentive listening attitude—was a man who instantly struck me as being singular among the throng around him. He might be sixty years of age; a powerfully built frame and expansive chest gave indication of physical strength and energy; but it was *the face* that impressed me. It was one of those that Rembrandt loved to paint; the grave serenity of strength in repose; the warm glow of life's autumn evening upon a countenance expressive of quiet dignity and intellectual power. The spacious dome of a massive head was covered with silvery—nay, snow-white hair, lending a venerable, though not an aged, aspect to the man. He was very plainly dressed; the blue cloth body-coat, with brass buttons, was perfectly American; the large high shirt-collar standing out from the lower part of a face entirely shaven; and a black silk neckerchief, loosely fastened around in the very carelessness of effect or appearance, was in perfect keeping with the simplicity of his *tout ensemble.* This was the Honorable D. S. Dickinson, the contemporary in politics of Webster, who found in him, in many a passage of arms, a foeman worthy of his steel. For some years Mr. Dickinson has remained in retirement from active public life, notwithstanding many efforts to induce him to reënter the arena. Yet it is shrewdly suspected that his counsel is not seldom sought and acted upon by the great ones of that party of which he once was so active and able a leader."

We now proceed to make a few extracts from Mr. Dickinson's public speeches. Here is an extract upon disunion:

"The spirit of sectional hate, which is now inculcated by the votaries of a corrupt and stultified Abolitionism, by bigots, zealots, fanatics and demagogues; in desecrated pulpits, in ribald songs, in incendiary presses and strife stirring orators, has already promoted a feeling of irritation which should fill the patriotic mind with apprehension and alarm. No feud is so bitter as that which exists between brethren—no persecution so relentless as that which pursues an estranged friend—no war so ruthless as one of domestic strife; and yet this evil genius, disguised with the garb of superior sanctity—the blear-eyed miscreant disunion—is walking up and down the earth like Satan loosed from his bondage of a thousand years, endeavoring to array one section of the Union against the other upon a question which was wisely disposed of by those who laid the broad and deep foundations of our government.

"With one hand it essays to tear out from the Constitution the pages upon which are written its holiest guaranties, and with the other, it seeks to erase from our nation's flag fifteen of the stars which help to compose the pride and hope and joy of every American. It would, in pursuit of its miserable and accursed abstractions, array man against man, brother against brother, and State against State, until it covered our fair land with anarchy and blood, and filled it with mourning and lamentation; until every field should be a field of battle, every hill-side drenched in blood, every plain a Golgotha, every valley a valley of dry bones; until fire should blast every field, consume every dwelling, destroy every temple, and leave every town black with ashes and desolation; until this fiendish spirit, compounding all the elements of fury and horror, would sweep over this fair and fertile portion of God's heritage, like the infuriated Hyder Ali on the Carnatic, leaving it one everlasting monument of barbarous vengeance."

In anticipation of the acquisition of territory from Mexico, on account of the Mexican war, the famous Wilmot proviso passed the House of Representatives at the heel of the session in 1846. As an antidote for the proviso, Mr. Dickinson introduced the following resolves into the Senate, Dec. 14, 1847:

"*Resolved,* That true policy requires the Government of the United States to strengthen its political and commercial relations upon this continent by the annexation of such contiguous territory as may conduce to that end, and can be justly obtained; and that neither in such acquisition nor in the territorial organization thereof, can any conditions be constitutionally imposed, or institutions be provided for or established, inconsistent with the right of the people thereof, to form a free, sovereign State, with the powers and privileges of the original members of the confederacy.

"*Resolved,* That, in organizing a territorial government for territory belonging to the United States, the principles of self-government upon which our federative system rests will be best promoted, the true spirit and meaning of the Constitution be observed, and the Confederacy strengthened, by leaving all questions concerning the domestic policy therein to the legislatures chosen by the people thereof."

In a speech of power, delivered in the Senate Jan. 15, 1848, he tried to demonstrate the correctness of the principle of these resolves. From this, the first speech made during the slavery controversy in favor of congressional non-intervention with slavery in the territories, we make the following extracts:

"The Republican theory teaches that sovereignty resides with the people of a State, and not with its political organization; and the Declaration of Independence recognizes the right of the people to alter or abolish and reconstruct their government. If sovereignty resides with the people and not with the organization, it rests as well with the people of a territory, in all that concerns their internal condition, as with the people of an organized State. And if it is the right of the people, by virtue of their innate sovereignty, to 'alter or abolish,' and reconstruct their government, it is the right of the inhabitants of territories, by virtue of the same attribute, in all that appertains to their domestic concerns, to fashion one suited to their condition. And if, in this respect, a form of government is proposed to them by the Federal Government, and adopted or acquiesced in by them, they may afterward alter or abolish it at pleasure. Although the government of a territory has not the same sovereign power as the government of a State in its political relations, the people of a territory have, in all that appertains to their internal condition, the same sovereign rights as the people of a State. . . .

"That system of government, whether temporary or permanent, whether applied to States, provinces, or territories, is radically wrong, and has within itself all the elements of monarchical oppression, which permits the representatives of one community to legislate for the domestic regulation of another to which they are not responsible, which practically allows New York and Massachusetts, and other Atlantic States, to give local laws to the people of Oregon, Minnesota and Nebraska, to whom and whose interests, wishes and condition, they are strangers."

The following extracts from a campaign speech in 1856, of Mr. Dickinson, will give the reader some idea of his wit and power before an out-door audience. He is speaking of the Pennsylvania election:

"In Pennsylvania every ill-omened bird in the nation had gathered and croaked. Every device that those bent on evil could conceive had been resorted to. Money had been spent with a lavish hand. All this had been done in order to induce the people of that State to favor the doctrines of the so-called Republican party. How well had she stood the test in the last great fight! There, fanaticism had been rebuked, hypocrisy had been unmasked, and villainy discomfited. The Democratic candidates had been placed in the field, and that being the home of Mr. Buchanan, the Republicans had strained every nerve to defeat him there. But how gallantly had old Pennsylvania come up to the work—how glorious the result! How had they tried and judged that party—that political mermaid—half-colored woman and half-scaly fish! The result reminded him of a conference between Mrs. Jones and Mrs. Smith. Mrs. Jones, calling on Mrs. Smith, said, 'Why, haven't you finished your washing yet?' To which Mrs. Smith replied, 'Oh! no, dear, we have a very great washing; it takes us a whole week to do our washing, and I don't think we can get it done in a week!' 'But, said Mrs. Jones, 'you haven't a *great* many clothes-lines, and they are not *very* long, and you don't seem to hang out any more clothes than other people.' 'Oh, no,' replied Mrs. Smith; 'but then you know what we hang out is a very small portion of what we wash.' So it was with the Republicans of Pennsylvania. What they hung out on election day was in miserable proportion to the amount of washing they had done. Proceeding, he said that the Democrats had hung out their banners—their principles were those of the Constitution, and their candidates were upon them. The Republicans, on the contrary, had but few principles, and scarcely any candidates. The Democratic candidates represented the principles of the Democratic party. And now of the general issue between the parties.

"What a spectacle! A slavery more base and abject than any African slavery that was ever dreamed of; an enslavement of white men, in order that their leaders may war against their brethren. How they would make up their dividend of profits he could not see. Their case would be similar to that of the man who thought he was going to get a great deal of money by his wife. She had often told him that when her father died, she would have considerable coming to her. Well, the old man died, and it turned out that he had left $9,000 and ten children. The husband tried to figure it up. He said, 10 from 9 you can't. He tried it again and said, 10 from 9 you can't. Turning to his wife, and greatly perplexed, he said, 'you told me that when the old man died, you would have something coming to you.' His wife replied that she had—that she had always understood her father had $9,000. 'So he has,' says the husband; 'but then he's got ten children—and 10 from 9 you can't. We won't get a d——d cent.' So it would be with the Republicans. They had resorted to political huckstering, such as had never before been heard of. They had run through every issue, and had talked thread-bare every principle. Kansas was now their great hobby. They said they did not care so much about other issues. But Kansas—bleeding

Kansas, absorbed their very souls. Kansas was to them what ale was to Boniface—it was meat, drink, washing and lodging. Now, though Kansas was an important section of the country, he did not think that it was worth while to upset the Government, whether slavery went there or not. The Democracy were willing to leave that question entirely with the people of that country. They had no fear from slavery there, even if it had all the evils pictured by the fanatics. New York could have slavery if it wished, so could all the other States, and all the Democracy wanted was that the people should do as they liked in the question, whether slavery should be there or no.

"In any event, slavery was not so bad or so baneful in its influences as the trickery that had been resorted to in Pennsylvania, and by the so-called Republicans. But, Kansas, bleeding Kansas, they cry continually. Why, they had run poor, bleeding Kansas until it was as dry as a turnip. It was to them what the lamp was to Aladdin. When he wanted to raise the wind, he rubbed his lamp, and when the Republicans wanted blood, they cried 'bleeding Kansas.' Kansas, to them, was like the Yankee's clock, that would strike whenever he told it to do so. But one day he told it to strike, and it didn't; he told it again, but still no strike. Finally, a voice was heard from behind the clock, saying, 'I can't strike—the string's broke.' To this pass has it come at length with the Republicans and their poor 'bleeding Kansas.' When they call for blood, the answer comes, 'The string's broke.'"

In a territorial speech in the United States Senate, January 12, 1848, Mr. Dickinson said:

"Our form of government is admirably adapted to extend empire. Founded in the virtue and intelligence of the people, and deriving its just powers from the consent of the governed, its influences are as powerful for good at the remotest limits as at the political centre.

"We are unlike all communities which have gone before us, and illustrations drawn from comparing us with them, are unjust and erroneous. The social order which characterizes our system is as unlike the military republics of other times, as is the religion of the Saviour of men to the impositions of Mahomet. Our system wins by its justice, while theirs sought to terrify by its power. Our territorial boundary may span the continent, our population be quadrupled, and the number of our States be doubled, without inconvenience or danger. Every member of the Confederacy would well sustain itself, and contribute its influences for the general good; every pillar would stand erect, and impart strength and beauty to the edifice. In matters of national legislation, a numerous population, extended territory, and diversified interests, would tend to reform abuses which would otherwise remain unredressed, to preserve the rights of the States, and to bring back the course of legislation from the centralism to which it is hastening. One-half the legislation now brought before Congress would be left undone, as it should be; a large portion of the residue would be presented to the consideration of State legislatures, and Congress would be enabled to dispose of all matters within the scope of its legitimate functions without inconvenience or delay.

"The present political relations of this continent cannot long continue, and it becomes this nation to be prepared for the change which awaits it. If the subjects of the British crown shall consent to be ruled through all time by a distant cabinet, Mexico cannot long exist under the misrule of marauders and their pronunciamentos, and this was as clearly apparent before as since the existence of the war. If, then, just acquisition is the true policy of this Government, as it clearly is, it should be pursued by a steady and unyielding purpose, and characterized by the sternest principles of national justice. It should not rashly anticipate the great results which are in progress, nor thrust aside the fruits when they are produced and presented. The national existence of Mexico is in her own keeping, but is more endangered at this time by her own imbecility and stubbornness—her national ignorance and brutality—than from the war we are prosecuting and all its consequences. She has been hastening to ruin for years upon the flood-tide of profligacy and corruption; and if she is now rescued, and her downfall arrested and postponed for a season, it may justly be attributed to the salutary influences of the chastisement she has received."

These general ideas upon the subject of territorial acquisition will indicate Mr. Dickinson's views upon the Cuban and Mexican questions of to-day.

JOHN BELL.

John Bell is a man of the old school in politics, an ancient southern Whig, who has preserved his whiggery intact, and has not been swallowed up in the Democratic party, but has rather sympathized to a great extent with the party in the North which has taken the place of the old Whig organization—the Republican party. Coming from a slave State, and himself a slaveholder, of course Mr. Bell does not belong to the Republican organization. He could not well do so without occupying an anti-slavery attitude in Tennessee. But he has acted in concert with the Republicans on most issues in Congress, and upon many of the issues which slavery has raised, he has taken sides with the North. In this manner he has gained the respect of his colleagues who go further than he does in opposition to slavery.

John Bell is an honest, upright man, and has been for years one of the ablest members of the U. S. Senate. He has evinced the highest courage in taking his stand against measures which were either proposed by politicians from his own section of the country, or were expected to inure to the benefit of that section. He came out boldly against the repeal of the Missouri Compromise, and the Kansas-Nebraska act, although in doing so he exposed himself at home, among his constituents, to the raking fire of his political enemies. He also opposed with great eloquence and vigor the Lecompton bill. For a southern senator to do these things requires pluck as well as principle, and we may be sure that John Bell lacks neither. His enemies will give him credit for both.

In his personal appearance in the Senate, Mr. Bell is noticeable. Though his hair is grey, the fire of his eye is undimmed, and the freshness of his countenance is youthful. Few men in the Senate speak so vigorously as he. His voice is sonorous and loud, and the energy of his tone, his style, and his gesticulation remind one of an orator of thirty. We remember very well how during the Lecompton debate in the Senate, Mr. Johnson, Bell's Democratic colleague, was replying with great severity to his speech against the Lecompton bill. A portion of his remarks were very personal, and must have somewhat irritated the brave old senator. Johnson was fresh from the stump, and its phrases and language were so beaten into his mind that he could not shake them off. So, frequently in the course of his speech in alluding to Mr. Bell, instead of saying "my colleague," he said "my *competitor*." This was done several times, when Mr. Bell half-rose in his seat, his face flushed red with his indignation, and hurled out at his colleague, "*Competitor! I am not the gentleman's competitor!*" No one who witnessed the scene will ever forget it. The Senate was convulsed with laughter.

Mr. Bell was born near Nashville, Tennessee, in February, 1797; his father being a farmer in moderate circumstances. He—the son—was educated at what is now Nashville University—afterward studied law, and was admitted to the bar in 1816. He then settled down in Franklin, Tennessee, from which place he was elected to the State Senate, in 1817, he then being but twenty years old. During the next nine years he forsook politics and confined himself to his profession, but in 1826 he ran for Congress, in opposition to Felix Grundy. He had the support of General Jackson, and triumphed by one thousand majority. The canvass was long and exciting, and Mr. Bell was justly proud of his victory. For fourteen consecutive years he remained in the House of Representatives from this district. When first elected he was a follower of Calhoun and an opponent of a Protective Tariff. He afterward, by reading and argument, saw fit to change his position in this respect, and has long been known as an advocate of the old Whig tenets—a high tariff, internal improvements, etc. etc. He was for ten years in the House, chairman of the committee on

Indian Affairs, was once chairman of the Judiciary committee. The breach between himself and Jackson was on the question of the removal of the deposits, and the result was that Mr. Bell went over to the Whigs. In 1834, he was made Speaker of the House of Representatives, his opponent being James K. Polk. The Whigs and a wing of the Democrats who disliked Van Buren voted for Mr. Bell, and elected him. Mr. Bell opposed Mr. Van Buren for removing men from office on acconnt of their politics, and he made a strong speech in the House against this policy. He refused to support Van Buren for the presidency and went in for Judge White, who carried the State of Tennessee. Mr. Bell was afterward reëlected to Congress from the Hermitage district, showing that the people even in Jackson's district supported him in the position he had taken. It was at this time that he had the courage to vote *in favor* of receiving anti-slavery politicians, when many northern politicians voted to strike down this right of the people under the most despotic forms of government. He also voted *against* Atherton's famous Gag Resolutions. In 1841, Gen. Harrison made him Secretary of War, but he resigned when Tyler came into power. He was soon elected to the United States Senate, where he remained till March 4th, 1859.

Mr. Bell supported the compromise measures of

1850—was opposed to the annexation of Texas—and, as we have remarked, opposed the Kansas-Nebraska act and the Lecompton Constitution. He is opposed to the *taking* of Cuba or buying it at an extravagant price—opposes all kinds of filibustering. We make a few extracts from Mr. Bell's great speech against the Lecompton bill. Upon Popular Sovereignty he thus expressed himself:

"What is the true doctrine on this subject? I had supposed that there could be no disagreement as to the true principles connected with the rights and powers of the people in forming a State Constitution; but since I have heard the speech of the senator from Georgia, I do not know what principle he agrees to. I say that in no disrespect; but I thought he was particularly wild, shooting *extra flammantia mœnia mundi*, on those high points of doctrine which he, in some parts of his speech, thought proper to enunciate. Does any person here deny the proposition, that the people of a territory, in the formation of a State Constitution, are to that extent—*quoad hoc*—sovereign and uncontrollable, though still owing obedience to the provisional government of the territory? Will any senator contend that the territorial legislature can either give to the people any power over that subject which they did not possess before, or withhold from them any which they did possess? The territorial legislature cannot dictate any one provision of the constitution which the people think proper to form. Who is prepared to contend that Congress can do anything more in this respect than a territorial legislature? It is usual for the territorial legislature, when the people desire to apply for admission into the Union, in the absence of an enabling act of Congress, to pass a law providing for the assembling of a convention to form a State Constitution. But that is a mere usage, resorted to when Congress has not thought proper to pass what is called an enabling act. What is an enabling act? Nothing more than to signify to the people of a territory, that if they shall think proper to meet in convention and form a State Constitution, in compliance with certain forms therein prescribed, to insure a fair expression of the people's will, Congress is prepared to admit them into the Union as a State.

"But such an act gives no more power to the people over the subject of a constitution than an act of a territorial legislature. But, suppose the people, either under an act of the territorial legislature or of Congress, meet in convention, by delegates chosen by the people, and form a constitution, what then? Has it any vitality as a constitution? Does it transform the territory into a State? Has it any binding force or effect, either upon individuals or upon the community? Nobody pretends that it has any such force. It is only after the acceptance of the constitution, and the admission of the territory into the Union as a State, that there is any vigor or validity in a constitution so formed. Before that time, it is worth no more than the parchment on which its provisions are written, so far as any legal or constitutional validity is concerned.

"But, upon principle, the people of a territory, without any act of the territorial legislature, without an enabling act of Congress, can hold public meetings and elect delegates to meet in convention for the purpose of forming a constitution; and when formed, it has all the essential attributes of a valid constitution, as one formed in any other way. Many senators contend that it is the inalienable and indefeasible right of the people of a State at all times to change their constitution in any manner they think proper. This doctrine I do not admit, in regard to the people of a State; but, in reference to the formation of a constitution by the people of a territory, there can be no question as to the soundness of this doctrine. They can form a constitution by delegates voluntarily chosen and sent to a convention, but what is it worth when it is formed? Nothing at all, until Congress shall accept it and admit the territory into the Union as a State under that constitution. It is worth no more in that case than in the case of a constitution formed under a territorial act or an act of Congress; but it is worth just as much."

Upon the repeal of the Missouri Compromise, and the effects which followed the act, he remarked:

"Four years ago, when it was proposed to repeal the Missouri Compromise—to adopt the principle of non-intervention, and concede to the people of the territories the right to settle the question of slavery in their own way—it was said by the advocates of the measure, that, as soon as the principles of it came to be understood, all agitation and discussion upon the subject of slavery in the territories would be localized—excluded from Congress—and the country would be left in undisturbed repose. So boldly and confidently were these views maintained, that the whole southern delegation in Congress, Whigs and Democrats, with seven or eight exceptions, together with many Democrats from the free States, came into the support of the measure. How were these bold predictions verified? In less than one month of the time during which the Kansas-Nebraska bill was pending in Congress, nearly the whole North was in a flame of resentment and opposition. Old men, of high character and great influence, who had for twenty years opposed the policy and designs of the Abolition faction in the North, suddenly became its allies and coadjutors. Thousands of the best citizens at the North, who had exerted all their energies to repress all opposition to the execution of the Fugitive Slave law of 1850, became suddenly converts to Free-Soilism. The religious feelings of whole communities became frenzied. The pulpit was converted into an engine of anti-slavery propagandism, and hundreds of thousands of sober-minded and conservative people at the North, who had never countenanced sectional strife on the subject of slavery, evinced that they had thrown off their conservatism, and were ready to array themselves under the banner of any party leader or faction, to check the progress of the South in what they considered its aggressive policy.

"After that demonstration of opposition at the North, but little more was said in debate of the tranquillizing character of the measure. But its most influential supporters from the South, becoming inflamed and irritated by the fierce invectives with which the measure was assailed, both within and out of Congress, became, in their turn, reckless (apparently at least) of all consequences, and seemed only bent on victory—on obtaining a triumph by passing the bill! It was in vain that they were admonished that they were adding largely to the abolition faction at the North; that they were increasing the free-soil element of political power in that section. They admitted no distinction between Abolitionists and Free-Soilers, and denounced all at the North who opposed the bill as Abolitionists and foes to the South. Some gentlemen declared that the screams of the Abolitionists were music to their ears. It was idle to warn men in such a tempest of passion, that, instead of sowing the seeds of peace, as they had promised, they were sowing dragons' teeth, that would spring up armed men. So intense did the feeling become on the subject, that some southern members of Congress, who had gone into the support of the bill on the idea that the Missouri restriction act was a violation of the treaty with France, and who would not have listened for a moment to the admission of aliens to the right of suffrage in the territories, lost sight of these views under the influence of the furor that was gotten up among the friends as well as the opponents of the measure; and they became even more determined champions of the bill when these grounds of their original adhesion were entirely swept away—one by the rejection of the Clayton amendment, and the other by the Badger proviso—than they were at the outset.

"There were, however, a few of the supporters of the bill who to the last contended that the intemperate demonstrations of opposition at the North were but the ebullitions of temporary excitement, which would subside as soon as the equitable and just principles of the bill should be exhibited in their practical operation in Kansas. On what flimsy grounds that delusion was indulged, and how soon and under what circumstances it vanished, I need not recount. The recollection of every patriot must still be painfully impressed with them. It is enough to say, that soon after these principles were put in operation in Kansas, disorder, anarchy, and civil war, ensued in rapid succession. It required the strong arm of the government of the United States and the interposition of the military force to sustain the territorial government; and even now, after the lapse of four years, we still find that the presence of a military force is necessary to maintain peace. So much for the effect of that measure on Kansas and the country. How has it been in Congress? Need I ask that question? Has not the subject of slavery in the territory been the absorbing subject of our thoughts and discussions at every session of Congress since the passage of the Kansas-Nebraska act? And as for the character and temper of the debates upon this subject, have they not, in asperity and fierceness, far exceeded those of any antecedent period of our history?

* * * * * * *

"I now ask the attention of the Senate to the effect of the experiment of localizing slavery agitation in the territories, made in 1854, in changing the complexion of parties both in Congress and in the country. In the Congress which passed the Kansas-Nebraska bill, we have seen that there was at the commencement of the session, in December, 1853, a Democratic majority of eighty-four in the House of Representatives, and only four Free-Soilers, and in the Senate a like number—so small, yet so distinct in their principles, that neither of the two great parties then known to the country knew well how to arrange them on committee.

"MR. HALE.—You left them off.

"MR. BELL.—The Whigs were afraid to touch them. Mr. Chase was a Democrat, and was so recognized by his brethren in the Senate, and was taken care of by them in arranging the committees; yet he was one of the gentlemen whom I have designated as Free-Soilers. Now, let us see what was the effect of the Kansas-Nebraska act on the elections which ensued in the fall of 1854, just on the heels of the adoption of that measure. One hundred and seven Free-Soilers were returned to the House of Representatives, and the Democratic party, instead of having a majority of eighty-four in that House, found itself in a minority of seventy-six; and in the Senate the number of Free-Soilers was increased to thirteen. Such was the complexion of the two houses of Congress in the 33d Congress, which assembled in December, 1855. Now, we find in the Senate twenty Free-Soilers. How many more they may have in the next Congress, will depend upon the disposition we make of the question *now before the Senate.* I call upon the senator from Georgia to say whether he will have that number limited or not. Does he want a sufficient number to prevent the ratification of any future treaty of acquisition? How long will it be before we have that number, if the southern Democracy persist in their present course? They would seem to be deeply interested in adding to the power of the Republican party.

"I consider that the most fearful and portentous of all the results of the Kansas-Nebraska act was to create, to build up a great sectional party. My friend from Ohio, who sits near me, [Mr. Wade] must allow me to say, that I regard his party as a sectional one.

"Mr. Wade.—Is not the other side a sectional party?

"Mr. Bell.—So far as they are confined to the South they are, but they say that they lap over.

"Mr. Wade.—Lap over further South still.

"Mr. Bell.—I consider that no more ominous and threatening cloud can darken the political horizon at any time. How formidable this party has already become, may be well illustrated by the fact that its representative candidate, Mr. Fremont, was only beaten in the last Presidential election by the most desperate efforts; and I feel warranted in saying, that but for the imminent prospect of his success, which shone out near the close of the canvass, Mr. Buchanan would not have attained his present high position."

From these extracts the reader will readily perceive the position of Mr. Bell upon the great political question of the day.

JOHN P. HALE.

John P. Hale comes of good old New England stock. His ancestors were the men who founded those New England institutions which are alike the glory of that section of the country and the whole nation. The grandfather of Mr. Hale—Samuel Hale—was a lawyer of ability and success, and he educated his son John—father of the present Mr. Hale—to the same profession. The father of Mr. Hale married a Miss O'Brien, daughter of Capt. Jeremiah O'Brien. Of this ancestor Mr. Hale is justly proud. The following true story is told of his gallantry at the beginning of the Revolutionary War:

"When the news of the struggle with the mother country reached Machias, in Maine (then a province of Massachusetts), on the 9th of May, 1775, an armed British schooner, the Margaretta, was lying in port, with two sloops under her convoy, loading with lumber in behalf of the king's government. An attempt was made to capture the officers of the Margaretta while they were at church, but they escaped on board, weighed anchor, and dropped down the river. On the 11th, a party of thirty-five volunteers was hastily collected, and, taking one of the lumber sloops, they made sail. The Margaretta, on observing their appearance, weighed and crowded sail, to avoid a conflict; the sloop proved to be a better sailor. As she approached, the schooner opened a fire with four light guns and fourteen swivels, to which the sloop replied with musketry, and soon the Americans boarded and captured the Margaretta. The loss of life in this affair was not very large, though twenty men on both sides are said to have been killed and wounded. It was the first blow struck on the water in the Revolutionary struggle, and it was characterized by a long chase, a bloody struggle, and a triumph.

"There was originally no commander in the sloop, but previously to engaging the Margaretta, Jeremiah O'Brien was selected for that station. Transferring the armament to a sloop, he engaged separately, and captured two English cruisers sent out from Halifax expressly to take him, and carried their crews as prisoners to Watertown, where the provincial Legislature of Massachusetts was assembled. His gallantry was so generally admired, that he was appointed a captain in the marine of the colony, and afterward distinguished himself as a continental officer. Two of his brothers, uncles of Mrs. John P. Hale, senior, were also noted for their nautical bravery."

Mr. Hale, the subject of this sketch, was born on

the 31st of March, 1806, at Rochester, New Hampshire. When a boy he, like most New England boys, attended the common district school of his neighborhood. When he grew up to be a young man, he was sent to Phillips Academy, at Exeter, where the well-known Dr. Abbott also educated Daniel Webster, Edward Everett, Lewis Cass and other distinguished men. In September, 1823, Mr. Hale entered Bowdoin College, and graduated with high honors in 1827. Among his associates in college were Hawthorne, Longfellow, Franklin Pierce, Prof. Stone, and S. S. Prentiss. In 1828, Mr. Hale selected his home, the town of Dover, where he now resides. There he went to study law in the office of D. M. Christie. He was admitted to the bar in 1830, and in 1834 his clients had become so numerous that he was obliged to take a partner. He was never so distinguished as a law-*student*, as for his popular argument with a jury. His forte was then, as now, in appealing directly to the hearts of men. By common sense, humor, pathos and sarcasm he won his cause. Mr. Hale was, we presume, a little more inclined to politics than to law, and if we may judge at all from his looks to-day, he was never over-fond of severe application, mental or physical, to labor.

In 1832, Mr. Hale was elected to represent Dover in the New Hampshire Legislature, and was a staunch Democrat. In 1834, General Jackson appointed him U. S. Attorney for the district of New Hampshire, an office which he filled creditably to himself. Mr. Van Buren continued him in this office, and he filled it till John Tyler removed him. This was a turning point in his history. He fell back to his old practice of the law; but in 1843, he was nominated and elected to Congress, to take his seat in the House of Representatives. A struggle was at that time beginning between the North and the South, and Mr. Hale, apparently to his certain defeat and humiliation, for New Hampshire was then overwhelmingly Democratic, took side with the North and freedom. He was renominated for Congress, but soon afterward he had the courage to come out in a letter denouncing the annexation of Texas. This, as a matter of course, brought down upon him the enmity of his old companions. The State Democratic Committee called a new convention in his district, set his nomination aside, and nominated John Woodbury in his place. It was at this juncture that Mr. Hale showed his nerve, and it is said that his spirited wife sustained him through the campaign with a courage and spirit second only to his own. Suffice it to say, that after an arduous campaign, Mr. Hale triumphed so far as to prevent his competitor from being elected. A majority was required to elect, and no candidate could get that majority. The next year Mr. Hale was sent again to the State Legislature to represent the town of Dover, and he was chosen Speaker of the House of Representatives. He presided so fairly and won so much upon the members, that before the adjournment took place, the Legislature elected Mr. Hale to represent the State, in part, for six years in the United States Senate! This was a great triumph. The man who had been set aside for his faithfulness to his own convictions of right, by party managers, was taken up by the State at large, and sent to represent New Hampshire in the Senate of the United States. His new position was an extraordinary one. He was about to take his seat in the Senate backed by no party, utterly alone, sent there for his individual merits, and not to advance the interests of any party.

A writer not agreeing or sympathizing with Mr. Hale in his peculiar anti-slavery views, speaks of this period of Mr. Hale's history in the following language:

"When Mr. Hale took his seat he was almost alone, and had to combat, single-handed, the political 'giants in those days.' Sometimes he was met with labored arguments, then subjected to bitter reproaches; at times those who were but 'his peers' would affect almost to ignore his presence, and again they would mercilessly denounce him as advocating doctrines dangerous to the liberties of the Republic

But the senator from New Hampshire was not to be intimidated or diverted from what he considered to be his duty. Adopting the *guerrilla* tactics, he manfully held his ground, and with felicitous humor, pungent retort, or keen sarcasm, made an impression upon the phalanx against which he had to contend. So high were his aims, and so conciliating were his manners, that before the close of his senatorial term, Mr. Hale had beaten down the barriers of prejudice, and fairly conquered sectional discourtesy. He was thus not only the standard-bearer, but the pioneer of the North in the Senate."

In 1853, the Democracy were in the ascendency in New Hampshire, and Mr. Atherton took Mr. Hale's seat in the Senate. Mr. Hale was persuaded at this time to locate himself in the city of New York, to practise his profession. Luckily, he did not give up his house at Dover, his family remaining there, and he paying his poll tax there.

In 1855, he was again elected to serve New Hampshire for an unexpired term; and in 1859, was reëlected for another whole term of six years. The same writer from whom we have just quoted, remarks further:

"Senator Hale is especially attentive to his constituents, and never neglects their interests for practice in the Supreme Court or other private business. He is, nevertheless, ever ready to address public assemblages on subjects in which he takes an interest. The sailors will never forget his efforts in procuring an abolition of flogging in the United States navy, in commemoration of which they presented him with a gold medal.

"From the commencement of Senator Hale's career up to the present time, he has been the untiring advocate of whatever he viewed as powerful for good, as calculated to meliorate the condition of man, or as likely to advance the general interests of the American Union, without prejudice to the rights of the section which he represents. He has ever firmly refused to bow before counterfeited images, or to scramble for place in the arena of party, but he has never declined to assume whatever burden of duty his friends counselled him to bear.

"In person, Senator Hale is burly, bluff-looking, with a clear eye, and a hearty grasp of the hand for his friends. His colloquial powers are of a splendid order, and he is a rare humorist, genial, sunshiny and kindly. He laughs with the foibles and shortcomings of the world—not at them; and his laugh is pure and silvery. Married in early life to Miss Lucy H. Lambert, of Berwick, Maine (a lady who combines rare attainments of mind, beauties of character, and personal charms), he has ever found his highest happiness in his own domestic circle, which is now graced by two accomplished daughters, just budding into womanhood. An evening spent with this estimable family is an event to be remembered with pleasure."

Mr. Hale has long been a favorite in the Senate with men of all parties. Whenever it is known beforehand that he is going to speak—no matter what the subject may be—he is sure to gather a crowded audience. He is one of the most popular men in the country, for his satire has never a spice of cruelty in it. His jolly humor, everlasting good nature, and natural love of fair play, make him friends wherever he is, no matter if he be among his bitterest southern enemies.

To gain any idea of the change which has taken place in the Senate since Mr. Hale took his seat in it, we must remember that then he stood up *alone* the champion of anti-slavery—unless we make an exception in favor of Mr. Seward—while now more than twenty Republican senators sit with him on the "opposition benches." To get a faint idea of the condition of the Senate when Mr. Hale entered it, let us go back to the 20th of April, 1845. The famous Drayton and Soyers slave case had just occurred, and Dr. Bailey and his paper, the "National Era," had been at the mercy of a mob for three days. Mr. Hale introduced into the Senate a bill relating to riots and unlawful assemblages in the District of Columbia. We will abridge the debate which ensued:

Mr. Foote, of Miss., made a very long speech on the general subject of slavery, and especially slavery in the District of Columbia. The attempt to legislate indirectly—that is, to sustain freedom of discussion in the District—against slavery, was an outrage upon the rights of the South. If any man gives countenance to this bill, he said, I pronounce him to be no gentleman—he would, upon temptation, be guilty of highway robbery on any of the roads of the Union. He charged that the abduction of the Drayton-Soyer slaves was instigated or countenanced by a member of the United States Senate—meaning Mr. Hale. This bill is intended to cover negro-robbery. The New Hampshire senator is endeavoring to get up civil war and insurrection. Let him go South. Let him visit the good State of Mississippi. I invite him there, and will tell him beforehand, in all honesty, *that he could not go ten miles into the interior before he would grace one of the tallest trees of the forest, with a rope around his neck, and if necessary*, I should myself assist in the operation!

Mr. Hale.—I did not anticipate this discussion, yet I do not regret it. Before proceeding further, let me say that the statement that I have given the slightest countenance to the recent "kidnapping of slaves is false."

Mr. Foote.—It had been stated so to me and I believed it. I am glad to hear the senator say he had no connection with the movement—some of his brethren doubtless had.

Mr. Hale.—The sneer of the gentleman does not affect me. While I am up, let me call the attention of the Senate to a man, who I am proud to call my friend, the editor of the "National Era." Mr. Hale read a card of Dr. Bailey's in the "Intelligencer," declaring his entire ignorance of the abduction of the slaves till they were returned.

Mr. Calhoun.—Does he make denunciation of the robbery?

Mr. Hale.—He had quite enough to do in defending himself, and it was no part of his duty to denounce others.

Mr. Calhoun.—I understand that.

Mr. Hale went on to refer to Mr. Foote's invitation of hanging in Mississippi, and would, in return for the hospitality, invite the senator to come to New Hampshire to discuss this whole subject, and he would there promise him protection and rights. He defended his bill as containing simply the plainest provisions of the common law; yet the South Carolina senator was shocked at his temerity.

Mr. Butler.—Will the senator vote for a bill, properly drawn, inflicting punishment on persons inveigling slaves from the District of Columbia?

Mr. Hale.—Certainly not; and why? Because I do not believe slavery should exist here.

Mr. Calhoun.—He wishes to arm the robbers and disarm the people of the district. . . . . . I will take this occasion to say, that I would just as soon argue with a maniac from Bedlam as with the senator from New Hampshire.

Mr. Hale went on calmly to reply to all these personalities by defending his bill. Mr. Foote again got the floor, and began to defend his threat of assassination. He never deplored the death of such men. The senator from New Hampshire will never be a victim. He is one of those gusty declaimers—a windy speaker—a ——

Mr. Crittenden.—I call the gentleman to order—and Mr. Foote was called to order by the presiding officer.

Later in the day, Mr. Douglas rose and congratulated Mr. Hale on the triumph he had achieved. The debate would give him ten thousand votes. He could never have represented a State on that floor but for such southern speeches as they had just listened to, breathing a fanaticism as wild and reckless as that of the senator from New Hampshire.

Mr. Calhoun.—Does the gentleman pretend to call me and those who act with me fanatics? We are only defending ourselves. The Illinois senator partially apologized. Mr. Foote was restive, however, and said that he must repeat his conviction, that any man who utters in the South the sentiments of the New

Hampshire senator, will meet with death upon the scaffold—and deserves it.

Mr. Douglas.—I must again congratulate the senator from New Hampshire upon the accession of five thousand more votes! and he is on for honors? Who can believe that *now* walks into the United States Senate, that such things could have been within so few years?

It would be easy to fill this volume with extracts from exciting and interesting debates in the Senate, in which Mr. Hale participated, but we have room only for a few paragraphs, to show his style and manner.

Jan. 19 and 21, 1857, Mr. Hale delivered one of his longest and ablest senatorial speeches upon Kansas and the Supreme Court. We subjoin a few extracts:

"I aver here that the object of the Nebraska bill was to break down the barrier which separated free territory from slave territory; to let slavery into Kansas, and make another slave state, legally and peacefully if you could, but a slave state anyhow. I gather that from the history of the times, from the character of the bill, from the measure, the great measure, the only measure of any consequence in the bill, which was the repeal of the Missouri restriction.

* * * * * *

"I say, then, sir, that the rule by which to judge of the intent, the object, the purpose of an act, is to see what the act is calculated to do, what its natural tendency is, what will in all human probability be the effect. Before the passage of the Kansas-Nebraska act, there stood upon your statute-book a law by which slavery was prohibited from going into any territory north of 36° 30′. The validity and constitutionality of that law had been recognized by repeated decisions of the courts of the several States. If I am not mistaken, I have a memorandum by me, showing that it had been recognized by the Supreme Court of the State of Louisiana. So far as I know, the constitutionality of that enactment was unquestioned, and the country had reposed in peace for more than a generation under its operation. By and by, however, it was discovered to be unconstitutional, and it was broken down. The instant it was broken down, slavery went into Kansas ; but still, gentlemen tell us they did not intend to let slavery in; that was not the object. Let me illustrate this. Suppose a farmer has a rich field, and a pasture adjoining, separated by a stonewall which his fathers had erected there thirty years before. The wall keeps out the cattle in the pasture, who are exceedingly anxious to get into the field. Some modern reformer thinks that moral suasion will keep them in the pasture, even if the wall should be taken down, and he proceeds to take it down. The result is, that the cattle go right in ; the experiment fails. The philosopher says ; 'Do not blame me ; that was not my intention ; but it is true, the effect has followed.' I retort upon him ; 'You knew the effect would follow ; and, knowing that it would follow, you intended that it should follow.'

* * * * * *

"This brings me to another part of my subject, in answer to a question which the honorable senator from Illinois (Mr. Douglas) propounded, when he asked if he was to be read out of the party for a difference on this point. I have great regard for the sagacity of that honorable senator, but I confess it was a little shaken when he asked that question ; is a man to be read out of the party for departing from the President on this great cardinal point ? Why, sir, he asks, is a man who differs from the President on the Pacific railroad to go out of the party ? Oh no, he may stay. If he differs on

Central America, very good; take the first seat if you please. You may differ with the President on anything and everything but one, and that is this sentiment, which I shall read; Mr. Buchanan shall speak his own creed. On the 19th of August 1842, in the Senate, Mr. Buchanan used this language:

" 'I might here repeat what I have said on a former occasion'—(you see it was so important he must repeat it)—'that all Christendom'—(mark the words)—'is leagued against the South upon this question of domestic slavery.'

"All Christendom includes a great many people. If that be true, and if you have got any allies, it is manifest they must be outside of Christendom, because Mr. Buchanan says all Christendom is against you; but still he leaves you some allies, and you will see—it is as plain as demonstration can make it—that your allies are not included in Christendom. Where are the allies? I will read the next sentence:

" 'They have no other allies to sustain their constitutional rights except the Democracy of the North.'

"There is a fight for you: all Christendom on one side, and the Democracy of the North on the other. That is not my version; it is Mr. Buchanan's. That is the way he backs his friends; for he went on, after having made this avowal, to claim peculiar consideration from southern gentlemen, and intimated that he might speak a little more freely, having previously indorsed them so highly as this. Well, sir, when all Christendom was on one side, and the Democracy of the North on the other, and the Democracy of the North growing less and less every day—a small minority in the New England States—how could the senator from Illinois be so unkind, or how could he doubt, if on this vital question he deserted the Democracy and went over to Christendom, as to how the question would be answered whether he was to be read out of the party? Read out, sir. That question was settled long ago. On this great vital question he is out of the party.

"I would not say anything unkind to that senator, nor would I say anything uncourteous in the world; but my experience in the country life of New England does present to my mind an illustration which I know he will excuse me if I give it. A neighbor of mine had a very valuable horse. The horse was taken sick, and he tried all the ways in the world to cure him, but it was of no avail. The horse grew worse daily. At last, one of his neighbors said: 'What are you going to do with the horse?' 'I do not know,' was the reply; 'but I think I shall have to kill him.' 'Well,' said the other, 'he does not want much killing.' You see, in ordinary times, and on ordinary questions, a little wavering might be indulged; but when it is on one question, and a great vital question, and all Christendom is on the one side, and the northern Democracy on the other, to go over from the ranks of the Democracy to swell the swollen ranks of Christendom, and then ask if he is to be read out!

"This omission to submit the constitution to the people of Kansas is not accidental. I am sorry to find, as I have found out this session, that the omission to put it in the original bill was not accidental. We have a little light on this subject from a gentleman who always sheds light when he speaks to the Senate—I mean the honorable senator from Pennsylvania [Mr. Bigler]. He says that this was not accidental, by any means. He has spoken once or twice about a meeting that was held in the private parlor of a private gentleman. There was a good deal of inquiry and anxiety to know what sort of a meeting that was. The gentleman who owns the house said he did not know anything about it. That is not strange. The hospitable man let his guests have the use of any room they chose. The honorable senator from Pennsylvania said this meeting was 'semi-official.' I do not know what kind of a meeting that was. I have heard of a semi-barbarous, a semi-civilized, and a semi-savage people ; I have heard of a semi-annual, and semi-weekly ; but when you come to semi-official, I declare it bothers me. What sort of a meeting was it ? Was it an official meeting ? No. Was it an unofficial meeting ? No. What was it ? Semi-official.

"I have never met anything analogous to it but once in my life, and that I will mention by way of illustration. A trader in my town, before the day of railroads, had taken a large bank bill, and he was a little doubtful whether it was genuine or not. He concluded to give it to the stage driver, and send it down to the bank to inquire of the cashier whether it was a genuine bill. The driver took it, and promised to attend to it. He went down the first day, but he had so many other errands that he forgot it, and he said he would certainly attend to it the next day. The next day he forgot it, and the third day he forgot it ; but he said, 'to-morrow I will do it, if I do nothing else ; I will ascertain whether the bill is genuine or not.' He went the fourth day, with a like result ; he forgot it ; and when he came home, he saw the nervous, anxious trader, wanting to know whether it was genuine or not ; and he was ashamed to tell him he had forgotten it, and he thought he would lie it through. Said the trader to him, 'Did you call at the bank ?' 'Yes.' 'Did the cashier say it was a genuine bill ?' 'No, he did not.' 'Did he say it was a bad one ?' 'No.' 'Well, what did he say ?' 'He said it was about middling—semi-genuine.' I have never learned to this day whether that was a good or a bad bill. They used to say, in General Jackson's time, that he had a kitchen cabinet as well as a regular one. This could not be a meeting of the kitchen cabinet, because it sat in a parlor. It was semi-official in its character also."

The speech closes with the following language in

reference to the Dred Scott decision of the Supreme Court:

"If the opinions of the Supreme Court are true, they put these men in the worst position of any men who are to be found on the pages of our history. If the opinion of the Supreme Court be true, it makes the immortal authors of the Declaration of Independence liars before God and hypocrites before the world; for they lay down their sentiments broad, full, and explicit, and then they say that they appeal to the Supreme Ruler of the universe for the rectitude of their intentions; but, if you believe the Supreme Court, they were merely quibbling on words. They went into the courts of the Most High, and pledged fidelity to their principles as the price they would pay for success; and now it is attempted to cheat them out of the poor boon of integrity; and it is said that they did not mean so; and that when they said all men, they meant all white men; and when they said that the contest they waged was for the right of mankind, the Supreme Court of the United States would have you believe that they meant it was to establish slavery. Against that I protest, here, now, and everywhere; and I tell the Supreme Court that these things are so impregnably fixed in the hearts of the people, on the page of history, in the recollections and traditions of men, that it will require mightier efforts than they have made or can make to overturn or to shake these settled convictions of the popular understanding and of the popular heart.

"Sir, you are now proposing to carry out this Dred Scott decision by forcing upon the people of Kansas a constitution against which they have remonstrated, and to which, there can be no shadow of doubt, a very large portion of them are opposed. Will it succeed? I do not know; it is not for me to say, but I will say this, if you force that, if you persevere in that attempt, I think, I hope the men of Kansas will fight.

I hope they will resist to blood and to death the attempt to force them to a submission against which their fathers contended, and to which they never would have submitted. Let me tell you, sir, I stand not here to use the language of intimidation or of menace; but you kindle the fires of civil war in that country by an attempt to force that constitution on the necks of an unwilling people; and you will light a fire that all Democracy cannot quench. Aye, sir, there will come up many another Peter the Hermit, that will go through the length and the breadth of this land, telling the story of your wrongs and your outrages; and they will stir the public heart; they will raise a feeling in this country such as has never yet been raised; and the men of this country will go forth, as they did of olden time, in another crusade; but it will not be a crusade to redeem the dead sepulchre where the body of the Crucified had lain from the profanation of the infidel, but to redeem this fair land, which God has given to be the abode of freemen, from the desecration of a despotism sought to be imposed upon them in the name of 'perfect freedom' and 'popular sovereignty.'"

ALEXANDER H. STEPHENS.

Mr. Stephens, of Georgia, has for years been a leading character in the politics of the country, and has been reckoned by all who know him, or of his acts in Congress, as one of the first men which the South has sent into public life. He is a native of Georgia, where he was born in the year 1812. His grandfather, the Hon. Alexander Stephens, was an Englishman and Jacobite, and came to this country about the year 1746. He joined the American Colonial army—was present at Braddock's defeat, and took a very active part in the Revolutionary War, and settled down, after it was over, in Pennsylvania. In 1795, he emigrated to Georgia, and finally settled down on the place now occupied by his grandson—the subject of this sketch—in Taliaferro County. He died on this place, in 1813, at the age of ninety-three. The year before, young Alexander was born, his mother dying while he was an infant. His father was comparatively poor, but was industrious and virtuous, so that he maintained a high reputation in the town of his birth. He died when Alexander was only fourteen years of age, leaving each of his children a trifle over four hundred dollars as their portion. Alexander was sickly and emaciated, and little was hoped of him. He had attended a common school in the neighborhood, and his uncle kept him still in attendance upon it. Of course this school was a very inferior one, not at all equal to one of the common schools of New England. But the boy learned enough there to excite his ambition, and he made known his desire to gain a classical education. He was without sufficient funds, but generous friends immediately came forward and furnished him with all the money he needed, which he would only accept as a loan. He now went to his studies alone, and in less than a year, without a teacher, fitted himself for a freshman class, and entered the Georgia University. After the usual four years' course, he graduated with unusually high honors. Having been an invalid since his birth, the severe application of his college course left him in a state of great prostration, and he was obliged to leave his studies and travel for his health. In May, 1834, he commenced the study of the law, and he was soon admitted to the bar. His first "case" was an action against a landlord for a stolen trunk—the trunk being his own. He gained his case and trunk easily. The next was a very important one. "A wealthy man was guardian of his grandchild, its mother having married to a second husband. In course of time, the mother desired possession of the child, which was resisted by the grandfather, who claimed it as legal guardian. The step-father, desiring to please his wife, came to young Stephens and engaged him as counsel to set aside the guardianship, older lawyers declining on the score of the hopelessness of the case, and perhaps a fear to encounter the learned array of counsel engaged on the opposite side. The trial came off before five judges, no jury being called. Owing to the respectability of the parties, and the novel scene of a sickly boy, without any legal practical experience, opposed to the most veteran lawyers at the bar, the case attracted unusual attention. The result was, that the guardianship was set aside, and the child was restored to the possession of its mother, and young Stephens at once took a prominent place at the bar, from that time, being engaged on one side or the other of every important case that was tried in the county."

Mr. Stephens' success was now so marked that he was sought after to remove to some prominent city, but he refused, preferring to remain with his old friends, and he was in a few years able, out of his earnings, to purchase his grandfather's estate, and settled upon it. The subjoined political sketch of Mr. Stephens is by one of his personal friends—Mr. Thorpe—and is in the main correct:

"In 1836, against his wishes, Mr. Stephens was

run by his friends for the legislature. On the Wednesday before the election he made his first stump-speech—this was followed by another on Saturday, and still another at the polls on election day. He was triumphantly returned against a bitter opposition. He signalized his appearance as a legislator in defence of the bill which proposed 'that Georgia should launch out in certain internal improvements,' and in spite of the formidable opposition, his speech probably saved the bill, and thus inaugurated the commencement of the present prosperity of the 'Empire State of the South.' In the six years which he remained in the legislature he took a most prominent part in all important matters, particularly the one which proposed a change in the Constitution. The instrument at the time in force said that it should only be amended by a bill passed by two-thirds of each branch of the legislature at two consecutive sessions.

"The difficulty seemed insurmountable, if opposition to a change existed in either branch of the legislature, and the opponents of the bill appeared to be impregnable. Stephens took the ground that when the constitution is silent upon the mode of its amendment, then the legislature can call a convention; that when a constitution points out a particular mode in which it may be amended, without excluding other modes, then the legislature may adopt some other mode than that pointed out; but when a constitution provides a mode for its amendment, and prohibits all other modes, then that mode only can be taken which is provided for. Jenkins, Crawford, Howard, and others, took the opposite side, opposed the bill, and voted for a convention; the universal opinion was that the convention could be called, and the convention was called by an overwhelming majority, which passed the proper amendments, but they were never ratified by the people.

"As a member of the legislature, he opposed the organization of the Court of Errors, believing that the judiciary as established was the best in the world, and that the change would only multiply difficulties, without gaining any additional certainty to the administration of the law; the bill was not passed while Mr. Stephens was in the legislature.

"In 1842, he went to the State Senate, opposed the Central Bank, and took an active part in the questions of internal improvements and districting the State, which then divided parties.

"In 1843, he was nominated for Congress, on a general ticket, and commenced the canvass with a majority of two thousand votes against him, and came out of the contest with thirty-five hundred majority; and as he discussed on the stump matters entirely relating to local interests, his eloquence and power undoubtedly carried the State. His entry into Congress was signalized by extraordinary circumstances; his right to a seat was denied. Stephens, in the discussion that ensued, made a speech in favor of the power of Congress to district the States, though he was elected in defiance of the law on a general ticket, and then left the House to decide upon his claims. He was permitted to take his seat.

"Up to this time Mr. Stephens was a prominent Whig, having been bred in that school of States' rights men of the South who sustained Harrison in 1840; but upon the question of the annexation of Texas coming up, he favored that bill, and for the first time affiliated with the Democracy. In the contest between Taylor and Cass, he supported Taylor. On the compromises of 1850, he was willing to support any measure that did away with Congressional restriction, leaving the territories to come into the Union with or without slavery. In the Mexican war, he stood beside Mr. Calhoun, and held that the troops should not be advanced; but after the war commenced, he sustained it with vigor.

"The guaranty that four slave States should be carved out of the territory of Texas was secured mainly by Mr. Stephens' untiring labor and foresight. In 1854, he advocated the Kansas bill, which declared null and void the Missouri restriction, for the purpose of carrying out the principle of 1850, advanced in the Utah and New Mexican bills. The year 1855 was the most interesting and critical period of his life, which he spent fighting the Know Nothing organization, in the commencement of which he found all his early friends and associates for the first time opposed to him. In the month of May, of this year, he wrote his celebrated letter against the order, addressed to Col. Thos. W. Thomas. The effect of it was overwhelming, not only in his own State, but in Virginia and the adjoining States. His position was sustained, and commencing with three thousand majority against him in his own district, he came out of the contest with nearly three thousand majority.

"When Mr. Stephens rises to speak there is a sort of electric communication among the audience, as if something was about to be uttered that was worth listening to. The loungers take their seats, and the talkers become silent, thus paying an involuntary compliment to Mr. Stephens' talents and high claims as a gentleman. At first his voice is scarcely distinguishable, but in a few moments you are surprised at its volume, and you are soon convinced that his lungs are in perfect order, and as his ideas flow, you are not surprised at the rapt attention he commands. His style of speaking is singularly polished, but he conceals his art, and appears, to the superficial observer, to be eloquent by inspiration. The leading characteristic of his mind is great practical good sense, for his arguments are always of the most solid and logical kind ; hence his permanent influence as a statesman, while his bright scintillations of wit, and profuse adornment, secure him a constant popularity as an orator. Possessed of a mind too great to be restrained by mere partisan influence, he has therefore the widest possible field of action, at one time heading a forlorn hope and leading it to victory, at another, giving grace and character to a triumphant majority. Common as it is to impugn the motives of many of our public servants, and charge them directly with corruption, Mr. Stephens has escaped without even the taint of suspicion, an inflexible honesty of purpose on his part, as a governing principle, is awarded to him by his veriest political foe."

Mr. Stephens' position in Georgia, in reference to calling a convention to frame a new constitution, is not very distinctly stated by Mr. Thorpe. A bill was introduced into the legislature providing for the calling of a convention to remodel the State constitution. Mr. Stephens opposed the bill because the constitution, as it then stood, provided that *only* by a two-thirds vote of both branches of the legislature, at two consecutive sessions, could any amendment be put upon the constitution. Mr. Stephens argued that, under these circumstances, it would be revolutionary to pass the bill calling a convention. But the bill passed—and a convention submitted various amendments to the people, all of which were repealed. Since then Mr. Stephens' views have been generally adopted by the people of Georgia, for the constitution has been amended in the mode pointed out in that document itself. Since then, too, Mr. Stephens' position has been sustained by the Supreme Court of the United States in the Dorr case.

We have noticed the fact that Mr. Stephens, when young and poor, was furnished with the means to procure an excellent classical and legal education. He repaid this money to the parties who so generously aided him when help was of so much importance to his welfare. Not only this: since he has himself been so successful, Mr. Stephens has been constantly engaged in helping poor young men to an education. He has carried *upward of thirty* young men through a collegiate or academic course within the last fifteen or twenty years, and has, in this way, repaid the generosity of his friends to him. This single incident will show what his character is for generosity.

Mr. Stephens is one of the most effective public speakers in the country, whether it be in the court-room, the legislative hall, or before the people. During the last Congress he was the leader of the Democracy in the House of Representatives, and by his management secured the admission of Oregon into the Union. Perhaps the finest speech he ever made in Congress was the closing one in the Oregon debate. We subjoin a few quotations.

One in reference to the anti-negro clause of the Oregon constitution :

"And those who profess to be the exclusive friends of negroes, as they now do, so far as that constitution was concerned, voted to banish them forever from the State, just as Oregon has done. Whether this banishment be right or wrong, it is no worse in Oregon than it was in Kansas. But, on the score of humanity, we of the South do not believe that those who, in Kansas or Oregon, banish this race from their limits, are better friends of the negro than we are, who assign them that place among us to which by nature they are fitted, and in which they add so much more to their own happiness and comfort, besides to the common well-being of all. We give them a reception. We give them shelter. We clothe them. We feed them. We provide for their every want, in health and in sickness, in infancy and old age. We teach them to work. We educate them in the arts of civilization and the virtues of Christianity, much more effectually and successfully than you can ever do on the coasts of Africa. And, without any cost to the public, we render them useful to themselves and to the world. The first lesson in civilization and Christianity to be taught to the barbarous tribes, wherever to be found, is the first great curse against the human family—that in the sweat of their face they shall eat their bread. Under our system, our tuition, our guardianship and fostering care, these people, exciting so much misplaced philanthropy, have attained a higher degree of civilization than their race has attained anywhere else upon the face of the earth. The Topeka people excluded them ; they, like the neighbors we read of, went round them; we, like the good Samaritans, shun not their destitution or degradation—we alleviate both. But let that go.

"Oregon has, in this matter, done no worse than the gentleman's friends did in Kansas. *I think she acted unwisely in it*—that is her business, not mine. But the gentleman from Ohio [Mr. Stanton] questions me, how could a negro in Oregon ever get his freedom under the constitution they have adopted? I tell him, under their constitution a slave cannot exist there. The fundamental law is against it. But, he asks, how could his freedom ever be established, as no free person of color can sue in her courts? Neither can they in Georgia; still our courts are open to this class of people, who appear by *prochein ami* or guardian. Nor is there any great hardship in this; for married women cannot sue in their own names anywhere where the common law prevails. Minors also have to sue by guardian or next friend. We have suits continually in our tribunals by persons claiming to be free persons of color. They cannot sue in their own names, but by next friend. They are not citizens; we do not recognize them as such; but still the courts are open; and just so will they be in Oregon, if the question is ever raised."

The closing portions of the speech give such a good idea of the style of Mr. Stephens' oratorical powers, that we must quote them:

"Let us not do an indirect wrong, for fear that the recipient from our hands of what is properly due will turn upon us and injure us. Statesmen in the line of duty should never consult their fears. Where duty leads, there we may never fear to tread. In the political world, great events and changes are rapidly crowding upon us. To these we should not be insensible. As wise men, we should not attempt to ignore them. We need not close our eyes, and suppose the sun will cease to shine because we see not the light. Let us rather, with eyes and mind wide awake, look around us and see where we are, whence we have come, and where we shall soon be, borne along by the rapid, swift, and irresistible car of time. This immense territory to the west has to be peopled. It is now peopling. New States are fast growing up; and others, not yet in embryo, will soon spring into existence. Progress and development mark everything in nature—human societies, as well as everything else. Nothing in the physical world is still; life and motion are in everything; so in the mental, moral, and political. The earth is never still. The great central orb is ever moving. Progress is the universal law governing all things—animate as well as inanimate. Death itself is but the beginning of a new life in a new form. Our government and institutions are subject to this all-pervading power. The past wonderfully exemplifies its influence, and gives us some shadows of the future.

"This is the sixteenth session that I have been here, and within that brief space of fifteen years, we have added six States to the Union—lacking but one of being more than half the original thirteen. Upward of twelve hundred thousand square miles of territory—a much larger area than was possessed by the whole United States at the time of the treaty of peace in 1783—have been added to our domain. At this time the area of our Republic is greater than that of any five of the greatest powers in Europe all combined; greater than that of the Roman empire in the brightest days of her glory; more extensive than were Alexander's dominions when he stood on the Indus, and wept that he had no more worlds to conquer. Such is our present position; nor are we yet at the end of our acquisitions.

"Our internal movements, within the same time, have not been less active in progress and development than those external. A bare glance at these will suffice. Our tonnage, when I first came to Congress, was but a little over two million ; now it is upward of five million, more than double. Our exports of domestic manufactures were only eleven million dollars in round numbers ; now they are upward of thirty million. Our exports of domestic produce, staples, etc., were then under one hundred million dollars ; now they are upward of three hundred million! The amount of coin in the United States, was at that time about one hundred million ; now it exceeds three hundred million. The cotton crop then was but fifty-four million ; now it is upward of one hundred and sixty million dollars. We had then not more than five thousand miles miles of railroad in operation ; we have now not less than twenty-six thousand miles—more than enough to encircle the globe—and at a cost of more than one thousand million dollars. At that time, Prof. Morse was engaged in one of the rooms of this Capitol in experimenting on his unperfected idea of an electric telegraph—and there was as much doubt about his success, as there is at present about the Atlantic cable ; but now there are more than thirty-five thousand miles in extent of these iron nerves sent forth in every direction through the land, connecting the most distant points, and uniting all together as if under the influence of a common living sensorium. This is but a glance at the surface ; to enter within and take the range of other matters—schools, colleges, the arts, and various mechanical and industrial pursuits, which add to the intelligence, wealth and prosperity of a people, and mark their course in the history of nations, would require time ; but in all would be found alike astonishing results.

"This progress, sir, is not to be arrested. It will go on. The end is not yet. There are persons now living who will see over a hundred million human beings within the present boundaries of the United States, to say nothing of future extension, and perhaps double the number of States we now have, should the Union last. For myself, I say to you, my southern colleagues on this floor, that I do not apprehend danger to our constitutional rights from the bare fact of increasing the number of States with institutions dissimilar to ours. The whole governmental fabric of the United States is based and founded upon the idea of dissimilarity in the institutions of the respective members. Principles, not numbers, are our protection. When these fail, we have like all other people, who, knowing their rights, dare maintain them, nothing to rely upon but the justice of our cause, our own right arms and stout hearts. With these feelings and this basis of action, whenever any State comes and asks admission, as Oregon does, I am prepared to extend her the hand of welcome, without looking into her constitution further than to see that it is republican in form, upon our well-known American models.

"When aggression comes, if come it ever shall, then the end draweth nigh. Then, if in my day, I shall be for resistance, open, bold, and defiant. I know of no allegiance superior to that due the hearthstones of the homestead. This I say to all. I lay no claim to any sentiment of nationality not founded upon the patriotism of a true heart, and I know of no such patriotism that does not centre at home. Like the enlarging circle upon the surface of smooth waters, however, this can and will, if unobstructed, extend to the utmost limits of a common country. Such is my nationality—such my sectionalism—such my patriotism. Our fathers of the South joined your fathers of the North in resistance to a common aggression from their fatherland ; and if they were justified in rising to right a wrong inflicted by a parent country, how much more ought we, should the necessity ever come, to stand justified before an enlightened world, in righting a wrong from even those we call brothers. That necessity, I trust, will never come.

"What is to be our future, I do not know. I have no taste for indulging in speculations about it. I would not, if I could, raise the veil that wisely conceals it from us.

'Sufficient unto the day is the evil thereof,' is a good precept in everything pertaining to human action. The evil I would not anticipate; I would rather strive to prevent its coming; and one way, in my judgment, to prevent it, is, while here, in all things to do what is right and proper to be done under the Constitution of the United States; nothing more, and nothing less. Our safety, as well as the prosperity of all parts of the country, so long as this government lasts, lies mainly in a strict conformity to the laws of its existence. Growth is one of these. The admission of new States, is one of the objects expressly provided for. How are they to come in? With just such constitutions as the people in each may please to make for themselves, so it is republican in form. This is the ground the South has ever stood upon. Let us not abandon it now. It is founded upon a principle planted in the compact of Union itself; and more essential to us than all others besides; that is, the equality of the States, and the reserved rights of the people of the respective States. By our system, each State, however great the number, has the absolute right to regulate all its internal affairs as she pleases, subject only to her obligations under the Constitution of the United States. With this limitation, the people of Massachusetts have the perfect right to do as they please upon all matters relating to their internal policy; the people of Ohio have the right to do the same; the people of Georgia the same; of California the same; and so with all the rest.

"Such is the machinery of our theory of self-government by the people. This is the great novelty of our peculiar system, involving a principle unknown to the ancients, an idea never dreamed of by Aristotle or Plato. The union of several distinct, independent communities upon this basis, is a new principle in human governments. It is now a problem in experiment for the people of the nineteenth century upon this continent to solve. As I behold its workings in the past and at the present, while I am not sanguine, yet I am hopeful of its successful solution. The most joyous feeling of my heart is the earnest hope that it will, for the future, move on as peacefully, prosperously, and brilliantly, as it has in the past. If so, then we shall exhibit a moral and political spectacle to the world something like the prophetic vision of Ezekiel, when he saw a number of distinct beings or living creatures, each with a separate and distinct organism, having the functions of life within itself, all of one external likeness, and all, at the same time, mysteriously connected with one common animating spirit pervading the whole, so that when the common spirit moved they all moved; their appearance and their work being, as it were, a wheel in the middle of a wheel; and whithersoever the common spirit went, thither the others went, all going together; and when they went, he heard the noise of their motion like the noise of great waters, as the voice of the Almighty. Should our experiment succeed, such will be our exhibition—a machinery of government so intricate, so complicated, with so many separate and distinct parts, so many independent States, each perfect in the attributes and functions of sovereignty, within its own jurisdiction, all, nevertheless, united under the control of a common directing power for external objects and purposes, may natural enough seem novel, strange, and inexplicable to the philosophers and crowned heads of the world.

"It is for us, and those who shall come after us, to determine whether this grand experimental problem shall be worked out; not by quarrelling amongst ourselves; not by doing injustice to any; not by keeping out any particular class of States, but by each State remaining a separate and distinct political organism within itself—all bound together for general objects, and under a common Federal head; as it were, a wheel within a wheel. Then the number may be multiplied without limit; and then, indeed, may the nations of the earth look on in wonder at our career; and when they hear the noise of the wheels of our progress in achievement, in development, in expansion, in glory and renown, it may well appear to them not unlike the noise of great waters; the very voice of the Almighty—*Vox populi! Vox Dei!* (Great applause in the galleries and on the floor.)

"THE SPEAKER.—If the applause in the galleries is repeated, the chair will order the galleries to be cleared.

"MANY MEMBERS.—It was upon the floor.

"MR. STEPHENS, of Georgia. One or two other matters only I wish to allude to. These relate only to amendments. I trust that every friend of this bill will unite and vote down every amendment. It needs no amendment. Oregon has nothing to do with Kansas, and should in no way be connected with her. To remand her back, as the gentleman from Kentucky (Mr. Marshall) proposes, to compel her to regulate suffrage as we may be disposed to dictate, would be but going back to the old attempt to impose conditions upon Missouri. There is no necessity for any census if we are satisfied, from all the evidence before us, that there are sixty thousand inhabitants there. Florida was admitted without a census. Texas was admitted, with two members on this floor without a census. So was California.

"To our friends upon this side of the house, let me say, if you cannot vote for the bill, assist us in having it voted upon as it is. Put on no riders. Give us no side-blows. Aid in keeping them off. Let the measure stand or fall upon its merits. If you cannot vote for the bill, vote against it just as it stands.

"I see my time is nearly out, and I cannot go into the discussion of other branches of the question; but may I not make an appeal to all sides of the house to come up to do their duty to-day? I have spoken of the rapid development of our country and its progress in all its material resources. Is it true that the intellectual and moral development of our country has not kept pace with its physical? Has our political body outgrown the heads and hearts of those who are to govern it? Is it so, that this thirty-fifth Congress is unequal to the great mission before it! Are we progressing in everything but mind and patriotism? Has destiny cast upon us a heavier load of duty than we are able to perform? Are we unequal to the task assigned us? I trust not. I know it is sometimes said in the country that Congress has degenerated. It is for us this day to show whether it is true or not. For myself, I do not believe it. It may be that the *esprit de corps* may have some influence on my judgment. Something may be pardoned to that. But still I feel that I address men of as much intelligence, reflection, talent, integrity, virtue and worth, as I have ever met in this hall; men not unfit to be the Representatives of this great, growing and prosperous Confederacy. The only real fitness for any public station is to be up to the requirements of the occasion, whatever that be. Let us, then, vindicate our characters as fit legislators to-day; and, with that dignity and decorum which have so signally marked our proceedings upon other great, exciting questions before, and which, whatever may be said of our debates, may be claimed as a distinguished honor for the present House of Representatives, let us do the work assigned us with that integrity of purpose which discharges duty regardless of consequences, and with a patriotism commensurate with the magnitude of the subject under all its responsibilities."

Mr. Stephens took very decided ground in favor of the Lecompton bill in 1857–8, and when that was likely to fail in favor of the English Compromise. He is also, while a Union man, very much in sympathy with the Southern Rights school of politicians, and has made two or three speeches in defence of filibusterism in the house. He has not entirely forgotten that he was once a Whig, for last winter he spoke in favor of, and supported heartily the French Spoliation bill. He is a very fair political opponent, doing everything in an open and frank manner, but a very shrewd tactician. He has rarely allowed himself to be led into excited, partisan or sectional speeches, and, therefore, has long been looked upon in Congress as an admirable party manager.

N. P. BANKS.

Few men in the country have, in these latter days of politics, been so uniformly successful, even when circumstances were untoward, as Governor Banks. He is known by the people as *a lucky man*. He succeeds in whatever he undertakes. He has risen from an obscure young man to be Speaker of the National House of Representatives, and Governor of one of the first States of the Union. What may not such a man expect if he be ambitious?

Mr. Banks was born in Waltham, Mass., January 30, 1816, where he received a common school education. At a very early age he was placed to work in a cotton-mill, in his native town, as a common hand. His father was an overseer in the same mill. Here he remained for some time, but not liking the business left the mill, and learned the trade of machinist. While thus engaged, a strolling theatrical company passed through Waltham, and young Banks was so much taken with their acting, that he learned to perform several parts himself. He succeeded so well that a tempting offer was made to him to follow the fortunes of the company. He was sufficiently wise to refuse the offer. There can be no doubt that to this dramatic corps Mr. Banks owes much of his after success. They taught him much of that gracefulness which, to this day, distinguishes him as an orator and a presiding officer.

Banks now joined a village lyceum and made himself a ready speaker—then delivered temperance speeches, and at last drifted into politics as a Democrat. He edited a village paper in Waltham, a Democratic paper, and Mr. Polk gave him an office in the Boston Custom House. In attending political meetings, Mr. Banks often acted as presiding officer, and it was soon discovered that he possessed a remarkable talent for such a post. In 1849, Mr. Banks was elected to the Massachusetts House of Representatives, and put himself down in the list of members as a "machinist." The very next year he turned to the law—in 1851 was chosen Speaker of the State Legislature, and was a prominent advocate of the coalition between the Democrats and Free Soilers. This was his first step out of the Democratic party toward Republicanism. The next year he was reëlected speaker, and in the autumn was elected to Congress. While in Congress, during his first term, he voted against the Kansas-Nebraska bill, though he was one of those Democrats who *voted to take the bill up*, a movement which insured its final success.

In 1854, Mr. Banks was taken up by the Americans and Republicans, and sent again to Congress, where, after a memorable *two months'* contest, yet fresh in the reader's memory, he was elected Speaker of the House of Representatives. No man has ever surpassed, if one has ever equalled him, as a speaker of that turbulent body, and he left the post with the highest honors. He was reëlected to Congress, but after taking his seat and remaining a month at Washington, he resigned it to assume the governorship of Massachusetts, to which office the people of the State had elected him by a tremendous majority.

He was reëlected in the fall of 1858 by a heavy majority, and at this time fills the Governor's chair. This, in a few words, is Governor Bank's political career. As a politician, he has shown himself shrewd, as a presiding officer prompt, graceful, commanding, and as an administrator, a governor, he has proved himself to be a man of rare genius. This, in fact, is Governor Bank's *forte.* He has a genius *for governing men*—that most rare of all gifts. He cannot be said to have made a political blunder in his life, speaking after the fashion of political men.

It is of great importance to the people what are the *political opinions* of such a man as Governor Banks. But he is so cautious, so reticent, that upon some points it is difficult to state his exact position. In a letter, addressed by Mr. Banks to the Republican Convention of Worcester—in the fall of 1857,

Mr. Banks states his opinions upon some of the prominent questions of the day. We will make a few extracts:

"My opinions upon all questions relating to the General Government of the States, have been made public during my connection with an office from which I have been but recently relieved, and also by my course in the late Presidential canvass. I resisted the repeal of the Missouri Compromise, and I am still opposed to that measure, as I am to all acts of the late and present administration, whether of an executive, legislative, or judicial character, which have been devised to maintain or to perpetuate the original purpose of that flagitious wrong; and I shall earnestly advocate the admission of Kansas into the Union of States, under its own charter of freedom. I am opposed to the further extension of slavery, or to the increase of its political power. I believe that the Constitution confers upon Congress sovereign power over the territories of the United States for their government; and that, in the exercise of its authority, it is its duty to prohibit slavery or polygamy therein. I shall support the most energetic measures which the Constitution admits, for the development of the moral and material interests of the American people, defend the sovereignty of the States against executive or judicial encroachment, and contribute all in my power for the restoration of the General Government to the principles of the fathers of the Constitution and the Union.

"I am opposed to the recent decision of the Supreme Court of the United States, not only upon the ground that it controverts the principles and overthrows all the precedents of our history upon the subject of slavery, but that it assumes to decide, as a judicial problem, the question whether slavery shall be established in this State, which has been, and ought to be, left as a political question for the people of the State to determine for themselves.

"It is pleasant for us at all times to recall the traditions of our fathers, to repeat their affirmation of principles, which seem to us to be self-evident truths, and which were announced to the world by men who were ready and able to support them in council, and to defend them in the field. But it is a pleasure that cannot be enjoyed apart from the conviction that it is for us an equal, if not a higher duty, vigilantly to course every means that will tend to insure and perpetuate their supremacy, on this continent at least. If it shall hereafter appear that our Government has departed therefrom, and joined itself to other and false political doctrines, I trust that it may never be said of the people of Massachusetts, that an unreasonable refusal of minor concessions, or their immaterial diversities of opinions—always the bane of republics—gave success and perpetual power to their opponents. No one can doubt that a vast majority of the people of the United States are opposed to the policy represented by the slavery propagandists; and still less can we doubt that it is their diversity of opinion in non-essentials that encourages the Government with hopes of success, and constantly defeats the purposes of the people. It is no less a shame for us, under such circumstances, to admit our incapacity to maintain our principles, than to acknowledge a defection from the faith of our fathers.

"In our age, with our lights, success is a duty. The graves of the past proclaim that failure must be the fault of the people, and not of their cause. But there will be no permanent failure. There was never a more auspicious hour for the friends of freedom than the present. To whatever policy the Government may now devote its energies, political power must soon fall into new hands. And when power shall pass into the hands of the young men of this age, I can entertain no doubt that, like the young men of a past age, to whom Jefferson appealed, and who were his constant supporters in the great battles of his day, for the suppression of the slave trade, and the ultimate supremacy of Liberty in the early councils of our people, they will give renewed life to a national policy of freedom, traditional and true, which must be the basis of all moral or material prosperity, and which is dictated alike by conscience and common sense. I rejoice with an inward joy, that the young men of Massachusetts, as it were by spontaneous movement, and with a true appreciation of their duty and power, have assumed a position and unfurled a flag that will be hailed in other States as a harbinger of a better age—a radiant star, that shall lead to new and decisive victories for the good old cause.

"The affairs of our State demand no less our attention. There is now an unusually favorable opportunity for the initiation of political changes of great importance, which cannot fail to be acceptable to all classes of people. Of these, restricted sessions of the legislature, and heavy retrenchment in State expenditures, are of lasting importance. Our people, constantly engaged in pursuits of commerce, manufactures, mechanic arts, and agriculture, have a right to demand of the Government that it shall meet, without evasion, the necessities of the time, and enable them, without following the constant changes of partisanship, to hold their servants to an immediate and direct responsibility."

It is not easy to say how closely Mr. Banks has been connected with Americanism in Massachusetts. It is very certain that he *used* Americanism, and that he guided it, but to what extent he has adopted, at any time, its doctrines, we cannot say. It has been said that Mr. Banks was opposed to the "Two Years'

Amendment" recently adopted by the voters of Massachusetts, but he failed to show his hand upon it one way or the other. The Americans, we believe, claim that Mr. Banks is one of them in principle, but upon what grounds we know not.

Mr. Banks, though formerly a Democrat, is understood to be in favor of a moderately protective tariff. He is, as the extracts we have quoted show, decidedly opposed to the extension of slavery, but does not occupy, as an opponent of slavery, such advanced ground as that upon which Mr. Seward stands. He is opposed to agitation upon the slavery question, except in self-defence, while Mr. Seward is for battle, open and decided, but constitutional, till slavery is driven from the continent.

JOSEPH LANE.

Gen. Lane occupies a somewhat prominent position before the country in reference to the Presidency. Not because he professes to be a leading statesman of the country, for it is but recently that he has become a national legislator, or participated, to any great extent, in national politics. But possibly for this very reason many eyes are turned toward him as a fit subject for the suffrages of the Charleston convention.

Joseph Lane is a native of North Carolina, and was born December 14, 1801. In 1804 his father removed his family to Kentucky, and in 1816 young Joseph crossed the Ohio, and entered a store in Warwick County, Indiana. What his opportunities were, in early life, for education, we do not learn, but that they were slight cannot be doubted—a common school education being all that was within his reach. The rest he procured for himself in the wide school of the world.

For several years Lane followed a mercantile life, marrying early, and changing his residence to Vanderberg County. He first tried the paths of public life as a member of the Indiana legislature, the people of Warwick and Vanderberg counties liking him so well that they invited him to become their representative in the State legislature. He proved himself to be a capable, and, indeed, popular legislator, so much so, that his constituents kept him in the Senate or House of Representatives of the State, off and on, for more than twenty years. He was always in the legislature a manager, rather than a talker. He has never claimed the title of orator, for he was not bred to it, nor ever had an aptness for it. But he showed at once that he possessed a genius for legislation, and was kept constantly by the people at the business. In the Indiana legislature, he strenuously opposed the project of repudiation which, in the dark days of Indiana, was supported by many of her citizens and politicians. His independent course against the proposed measure of dishonor, was all that saved the State from the terrible step, and this fact is generally admitted by her people, irrespective of their politics.

The military career of Gen. Lane now began, and is sketched by one of his friends in the following language:

"In the Mexican war, Gen. Lane was among the first to respond to the call for volunteers, by enlisting as a private in the 2d Indiana regiment, of which he was subsequently elected colonel. He, however, took the field with the rank of brigadier general, having been commissioned by President Polk, at the solicitation of the Indiana Congressional delegation. His subsequent conduct fully justified this honor. Soon after reaching Mexico, he was appointed by General Butler civil and military governor of Saltillo, but after the battle of Monterey, received orders to join General Taylor with his brigade. He was first under fire at the terrible battle of Buena Vista, on the 22d and 23d of February, 1847, and particularly distinguished himself in the furious encounters of the second day. With a command reduced to 400 men, by details sent to check a flank movement of Santa Anna, General Lane maintained the position he occupied against an attack of 6,000 Mexicans. It appears almost incredible that he was enabled to roll back such an overwhelming force. When Santa Anna made his last desperate attack on the Illinois and Kentucky regiments, General Lane, at a critical moment, hastened to their support, and his timely aid enabled the column to reform and return to the contest, and thus contributed largely to the victory that crowned the American arms. In September, 1847, General Lane was transferred to Scott's line. On the 20th of September he took up his line of march for the capital at the head of a column of volunteers, including some horse, and two pieces of artillery, and amounting in all to about 2,500 men. On the way,

Major Lally joined him with 1,000 men, and at Jalapa his force was further augmented by a company of mounted riflemen, two companies of infantry (volunteers), and two pieces of artillery. At this time the gallant Colonel Childs, U. S. A., was holding out Puebla, against a siege conducted by Santa Anna in person. Foiled in this effort, the Mexican general moved toward Huamantla, with the purpose of attacking General Lane's column in the rear, simultaneously with another attack from the direction of Puebla. But General Lane, who, throughout the campaign, exhibited the highest military qualities, penetrated the design of the enemy, and leaving a detachment to guard the wagon trains, diverged from the main road and marched on to Huamantla, which he reached on the 9th of October. The Mexicans, dismayed at his unexpected appearance, hung out white flags, and the Americans began to enter the city.

"The treacherous Mexicans, however, opened a fire on his advanced guard, under Captain Walker, and a terrible contest took place in the plaza. General Lane, in the meanwhile, was engaged with the reinforcement brought up under Santa Anna; but after a furious battle, the Americans were victorious, and the stars and stripes waved in triumph over Huamantla. The remains of the Mexican force fell back on Atlixo, where they were rallied and reinforced by General Rea. General Lane, coming up after a long and fatiguing march, found the enemy strongly posted on a hill-side about a mile and a half from the town, and immediately gave them battle. After a desperate conflict, the Mexicans gave way, and threw themselves into Atlixo. At nightfall, General Lane established his batteries on a commanding eminence, and opened his fire on the town; but the Mexican troops having retreated, the civil authorities immediately surrendered the place, and the Americans took possession of it. Throughout the remainder of the campaign, General Lane was in active service, and contributed greatly to its fortunate issue. His operations exhibited a striking combination of intelligence and daring. With a Napoleonic celerity of movement, he appeared almost ubiquitous. Wherever and whenever his presence was most needed, then and there did the 'Marion of the Mexican war' make his appearance. The long marches executed by his command excited the admiration of military men as much as their chivalric daring in the field. General Lane succeeded in infusing into his troops his own spirit of patient toil and brilliant valor. After marching many leagues under a broiling sun, reflected from arid plains and rocks, through rugged defiles and lonely valleys, the presence of the enemy always found them ready to rush into battle, resistless and undaunted. Far away from the scenes of strife, we read of General Lane's exploits with mingled admiration and astonishment, and the barbarous names of Tlascala, Matamaros, Galaxa, Tulaucingo, became 'familiar in our mouths as household words,' when illustrated by the valor of the American general. The story of his deeds read like a romance, and there was that in the character of the gallant volunteer which enlisted the warmest sympathy. He was the true type of the American citizen soldier, abandoning the tranquil delights of home, and the honors of a civic career, for the toils and dangers of war, at the call of his country, and learning the military art by its exercise. To the fiery and impetuous valor which distinguishes the French soldier, General Lane united the stern resolution which characterized the old Roman warrior, but he repudiated the Roman military maxim, 'Woe to the vanquished!' as unworthy of an American officer. The wounded enemy received as much attention at his hands as a wounded comrade, and as he had communicated to his men his spirit of endurance and valor, so he impressed them by his example of humanity and moderation in victory. In July, 1848, General Lane returned to the United States, and was appointed by President Polk, Territorial Governor of Oregon. After a perilous journey, he reached his post in March, 1849, and immediately organized the government. After being superseded by Governor Gaines, under Taylor's administration, he was elected by the people of Oregon, with whom he was universally popular, as delegate to Congress. In 1853, the outrages of the Indians in the southern part of Oregon, called him once more to the field at the head of a small force of volunteers and regular troops, and after a desperate battle near Table Rock, in which he was severely wounded, he succeeded in forcing them into submission and peace."

General Lane labored faithfully to bring Oregon into the Union, and at last succeeded, for in February, 1859, the Oregon bill passed the House of Representatives, and he having been elected senator of the young State took his seat in that body, and chose the long, or six years' term.

General Lane has taken little part, as we have said, in the recent party politics of the day, though, in the winter of 1857–8, he did make a speech in defence of the Lecompton Constitution. He was not however ultra in his sentiments. We quote his speech, which was short, on the admission of Oregon into the Union. It will be seen that portions of the speech relate to General Lane's personal history:

"Mr. Speaker, I have not yet had an opportunity of addressing myself to the House in behalf of the admission of Oregon. It is a matter of very great importance to the people of that territory, and of the whole country. I would not now trespass on the time of the House, were it not for the purpose of making a personal explanation.

"I find in the 'Oregon Statesman,' a paper published at

Salem, Oregon, a letter purporting to have been written from this city, bearing date the 17th of June last, in which it is charged that I had managed to prevent action on the admission bill, for the purpose of obtaining double mileage if elected to the Senate. If that letter had not been published in a Democratic paper, I would not have noticed it; but as it has been, I feel it my duty to say, that if the letter was written here, the writer of that letter knew very little about me.

"Money, I thank God, has not been a consideration with me in the discharge of my official duty. It has had no influence over my action, official, moral, political, or social. I have never coveted money. I desire only the reputation of an honest man; and that I intend to deserve always, as I have deserved hertofore that reputation. I did all I could to bring Oregon in; and when I found we could not, I said to you, Mr. Speaker, I said to the Sergeant-at-Arms of the Senate, I said to the Sergeant-at-Arms of the House, that if elected and admitted to the Senate, I would not take double mileage, or double compensation. Throughout all my official action, I have studied the strictest principles of economy toward the Government. When I was appointed Governor of Oregon territory, in 1848, I paid for my own outfit, and travelled across the plains to the territory of Oregon without the cost to the Government of a single cent. When I arrived at San Francisco, I had to make the trip from there to Oregon by water. I had run out of money, and I borrowed enough to pay my passage to Oregon City, and I paid it as soon as I earned it out of my salary. Though I was offered a free passage by the quartermaster, who went out in the same vessel with a small detachment of troops, and who thought I was entitled to a free passage, yet I declined to accept the offer.

"Then, in the discharge of my duties of Governor, in the management of Indian affairs, I can say, that, for the smallness of those expenses, there is no parallel to my administration in that respect. During the time I was Governor of Oregon, and *ex officio* superintendent of Indian affairs, I visited fifty-odd tribes of Indians, and gave them presents, small in amount, it is true, but such as were necessary to keep them in a good disposition toward the whites; and that for the whole amount of expenses in travelling, I made not a cent of charge. My accounts show not a single charge against the Government; and the whole amount of expense, of whatever nature, for the whole eighteen months that I visited those tribes tribes of Indians, was less than three thousand dollars. I mention these things in the way of a personal explanation against the charges of a letter-writer.

"MR. KILGORE.—I wish to ask the gentleman from Oregon a question. I understood him to remark that he would not have noticed the matter had it been published in a Republican paper. Will the gentleman let us know why he would not have noticed it if it had been published in a respectable Republican newspaper?"

"MR. LANE.—The Republican papers have taken the liberty so often of giving me so many hard raps that I have got used to it, and I would not have taken it to heart. But this appears in a Democratic paper, and in a paper that has had the Government public printing. This is a fire in the rear that I do not like.

"I will say this: that I have had no cause of complaint of letter-writers since I have been a delegate upon this floor. Very few of them have taken the trouble to notice me favorably, and I am sure I never should desire them to notice me unfavorably; but I will say in vindication, or rather to the credit of the letter-writers in this city, that I do not believe that this letter was written in Washington. I believe it was written in Oregon territory, and with a view, in my absence, to affect my character as a public servant and as an honest man, and with a view to prejudice the admission of

Oregon; and perhaps in order that the editor of this Democratic paper might still have the benefit of his thousands of dollars annually for the public printing.

"I have said this much about the letter-writers; and now I must be allowed, as I feel the deepest interest in the admission of Oregon, to say a few words upon this subject.

"Mr. Gooch.—I wish to ask the gentleman from Oregon if, in case Oregon is admitted and he has a vote at either end of this Capitol, he will vote to relieve Kansas from the effect of the English bill, so called, and let her present herself for admission when she chooses?

"Mr. Lane.—I do not come here to make any bargain, contract, or promises. I am an honest man; and if I am permitted to go into the Senate I shall exercise a sound discretion and judgment, and with a strong desire to promote the general good, prosperity and welfare of a country that I love more than life; and I believe that my official action through life is a guaranty that in all matters I will do what I believe to be right.

"Now, Mr. Speaker, Oregon territory is peculiarly situated. I think if there ever was a case in this country where a people were entitled to the care, the protection, and aid of this Government, it is the people of that territory. They went out there at a very early day. I heard with pleasure, from gentlemen on the other side of the House, a partial history of the early settlement of that country. As early as 1832, 1833, and 1834, and from that time down to 1839 and 1840, the missionary societies of this country took it into their heads very wisely to establish missionaries upon the Pacific. They sent out good and educated men, men who had a strong desire to civilize the savages, to inculcate religious principles among them, and encourage habits of industry and civilization. Their missions were assisted by many old trappers, who, though they had spent many years in the mountains, in pursuit of game and furs, were yet men who had noble and pure hearts, and who readily offered such aid and assistance as was in their power. Settlements grew up around the missionary posts. Every effort was put forth by these good people to influence the habits of the savages. They were urged to be led upon the paths of Christianity and civilization.

"In 1841, these settlements had been extended all over the country, and their welfare depended upon order and good government. They, therefore, organized themselves into a temporary provisional government. A board was appointed to enact laws, and judges were selected for the decision of all matters in dispute. That provisional government continued until 1843, when a regular form of government was adopted. George Abernethy was elected Governor. A Legislative Assembly was created, judges were appointed, and all the operations of a government went on as smoothly as they do in any of the territories of the United States. A post-office department was established, and mail service was performed throughout the territory. Communication thus was kept up with all sections of the Union and Oregon. That government continued until 1848, when, by act of Congress, the laws of the United States were extended over Oregon, and a territorial government was voted to her. When I arrived there, in the winter of 1848, I found the provisional government I have referred to, working beautifully. Peace and plenty blessed the hills and vales, and harmony and quiet, under the benign influence of that government, reigned supreme throughout her borders. I thought that it was almost a pity to disturb the existing relations—to put that government down and another up. Yet they came out to meet me, their first Governor under the laws of the United States. They told me how proud they were to be under the laws of the United States; and how glad they were to welcome me as holding the commission of the General Government. Why, sir, my heart waxed warm to them from that day.

"Mr. Speaker, can any man upon this floor reconcile it with the common dictates of justice to deny to this people a State government? They are law-abiding; they have population; they are competent for self-government: wherein is it that they are deficient? My friend from Tennessee [Mr. Zollicoffer] said that he voted for Kansas because of fear of disturbances; because, forsooth, they were outlaws and bad men. Would not that be a reward for defiance of the law?

"Mr. Zollicoffer.—The statement of the gentleman from Oregon does me a great injustice. On the Kansas question there was great excitement, connected with the question of slavery, which agitated the public mind of the whole Union to such an extent that I regarded it my duty to aid to bring Kansas into the Union, and at once settle the agitation attaching to that territory. This consideration was, to my mind, paramount to that of population.

"Mr. Davis, of Mississippi.—I desire to ask the gentleman from Oregon whether, from his knowledge of the country, he believes there are ninety-three thousand four hundred and twenty people there?

"Mr. Lane.—I do. From my knowledge of the country, from the rapid increase of population there, I believe that there are ninety-three thousand four hundred and twenty inhabitants there; ninety-three thousand four hundred and twenty white people, no Chinamen or negroes counted. I am not only satisfied of that, but I can show, I think, that Oregon, before the apportionment in 1870, will stand here with her representatives representing three hundred thousand people.

"Mr. Speaker, she comes here with a constitution regularly framed, and adopted by her people. It is the wish of those people that they shall assume the responsibilities of State government. Are they not entitled to it? Now I would ask the friends of her admission to vote down all amendments. If the bill is to stand, let it stand as it came from the Senate. If it is to fall, then let it fall upon that bill. Do not refuse her request by indirection; let the issue be fairly and openly made. She has been fair and honest in her dealings with us, and why should we be otherwise to her? My northern friends will believe me when I say that the rights of every State of the Union are as dear to me as those of Oregon. If I have a seat in Congress, I will be, at all times, prompt to resent any trespass on the rights of the States as secured by the Constitution. My affection rests on every inch of this Union—East and West, North and South. The promotion of the prosperity of this great country is the strongest desire of my heart. I then ask gentlemen, on all sides of the House, on what principle of justice or right, the application of Oregon can be refused?"

In his personal appearance Mr. Lane is dignified and commanding. He is uniformly good natured and his intimate friends assert that in his judgments of men and political parties he is very fair. He is tall, with a fine forehead, greyish hair, and florid complexion. As a speaker, we have remarked, he is not distinguished, though he is perfectly at his ease while delivering a speech in Congress.

JOHN McLEAN.

JOHN McLEAN, or rather Judge McLean—for by the last name he is everywhere known—has been member of Congress, Post Master-General, General Land Office Commissioner, Judge in the State of Ohio, and finally Judge of the Supreme Court of the United States. We can add that the man so prominent, so successful, is worthy of all his advancement, for he has ever been a man of unswerving integrity, and of lofty character. He was born in Morris County, New Jersey, on the 11th of March, 1785. Four years later, his father, who was poor, removed to the West—first to Morganstown, Virginia, next to Jessamine, Kentucky, and finally to what is now Warren County, Ohio. This was then a wild country, and the hardy pioneer went at work and cleared up a farm in it, whereon he resided forty years, and died in the home which he had made in the wilderness. Here, too, lived John McLean, the subject of this sketch, and worked upon the farm which he afterward owned. There were few opportunities within his reach to obtain a good education—this was at the beginning of the present century—

but to such schools as were to be found near home he was sent, and made such rapid progress that when he was sixteen years of age he was put under the care of a neighboring clergyman that he might study the languages, and as his father's means were still somewhat limited, he entirely supported himself and paid his tuition expenses by his labor. He was already ambitious, and determined to study the law. When he was eighteen years old, he made an engagement to write in the clerk's office of Hamilton County, in Cincinnati, and entered the law office of Arthur St. Clair, then an eminent lawyer of Cincinnati. His writing in the clerk's office supported him, though he was obliged to practise the closest economy. He took part in a debating society, and by practice fitted himself for his future business. In the spring of 1807, he married a Miss Edwards—before he was admitted to the bar—which was doubtless in the eyes of all his prudent friends a very foolish act. But so it did not turn out to be. Miss Edwards made him an excellent wife, and the early marriage saved him from vice and dissipation into which so many young men of his profession plunge at his age. In the fall of the same year, Mr. McLean was admitted to the bar, and returned to Warren County, where he speedily secured a large legal business.

In 1812, he became a candidate for Congress, his district then including Cincinnati. He had two competitors, but was chosen by a large majority. One of his friends writes:

"From his first entrance upon public life, John McLean was identified with the Democratic party. He was an ardent supporter of the war, and of the administration of Mr. Madison, yet not a blind advocate of every measure proposed by the party, as the journals of that period will show. His votes were all given in reference to principle. The idea of supporting a dominant party, merely because it was dominant, did not influence his judgment, or withdraw him from the high path of duty which he had marked out for himself. He was well aware, that the association of individuals into parties was sometimes absolutely necessary to the prosecution and accomplishment of any great public measure. This he supposed was sufficient to induce the members composing them, on any little difference with the majority, to sacrifice their own judgment to that of the greater number, and to distrust their own opinions when they were in contradiction to the general views of the party. But as party was thus to be regarded as itself, only an instrument for the attainment of some great public good, the instrument should not be raised into greater importance than the end, nor any clear and undoubted principle of morality be violated for the sake of adherence to party. Mr. McLean often voted against political friends;

yet so highly were both his integrity and judgment estimated, that no one of the Democratic party separated himself from him on that account. Nor did his independent course in the smallest degree diminish the weight he had acquired among his own constituents.

"Among the measures supported by him, were the tax bills of the extra session at which he first entered Congress. He originated the law to indemnify individuals for property lost in the public service. A resolution instructing the proper committee to inquire into the expediency of giving pensions to the widows of the officers and soldiers who had fallen in their country's service, was introduced by him; and the measure was afterward sanctioned by Congressional enactment. By an able speech he defended the war measures of the administration; and by the diligent discharge of his duties in respect to the general welfare of the country, and the interests of his people and district, he continued to rise in public estimation. In 1814, he was re-ëlected to Congress by the unanimous vote of his district, receiving not only every vote cast in the district for representative, but every voter that attended the polls voted for him—a circumstance that has rarely occurred in the political history of any man. His position as a member of the committee of foreign relations and of the public lands, indicates the estimation in which he was held, and his familiarity with the important questions of foreign and domestic policy which were in agitation during the eventful period of his membership."

In 1815, he was urgently solicited to become a candidate for the U. S. Senate, but he declined. He was then but thirty years of age. In 1816, he was unanimously elected judge of the Supreme Court of the state of Ohio and he resigned his seat in Congress. While in Congress he voted for a bill giving to each member a salary of $1,500 a year instead of the per diem allowance.

Judge McLean presided on the bench in Ohio for six years, during which time he won for himself an enviable judicial reputation. In 1822, he was appointed commissioner of the general Land Office by President Monroe; and in 1823, he entered the cabinet as Postmaster General. As Postmaster General he secured a fine reputation, improving its finances and in every possible way improving the postal facilities of the country. By an almost unanimous vote of Congress his salary was increased from $4,000 to $6,000.

"The distribution of the public patronage of his department exhibited in another respect his qualities as an executive officer, and manifested the rule of action that has always marked his character. The principle upon which executive patronage should be distributed, has been one of the most important questions in this government, and has presented the widest variation between the profession and practice of individuals and parties. In the administration of the post-office department by Judge McLean, an example was presented in strict consistence with sound principles of republican government, and just party organization. During the whole time that the affairs of the department were administered by the judge, he had necessarily a difficult part to act. The country was divided into two great parties, animated by the most determined spirit of rivalry, and each bent on advancing itself to the lead of public affairs. A question was now started, whether it was proper to make political opinions the test of qualification for office. Such a principle had been occasionally acted upon during the preceding periods of our history; but so rarely, as to constitute the exception, rather than the rule. It had never become the settled and systematic course of conduct of any public officer. Doubtless every one is bound to concede something to the temper and opinions of the party to which he belongs, otherwise party would be an association without any connecting bond of alliance.

"But no man is permitted to infringe any one of the great rules of morality and justice, for the sake of subserving the interests of his party. It cannot be too often repeated, nor too strongly impressed upon the public men of America, that nothing is easier than to reconcile these two apparently conflicting views. The meaning of party, is an association of men for the purpose of advancing the public interests. Men thrown together indiscriminately, without any common bond of alliance, would be able to achieve nothing great and valuable; while united together, to lend each other mutual support and assistance, they are able to surmount the greatest obstacles, and to accomplish the most important ends. This is the true notion of party. It imports combined action; but does not imply any departure from the great principles of truth and honesty. So long as the structure of the human mind is so varied in different individuals, there will always be a wide scope for diversity of opinion as to public measures; but no foundation is yet laid in the human mind for any material difference of opinion, as to what constitutes the great rule of justice.

"The course which was pursued by Judge McLean was marked by the greatest wisdom and moderation. Believing that every public officer holds his office in trust for the people, he determined to be influenced by no other principle in the discharge of his public duties, than a faithful performance of the trust committed to him. No individual was removed from office by him, on account of his political opinions. In making appointments where the claims and qualifications of persons were equal, and at the same time one was known to be friendly to the administration, he felt himself bound to appoint the one who was his friend. But when persons were recommended to office, it was not the practice to name, as a recommendation, that they had been or were warm supporters of the dominant power. In all such cases, the man who was believed to be the best qualified was selected by the department."

In 1829, General Jackson appointed Mr. McLean to the bench of the Supreme Court of the United States, he having previously declined the War and Navy Departments, although the two men differed somewhat in their ideas of public policy. In January, 1830, he took his seat upon the bench, and since that time the only indications of Judge McLean's opinions on the political issues of modern times which the public could notice, have been afforded by his published decisions involving the question of slavery. Some years since, the private friends of Judge McLean were aware that he sympathized very deeply with the Anti-Slavery reformers of the West and North, and that he did not approve of the political principles of the Democratic party, as laid down in their regular platforms, on this subject. He may be safely set down as a conservative opponent of negro slavery, and its extension into the territories of the republic. In the last Presidential election he voted for John C. Fremont, which would seem to settle the question as to his political affinities. He is a Republican.

From Judge McLean's opinion, delivered in the Dred Scott case, we gather his views upon some of the more prominent political issues of the day:

"As to the locality of slavery. The civil law throughout the continent of Europe, it is believed, without an exception, is, that slavery can exist only within the territory where it is established; and that, if a slave escapes, or is carried beyond such territory, his master cannot reclaim him, unless by virtue of some express stipulation.

"There is no nation in Europe which considers itself bound to return to his master a fugitive slave, under the civil law or the law of nations. On the contrary, the slave is held to be free where there is no treaty obligation, or compact in some other form, to return him to his master. The Roman law did not allow freedom to be sold. An ambassador or any other public functionary could not take a slave to France, Spain, or any other country in Europe, without emancipating him. A number of slaves escaped from a Florida plantation, and were received on board of ship by Admiral Cochrane; by the King's Bench, they were held to be free.

In the great and leading case of Prigg *v.* the State of Pennsylvania, this court say that, by the general law of nations, no nation is bound to recognize the state of slavery, as found within its territorial dominions, where it is in opposition to its own policy and institutions, in favor of the subjects of other nations where slavery is organized. If it does it, it is as a matter of comity, and not as a matter of international right. The state of slavery is deemed to be a mere municipal regulation, founded upon and limited to the range of the territorial laws. This was fully recognized in Somerset's case, which was decided before the American Revolution.

"There was some contrariety of opinion among the judges on certain points ruled in Prigg's case, but there was none in regard to the great principle, that slavery is limited to the range of the laws under which it is sanctioned.

"No case in England appears to have been more thoroughly examined than that of Somerset. The judgment pronounced by Lord Mansfield was the judgment of the Court of King's Bench. The cause was argued at great length, and with great ability, by Hargrave and others, who stood among the most eminent counsel in England. It was held under advisement from term to term, and a due sense of its importance was felt and expressed by the Bench.

"In giving the opinion of the court, Lord Mansfield said:

"'The state of slavery is of such a nature that it is incapable of being introduced on any reasons, moral or political, but only by positive law, which preserves its force long after the reasons, occasion, and time itself, from whence it was created, are erased from the memory; it is of a nature that nothing can be suffered to support it but positive law.'"

In relation to the connection between the Federal Government and slavery, Judge McLean remarks:

"The only connection which the Federal Government holds with slaves in a State, arises from that provision in the Constitution which declares that 'No person held to service or labor in one State, under the laws thereof, escaping into another, shall in consequence of any law or regulation therein, be discharged from such service or labor, but shall be delivered up, on claim of the party to whom such service or labor may be due.'

"This being a fundamental law of the Federal Government, it rests mainly for its execution, as has been held, on the judicial power of the Union; and so far as the rendition of fugitives from labor has become a subject of judicial action, the federal obligation has been faithfully discharged.

"In the formation of the Federal Constitution, care was taken to confer no power on the Federal Government to interfere with this institution in the States. In the provisions respecting the slave trade, in fixing the ratio of representation, and providing for the reclamation of fugitives from labor, slaves were referred to as persons, and in no other respect are they considered in the Constitution.

"We need not refer to the mercenary spirit which introduced the infamous traffic in slaves, to show the degradation of negro slavery in our country. This system was imposed upon our colonial settlements by the mother country, and it is due to truth to say that the commercial colonies and States were chiefly engaged in the traffic. But we know as a historical fact, that James Madison, that great and good man, a leading member in the Federal Convention, was solicitous to guard the language of that instrument so as not to convey the idea that there could be property in man.

"I prefer the lights of Madison, Hamilton, and Jay, as a means of construing the Constitution in all its bearings, rather than to look behind that period, into a traffic which is now declared to be piracy, and punished with death by Christian nations. I do not like to draw the sources of our domestic relations from so dark a ground. Our independence was a great epoch in the history of freedom; and while I admit the Government was not made especially for the colored race, yet many of them were citizens of the New England States, and exercised the rights of suffrage when the Constitution was adopted, and it was not doubted by any intelligent person that its tendencies would greatly ameliorate their condition.

"Many of the States, on the adoption of the Constitution, or shortly afterward, took measures to abolish slavery within their respective jurisdictions; and it is a well-known fact that a belief was cherished by the leading men, South as well as North, that the institution of slavery would gradually decline, until it would become extinct. The increased value of slave labor, in the culture of cotton and sugar, prevented the realization of this expectation. Like all other communities and States, the South were influenced by what they considered to be their own interests.

"But if we are to turn our attention to the dark ages of the world, why confine our view to colored slavery? On the same principles, white men were made slaves. All slavery has its origin in power, and is against right."

In reference to the power of Congress to prohibit slavery in the territories, we quote the subjoined paragraphs from Judge McLean's opinion:

"On the 13th of July, the ordinance of 1787 was passed, 'for the government of the United States territory northwest of the river Ohio,' with but one dissenting vote. This instrument provided there should be organized in the territory not less than three nor more than five States, designating their boundaries. It was passed while the federal convention was in session, about two months before the Constitution was adopted by the convention. The members of the convention must therefore have been well acquainted with the provisions of the ordinance. It provided for a temporary government, as initiatory to the formation of State governments. Slavery was prohibited in the territory.

"Can any one suppose that the eminent men of the federal convention could have overlooked or neglected a matter so vitally important to the country, in the organization of temporary governments for the vast territory northwest of the river Ohio? In the 3d section of the 4th article of the Constitution, they did make provision for the admission of new States, the sale of the public lands, and the temporary government of the territory. Without a temporary government, new States could not have been formed, nor could the public lands have been sold.

"If the 3d section were before us now for consideration for the first time, under the facts stated, I could not hesitate to say there was adequate legislative power given in it. The power to make all needful rules and regulations is a power to legislate. This no one will controvert, as Congress cannot make 'rules and regulations,' except by legislation. But it is argued that the word territory is used as synonymous with the word land; and that the rules and regulations of Congress are limited to the disposition of lands and other property belonging to the United States. That this is not the true construction of the section appears from the fact that in the first line of the section 'the power to dispose of the public lands' is given expressly, and, in addition, to make all needful rules and regulations. The power to dispose of is complete in itself, and requires nothing more. It authorizes Congress to use the proper means within its discretion, and any further provision for this purpose would be a useless verbiage. As a composition the Constitution is remarkably free from such a charge.

"The prohibition of slavery north of 36° 30′, and of the State of Missouri, contained in the act admitting that State into the Union, was passed by a vote of 134, in the House of Representatives, to 42. Before Mr. Monroe signed the act, it was submitted by him to his Cabinet, and they held the restriction of slavery in a territory to be within the constitutional powers of Congress. It would be singular, if, in 1804, Congress had the power to prohibit the introduction of slaves in Orleans territory from any other part of the Union, under the penalty of freedom to the slave, if the same power embodied in the Missouri Compromise could not be exercised in 1820.

"But this law of Congress, which prohibits slavery north of Missouri and of 36° 30′, is declared to have been null and void by my brethren. And this opinion is founded mainly, as I understand, on the distinction drawn between the ordinance of 1787 and the Missouri Compromise line. In what does the distinction consist? The ordinance, it is said, was a compact entered into by the confederated States before the adoption of the Constitution; and that in the cession of territory, authority was given to establish a territorial government.

"It is clear that the ordinance did not go into operation by virtue of the authority of the confederation, but by reason of its modification and adoption by Congress under the Constitution. It seems to be supposed, in the opinion of the court, that the articles of cession placed it on a different footing from territories subsequently acquired. I am unable to perceive the force of this distinction. That the ordinance was intended for the government of the northwestern territory, and was limited to such territory, is admitted. It was extended to southern territories, with modifications by acts of Congress, and to some northern territories. But the ordinance was made valid by the act of Congress, and without such act could have been of no force. It rested for its validity on the act of Congress, the same, in my opinion, as the Missouri Compromise line.

"If Congress may establish a territorial government in the exercise of its discretion, it is a clear principle that a court cannot control that discretion. This being the case, I do not see on what ground the act is held to be void. It did not purport to forfeit property, or take it for public purposes. It only prohibited slavery; in doing which, it followed the ordinance of 1787."

In 1840, Judge McLean lost his wife, and in 1843, married his present wife, Mrs. Sara Bella Garrard of Cincinnati. In his personal appearance, Judge McLean is imposing, for he is tall and well proportioned, and his face is one of the finest among the list of American jurists. As a judge, he is above reproach; and as a Christian—he is a member of a Christian church—he has won the esteem of all who know him in that relation.

HENRY A. WISE.

Governor Wise is certainly one of the ablest of the southern democrats. He may lack judgment and that balance of character which is necessary in the truly great man; but he is a decided genius. Whatever he has attempted he has accomplished, thus far, from his wonderful energy and activity. Whether he has reached that bound in his political triumphs beyond which he cannot pass, remains to be seen. We will very briefly glance at his past history and his present views upon the great political issues of the country.

Henry A. Wise was born in Drummond Town, Accomack County, Virginia, December 3, 1806. He was a precocious lad, for he graduated at Washington College, Pa., when he was but nineteen years old. He then studied law, and was admitted to the bar of Winchester, Va., in 1828. With a western fever in his bones, and desirous of a new field in a new country, he emigrated to Nashville, Tennessee, where he practised law for two years. He soon grew homesick for old Virginia, and returned to Accomack County. The district showed its estimation of the young man by returning him to Congress in 1833. He continued to represent it in the House of Representatives for ten years. In 1843, he resigned his place and took the mission to Brazil. He remained there for a Presidential term. In 1848, he was a Presidential elector in Virginia; in 1850, was a member of the Reform Convention which adopted the present constitution of the State. In 1852, he was again a Presidential elector, and in 1855 was nominated by his party as their candidate for Governor. This caucus will always be remembered and will give him unfading political laurels. The contest was probably one of the most exciting, close, and bitter, which ever took place, even in Virginia. The Know Nothings, or Americans, were then in the height of power and were sanguine of success. Mr. Wise took the stump with the prophets against him, and in fact with a general impression abroad that he would be defeated. He carried on the year's canvass as no other man beside Henry A. Wise could have done it. He bearded Americanism in its den—forced it upon its own territory—and triumphed in the popular vote by thousands. However rash and extravagant his speeches were, he had that overwhelming enthusiasm and vigor, which carried down all opposition, and placed him in the Governor's chair.

As a politician, Governor Wise has always been

true to the Virginian school. Rigidly in favor of State rights, and as rigidly opposed to protective tariffs—in short, bitterly anti-Whig in all his opinions. On the slavery question, from the outset, he has been ultra pro-slavery, though he was opposed to the Lecompton policy of Mr. Buchanan's administration. He has favored internal improvements in Virginia, and has in this respect differed from Mr. Hunter. This is the bright feature in Governor Wise's political character. He never was an old fogy, but is brimful of originality and reform. To see what is Governor Wise's position on many of the issues of the day, we will quote a few passages from his letter of January 3, 1859, to Hon. David Hubbard:

"Now, I have raised my warning of late against this weakness and wickedness on our part. I have tried to protect my widowed mother, the South, by giving honest filial counsel against the whole household. The Reubens have tried to sell me into Egypt for my 'dreaming.' But I am, nevertheless, loyal to the house of my father and loving to my misguided brethren, and I mean to redouble my efforts the more to save the house of Israel. If I must be driven out as a dreamer, I will, at least, preserve 'mine integrity,' and time and the day of famine will show whose counsel and whose course will have saved the household and fed it, and all the land of the stranger too. Aye; and is democracy as well as the South to have no out-spoken, honest counsellor? Are we to be given over to the federal gods of Pacific railroads? Are we to *out-Yazoo Yazoo*? To out-Adams Adams in putting internal improvements by the General

Government on the most Omnipotent and indefinitely stretching power of all powers of the Federal Government—*the war power*? Are we to abolish *ad valorem* and adopt the specific duties to supply a tariff for revenue, the standard of which is already eighty-one millions of expenditure on three hundred and twenty-one millions average rate of importations? Are we to increase eighty-one millions of expenditure to the unknown limitless amount required for railroads across this continent; for post-offices that don't pay expenses; for pensions unheard of in character and amount; for a land office which gives away three acres for every one sold, and brings us in debt; for increase of a standing army such as our frontiers and Indian wars and protectorates of foreign territory propose; and, therefore, for such a navy as Isthmian wars with no less than eight powers of the earth—England, Spain, France, Mexico, Nicaragua, Costa Rica, New Granada, and Paraguay—demand if threatened only? Is protection to be turned into prohibition? If so, what is a 'direct tax?' Is land tax the only one which can be 'apportioned?' Are the landowners to pay all the cost of the crusade of Congress and manifest destiny? Is strict construction and are State rights to be abandoned, and are we to give up State corporations to the bankruptcies of a federal commission? Where would have been our people and their effects last year if a federal power could have put our State banks into a course of liquidation under a commission of bankruptcy? Is the South, is any portion of our community, in a situation to rush into wars—wars invited by the President with three European and five American powers? And are we to be a grand consolidated, elective, North and South American imperialism? The question is not, 'Will the Union be dissolved?' That is a settled question. But the question is, 'Is the old Virginia democratic faith to be abandoned, and are we to rush on with the President into a full scheme of federal policy which in its outline and filling up, exceeds any federalism, in all its points, which a Hamilton, or Adams, or any other latitudinarian, ever dared to project or propose?

"For my part, I take ground now firmly and at once against the war power. I am for the Washington policy of peace, and against all entangling alliances and protectorates, and the Jackson rule of 'demanding nothing but what is right, and submitting to nothing that is wrong,' and for preserving and protecting the South and whole country from ambitious and buccaneering wars, of which the landed and planting interests would have to bear the burden, at a great sacrifice of present prosperity. I am against internal improvements by the General Government, more than ever since their construction is put on the war power. If we could beard England up to 54° 40′, ten years ago, without a road or known route to Oregon, why can't we wait for emigrants to beat a path on their way to gold mines, and hold California, without cutting a military road in time of peace? I am for retrenchment and reform of all expenditures, and for revenue only for economical administration, on a scale of pure, old-fashioned republican simplicity, discriminating no more than is necessary to prevent prohibition on non-dutiable articles. I am for free trade, and the protection it affords is demonstrably ample for a people of enterprise and art like ours. I am against State-bank bankruptcy, and all sorts of bankruptcy whatever. The Federal Government shall never declare again that honest debts shall be paid by gulping and oaths, with my consent. But my paper is run out.

"The President bids high. To filibusters he offers Cuba and the Isthmus and North Mexico; to the West a Pacific Railroad; to the North protection to iron and coarse woollens; and to the great commercial countries the power of centralization by obvious uses and abuses of a bankrupt act to supply to State banks. Yesterday Biddle was a monster, and to-day a few Wall street bankers can expand and contract upon us more like a vice than he did; and what would they not do if they could force the poor provinces when they pleased into bankruptcy?"

In his later letter—to Mr. Samford, of Alabama—Gov. Wise gave his opinion of the Douglas "non-intervention" doctrine in unmistakable language. He says:

"Intervention for protection, by the United States, through Congress, is all-pervading. It penetrates into States, territories, districts and other places throughout the United States, and is one of the most vitally essential attributes of our blessed Federal Union.. No doctrine could be more repugnant to its benign spirit, none more destructive of federal immunities and privileges, and none more fatal to State rights and the safety of individual persons and their property, than this new light of "Non-Intervention" to protect all and everything in the jurisdiction of the United States. It is a question which cannot be retired from discussion in Congress, where it rises up every day in every form, and where it must be met with intelligence, integrity and courage. It cannot be renounced or smothered, or the Government must relinquish its dominion over every subject of its jurisdiction.

"And this doctrine of 'Non-Intervention for Protection' is only equalled in danger and destructiveness by that correlative error of some minds in these days: 'That Congress may not intervene to protect; for if it has the power to protect, it has the power to destroy.' This is a *non sequitur*, and a weak fallacy and gross delusion. The power and duty to protect is the power and duty not only not to destroy, but something far greater—it is the duty to intervene against invasion and violence. The whole American system of government throughout is one to protect against destruction. Because Congress may and shall provide the writ of habeas corpus, trial by jury, freedom of speech or of the press, etc., etc., shall it, therefore, be said to possess the power to withhold, deny or destroy either or all of these rights?

"But, say some, *cui bono?*—if a majority of Congress are opposed to the protection of the right, what use is there in claiming the mere abstraction of the right? I reply that there is great use and practical effect in it too.

"The proposition of non-intervention is: 'By the Compromise of 1850, the Kansas Nebraska act, and other declarations of its will, Congress renounced the exercise of any direct jurisdiction over the territories, and delegated its power to the local legislatures.' But it concedes that Congress could bestow no authority on the local legislatures of which it was not itself possessed'—in other words, "Congress cannot delegate more power than it possesses itself; and it has none to prohibit slavery. Very well, and so good as to the power. But there is a positive duty to be discharged as well as a power not to be exercised. Suppose the territorial legislature attempts to prohibit slavery, and thus do what Congress itself cannot do in the territories. Has Congress renounced its jurisdiction in the case? Could it or can it do so? If not, what is its duty? Does non-intervention renounce this duty of protection, in such a case, or not? It replies that this claim upon Congress to discharge this duty will be vain. Why? There is a dead majority against us in Congress, and they will not heed the appeal to the legislative department for protection.

"Well, but the case supposes a like dead majority and an aggressive majority against us in the territorial legislature too.—What then? There is no refuge of safety from a majority against us in territorial legislatures. Non-intervention quickly answers this dilemma, by saying: 'let the courts determine between us and our adversaries.' This is what is called 'remitting' the question to the judiciary, which may decide as well as the Congress or the Executive. —True, the judiciary may and must decide, anyhow, in either case, for that was no discovery of Mr. Calhoun, but a Constitutional function, which has ever belonged to the courts, and of which Congress and the Executive and the Territorial authorities cannot deprive them; and, without any remission by Congress, the judiciary department has the power of deciding upon the validity of laws. And it can as well and more directly pass upon the validity of laws enacted by Congress itself as upon the validity of those enacted by the territorial legislatures. If Congress passes an unconstitutional law, we can go to the courts, just as easy as if the law was passed by its delegate, the territorial Legislature. And if Congress does not renounce its direct jurisdiction and delegate it to the territorial legislature, then the latter will have no power to annoy the slave property locally by its abuse of delegated power; and the territorial legislature is more apt to pass a prohibition than Congress is, for very obvious reasons. The eye of the whole nation is immediately upon Congress, and no positive code is required to establish its power and duty to protect persons and property. The Constitution itself dictates and enjoins both. And it is first of all necessary, that neither the power nor the duty shall be practically denied, embarrassed or obstructed, by the enactment of unconstitutional laws of prohibition. Positive legislation is more apt to be passed against slavery by local than by national laws. In any practical view, then, we are attempting to shear a lion instead of a wolf. Non-intervention is simply absurd and impossible, and it is worse than impracticable.

* * * * * * * * * *

"Such are the teachings to me of our past history, and I

trust that I have now demonstrated in the second place: 'That the inhabitants or people of a territory are sovereign to form themselves a constitution and State government as I have shown in the first place, that in their territorial condition they are within the entire control and jurisdiction, or under the entire rule or regulation of Congress, subject to the Constitution of the United States, and that the citizens of each and all of the States are alike equally entitled to protection in all the privileges and immunities of persons and property, common to equal confederates.

"And this right and this duty of protection is not to be evaded or avoided either by the false *ad captandum* clamor that a code is required to be enacted by Congress for the protection of slave property. This is but to cast odium upon slavery, by creating the impression that a discrimination is necessary to distinguish it above what is due to other personal and proprietary rights. On the contrary, no such code is required to create either the right or the duty of protection, and no law is necessary to distinguish slave property from any other property. All persons and all property, equally and alike, require only not to be assailed and destroyed in, or excluded from the common territories. Every species of rights requires laws, it is true, suited to its character and to its case. Personal property, for example, must have a law that it shall not be 'taken and carried away;' and land, which cannot be 'taken and carried away,' must have a law that it shall not be trespassed upon in some other way; and so with slaves and everything else, they must have provisions according to their kind. But the Constitution of the United States, and the laws of Congress heretofore organizing territories are sufficient, and if amendments of the laws are required, it is the duty of Congress to see that they are provided, of the Executive of the United States to see that they are executed, and of the judiciary to decide upon the rights under the laws. The slave States should never pretend to any peculiar privileges, and do not, so far as I know. They ask only that their rights shall not be assailed and invaded, and, if they be assailed, that they may be protected as other personal and proprietary rights are protected ; that they may have equal, confederate, federal privileges and immunities, and they ask for no special or peculiar code. . . . . .

"To escape danger or disaster to themselves, your Congress, and Executives, and judiciary, and State legislatures, shall not, with my consent, be allowed to drop the reins of government and leap from the seats of power and responsibility, and renounce the duty of protection and preservation to all within their care by the ignoring and stultifying and disqualifying plea of negation—'*Non-intervention.*' There are too many elements of discord in this country which require to be restrained by the most active and positive, but prudent intervention. These resolutions of Vermont, the tendency of which is either to drive one section of the States out of the Union, or to degrade and subjugate them in it, are an example. If anything can be worse than disunion to the United States, it would be the more dire alternative of degrading and subjugating any one State by forcing her submission to unequal laws and dishonorable conditions in the confederacy. The state or section of states thus subdued and humbled, would be unworthy of the union with other free republics, and such a union would be no longer what union now is. It should, then, be the watchful concern of all to maintain and support the honor, dignity, and equality of each ; and equality alone can reciprocally maintain the strength of all. If first one and then another may be subdued, finally all but one will become subject to that one, central and consolidated. This should always combine the majority of States to support the weaker portion of the Union against the very appearance of oppression."

Such is the position of Gov. Wise on the slavery question. He is radical in his views, demanding the fullest protection from the courts and Congress for the protection of slavery. The faults as well as the virtues of Gov. Wise he carries openly in his face; if he is bold and imprudent, so he is frank and truthful. There is no deceit in him, and his political enemies know the worst when they know anything of his views or his course.

R. M. T. HUNTER.

Senator Hunter is a contrast, in almost every one of his traits of character, to Governor Wise. The Governor is voluble—he writes letters thirty columns long upon the condition of the country. Senator Hunter is reticent. The Governor is, say his enemies, rash. Mr. Hunter is cautious and prudent to a fault. Governor Wise, again, is a reformer in his way—Senator Hunter is set down as an "old fogy" in politics. Yet both are Democrats, and agree in essentials, as a matter of course.

Few members of the Senate enjoy to such an extent the respect of the entire body as Mr. Hunter. His manners, his bearing, his style of speaking, and his deportment in social circles, are such as to win him the esteem of all who know him, even in spite of political opposition.

In the Senate, he resembles some quiet unpretending farmer, who might have come up from a rural district, to sit in a State legislature. He dresses plain, is dignified without the least particle of pretension; speaks plainly, slowly, but clearly. Never tries to ride down a political opponent by declamation, but coolly *argues* the point of difference. During the most exciting debates he keeps his temper, and though in political matters, especially upon the slavery question, he is ultra-southern in his views, he is so watchful, so prudent, so mild in his speech, that he contrives to win the esteem of his northern associates, and to be very popular with them.

Mr. Hunter is a native of Essex County, Va., was liberally educated, and adopted the law as a profession. His first political experience was gained in the Virginian State Legislature, where he remained three years; but in 1837, he was elected to Congress as a member of the House of Representatives, where he remained four years. In 1845, he was reëlected to Congress, and was made Speaker of the Twenty-sixth Congress. In 1847, he was elected United States' Senator, where he still remains, and has been for years the able Chairman of the Finance Committee.

Mr. Hunter's political views are known to the country at large. He is a southern Democrat, with the views of a southern democratic politician—anti-tariff, of course—anti-homestead law—in the last Congress voting in the Senate against bringing up the bill for consideration. His views on Popular Sovereignty, we will give, shortly, from his own lips. He supported the Lecompton bill through thick and thin, though he did it as he does all his work, in a modest, quiet way, without bluster, or any attempt to intimidate.

In the non-intervention debate of March, 1839, Senator Hunter gave his views of the question under discussion, in the following language:

"It is with extreme reluctance that I say a word on this subject so unhappily sprung up on the appropriation bill, of which I stand here as the guardian, a very insufficient one, as it seems; but the course of the debate has made it necessary for me, in my own vindication, to say a word or two in regard to this Nebraska-Kansas act.

"I differ from the senator from Illinois in regard to the bill, the history of its inception, and what was intended by it. As I understand it, we stood in this position: the southern senators, I believe, almost without an exception, who spoke upon that question—I know I did for one, as I have always done from the time I first made my appearance on this floor—maintained that the South had the right, under the Constitution, of protection of this property in the Territories; on the other hand, senators from the free States denied that right. None of them would vote to give it to us; but there were a portion of the northern democracy who were willing to do this; they were willing to repeal the Missouri restriction, and establish a territorial government there. A bill was immediately drawn which left this right to the territories to legislate for the prohibition of slavery in abeyance. It neither affirmed nor disaffirmed the power of the territorial legislature to legislate upon this subject of slavery; but it provided very carefully and cautiously that any question arising out of it might be referred to the judiciary. . . . .

The case then stood thus: whilst the southern men maintained on one side (and I was amongst them) that they had the right to the protection of their property under the Constitution, those from the free States maintained the opposite opinion. There could have been no accord between them on that point; but the southern men, with some objection and reluctance, in order to harmonize, did agree, as the only mode of getting the Missouri Compromise repealed, if the territorial legislature attempted to exercise the power, that the court should decide; and this they could do with perfect consistency, because they provided that whatever powers were delegated to the territorial legislature should be exercised under the Constitution. In their opinion, the Constitution not only prohibited Congress from delegating a power to abolish slavery to the territories, but from exercising it itself. Whilst they maintained that Congress had the power to govern in the territories, they maintained that there was an obligation on Congress, imposed by the equality of the States, that they should not prohibit the institutions of one State while they allowed those of another; and that was the mode in which it was passed. The bill in itself was, in my opinion, a compromise in which neither sacrificed principles, but left the whole question in abeyance to be decided by the courts without taking from Congress the power to resume jurisdiction, if they should choose to do so afterward. They retained as much good as they could without raising those questions upon which there could have been no accord of opinion.

"Now, sir, I say it never was understood, so far as I had anything to do with the bill, by the southern men who maintained the class of opinions of which I am speaking, that they were conferring on the territorial legislature the absolute power to deal with this subject. They did not; but they were secured to vote for a bill which would organize a territorial Legislature which should leave this question in abeyance, and this bill decided nothing, but only provided that the question should go to the courts, to be decided under that jurisdiction.

"Nor did the bill—although everybody consented to strike out the phrase to which the senator from Illinois alludes—nor did the bill ever mean to say that Congress absolutely gave up jurisdiction over the subject. Inasmuch as it was a common point which accomplished good, which repealed what all the branches of the Democracy thought unconstitutional—the Missouri Compromise—they passed a bill which did that, without deciding absolutely on other differences of opinion, but merely providing a tribunal to decide them when they should come up."

That Senator Hunter stated the truth in reference to himself is evident from the subjoined quotation from a speech of his, delivered during the discussion of the Kansas-Nebraska act in 1854:

"But it has been often said by those who admit that Congress has the power of governing the territories, that it is a power to be exercised, not in reference to the rights of the States, but in reference to the good and welfare of the people of the territories. Now, if in exercising this power we are to be confined to the single consideration of the good and welfare of the people of the territories, then, I say, the whole subject of government ought to be left to the people of the territories. That is the true American principle. If the only consideration which is to apply to their government be the good and welfare of the people of the territories, then they ought to determine all questions in regard to their domestic institutions and laws. But, in my opinion, the government of these territories ought to be administered with the double object of securing the rights of the States as well as those of the people of the territories, and to these last should be given all the rights of self-government which are consistent with the limitation, that they shall not interfere with the equal rights of the States, or violate the provisions of the Constitution. With those limitations, all the power that could possibly be given to the people of that territory, ought to be given to them. All that portion of the power which is to be exercised with a view to their interests, ought to be exercised as they wish it. That, in my opinion, is the true principle.

"I know we have most high, distinguished, and respectable authority for the opinion that the people of the territories have a sort of natural right to exercise all power within those territories. It is not my purpose to raise an issue upon that question. I do not mean to argue it. I do not wish to raise an issue with the friends of this bill, with those whom I am assisting, and who are assisting me, to pass this measure. Nor will I do it unless it should be absolutely necessary, which is not now the case. For, happily, the bill is so framed that it can be maintained, not only by those who entertain such opinions as I have referred to, but by those, also, who entertain opinions like my own. The bill provides that the legislatures of these territories shall have the power to legislate over all rightful subjects of legislation, consistently with the Constitution. And if they should assume powers which are thought to be inconsistent with the Constitution, the courts will decide that question, whenever it may be raised. There is a difference of opinion amongst the friends of this measure, as to the extent of the limits which the Constitution imposes upon the territorial legislatures. This bill proposes to leave these differences to the decision of the courts. To that tribunal I am willing to leave this decision, as it was once before proposed to be left, by the celebrated compromise of the senator from Delaware (Mr. Clayton), a measure which, according to my understanding, was the best compromise which was offered upon this subject of slavery. I say, then, that I am willing to leave this point, upon which the friends of this bill are at difference, to the decision of the courts."

This position cannot be misunderstood. It is that the Supreme Court may overturn the action of territorial legislatures. But does Senator Hunter advocate, as Governor Wise does, Congressional intervention *to enforce* the decisions of the Supreme Court? Upon this point he is silent; though, from the language he uses, it is evident enough that as a matter of right he would claim the interference of Congress for this purpose—but, considering the fact that there is not the slightest chance that Congress could ever be brought to vote such protection, he may *as a matter of policy* relinquish the demand.

HENRY WILSON.

HENRY WILSON was born on the 16th of February, 1812, at Farmington, New Hampshire. His parents being poor, with a large family of children to support by their labor, he, with their consent, at the age of ten years, apprenticed himself to Mr. William Knight, a farmer of his native town, a man remarkable for his industry and habits of rigid economy. He remained with Mr. Knight till the age of twenty-one, and for these eleven years of incessant toil, he received one yoke of oxen, and six sheep. During this period, he was annually allowed to attend the public school four weeks. Throughout these years of unremitting, severe, and scantily-rewarded toil, he devoted his Sabbaths, and as much of his evenings as he could command, to reading. Too poor to purchase lights, he was forced to read by the dim light of wood fires; and after other members of the family had retired to rest, though weary with the toils of the day, he spent the hours in reading, which they employed in sleep. During his apprenticeship, he read more than seven hundred volumes of history and biography, most of which were selected and loaned to him by the wife of the Hon. Nehemiah Eastman, a gentleman who was a member of Congress during the first years of John Quincy Adams' administration. Mrs. Eastman was the sister of Hon. Levi Woodbury, and a lady of rare intelligence. To the judicious kindness of this accomplished lady, who thus early discovered and appreciated his talents, he was indebted for the means of acquiring a fund of solid and useful knowledge, and of forming habits of study and reflection, which have largely contributed to his subsequent success. To Judge Whitehouse, of his native town, he was also largely indebted for the use of many valuable books. Poverty and toil were the companions of his boyhood. His means of mental culture were very limited, and his education, on attaining his majority, was very deficient; yet very few young men at the age of twenty-one were better read in history, especially in the history of the United States, England, and modern France.

After attaining his majority, Mr. Wilson, for eight months, worked on a farm, receiving nine dollars a month.

Hoping to better his condition, in December, 1833, he left Farmington, and, with a pack on his back, made his way, on foot, to the town of Natick, Massachusetts, his present residence. Here he hired himself to a shoemaker, who agreed, for five months' service, to teach him the art of bottoming shoes. At the end of six weeks, Mr. Wilson bought his time, and went to work on his own account, at which employment he continued for more than two years, working so hard and incessantly that his health became seriously injured, and he was at length compelled to quit for a time the shoemaker's bench; and in May, 1836, he made a visit to Washington, where he remained for several weeks in regular attendance upon the debates in Congress. During his stay at the metropolis, Pinckney's Gag Resolutions were passed by the House of Representatives, and Calhoun's Incendiary Publication bill passed the Senate by the casting vote of the Vice-President, Martin Van Buren. The exciting debates to which he listened during this memorable period, and the scenes which he witnessed at Williams' slave-pen, to which he paid a visit, made Henry Wilson an anti-slavery man, and he returned to New England with the fixed resolution to do all in his power to advance the anti-slavery cause, and overthrow the influence of slavery in the nation. How steadily he has adhered to that resolution, his subsequent career bears ample witness.

From Washington, Mr. Wilson returned to New Hampshire, and entered Stafford Academy as a student, on the first of July, 1836. In the autumn of that year, he attended the academy at Wolfsborough; and during the winter of 1837, taught school in that town. In the spring of 1837, he entered Concord Academy, where he remained six months. While there, he was chosen a delegate to the Young Men's Anti-slavery State Convention, before which body he made his first public speech in behalf of freedom. In the autumn, he returned to Wolfsborough Academy, and at the close of the academic term, went again to Natick, Mass., where he taught school during the winter of 1837–8. He had intended to continue for some time longer at school, and to commence a course of classical studies, but the failure of a friend, to whom he had intrusted the few hundred dollars his own hands had earned, left him penniless, and he was compelled to change his plans of life.

In the spring of 1838, he engaged in the shoe manufacturing business, in which he continued till the autumn of 1848. During these ten years he annually manufactured from 40,000 to 130,000 pairs of shoes, a large portion of which he sold to southern merchants. One of his southern customers, who owed him more than a thousand dollars, having failed, wrote to him that he could pay him fifty per cent. of his debt, and asked to be discharged. On examining his statement, Mr. Wilson found that several slaves were included in his assets. Here was a question to test his anti-slavery professions. Mr. Wilson promptly signed the papers discharging him from all obligations, and wrote to him, never to send him a dollar of the dividend if it included the money received for slaves.

In November, 1839, Mr. Wilson was a candidate for representative to the legislature from the town of Natick, but being a zealous temperance man, and an advocate of the fifteen-gallon law, he was defeated by the opponents of that measure. In the spring of 1840, he took the stump for General Harrison, and during that memorable campaign, made upward of sixty speeches. In 1840, he was married to Miss Harriet M. Howe, of Natick. In 1840, and again in 1841, the people of Natick elected him their representative to the legislature. In 1842, he was a candidate for the State Senate, for Middlesex County, but in that year the Whig ticket was defeated. The next year, however, and in that following, 1844, he was chosen senator.

During the session of 1845, the State was deeply agitated by the discussion of the annexation of Texas. In February of that year, a State convention was called to be held in Faneuil Hall, to protest against the annexation. Mr. Wilson drew up the paper calling the convention, for the signatures of the members of the legislature, and applied to every Whig member for his name. The president of the Senate, Hon. Levi Lincoln, and other Whig members, refused to sign the call. Mr. Abbot Lawrence, Mr. Nathan

Appleton, Mr. John Davis, Mr. Winthrop, and other eminent Whigs also declined to unite in, or to approve the movement. This was the beginning of that division among the Whigs of Massachusetts on the slavery question, which resulted in an open rupture in 1848, and finally in the utter overthrow of that great and powerful party in Massachusetts.

In September, 1845, Mr. Wilson got up a call for a mass convention, in Middlesex County, to oppose the admission of Texas as a slave State. The call was responded to by the people, and at an adjourned meeting in Cambridge, over which Mr. Wilson presided, a state committee was appointed, composed of men of all parties, to procure signatures to petitions against the admission of Texas. Sixty-five thousand names were procured in a few weeks, and Henry Wilson and John G. Whittier were appointed to carry the petitions to Washington.

In the autumn of 1845, Mr. Wilson declined being a candidate for the Senate, and was chosen Representative from the town of Natick. In the legislature he introduced a resolution announcing the unalterable hostility of Massachusetts to the further extension and longer existence of slavery in America, and her fixed determination to use all constitutional and legal means for its extinction. In spite of the coldness and opposition of several leading Whigs, this resolution was adopted by ninety-three majority in the House, but was lost in the Senate by four votes. Mr. Wilson made an elaborate speech in its behalf, and Mr. Garrison, in the "Liberator," pronounced it the fullest and most comprehensive speech upon the slavery question, ever made in any legislative body in this country. In 1846, Mr. Wilson declined to be again a candidate for the legislature.

In 1843, the officers of the First Regiment of Artillery elected Mr. Wilson its Major without his knowledge. He accepted the position, and in June, 1846, he was chosen Colonel, and was elected Brigadier General of the Third Brigade in August, which position he continued to hold for five years.

In March, 1848, a Whig district convention was held at Dedham, to nominate a candidate for Congress to fill the vacancy occasioned by the death of John Quincy Adams. Henry Wilson, Horace Mann, and William Jackson, were the leading candidates. After three ballotings Mr. Wilson declined being considered a candidate, and Mr. Mann was nominated. The convention, at the same time, by an almost unanimous vote, elected Mr. Wilson a delegate to the National Whig Convention. That the vote was not unanimous was owing to the fact that he had stated in public and in private that if General Taylor should be fixed upon by the Whig party as its candidate, unpledged to the Wilmot Proviso, he not only would not support him, but would do all in his power to defeat him.

When General Taylor was nominated, and the Wilmot Proviso voted down by the Whig National Convention, in June, 1848, General Wilson, and his colleague, Hon. Charles Allen, denounced the action of the convention, and left it. Gen. Wilson then got up a meeting of a few northern men, which was held in the evening, to consider what steps should be taken.

Gen. Wilson called the meeting to order, and after stating its purposes, moved the appointment of a committee to call a convention of the opponents of the Slave Power. The committee was accordingly appointed, and united with others in calling the Buffalo Convention, which nominated Mr. Van Buren and Mr. Chas. Francis Adams.

In the summer of 1848, General Wilson purchased the "Boston Republican" a free-soil newspaper, which he edited from January, 1849, to January, 1851, during which two years he gave his whole time to the free-soil cause, and spent more than seven thousand dollars of his own property, in the support of the newspaper, whose continued existence was deemed essential to the welfare of the party of which it was the organ. In 1849, he was chosen chairman of the Free-soil State Committee, in which capacity he acted for four years. In the fall of 1849, a coalition was formed between the free-soilers, and the Democrats of Middlesex County, for the election of senators, and General Wilson was pressed by both parties to stand as a candidate for the Senate, which he steadfastly refused to do. He was, however, in that year, chosen a representative from the town of Natick. When the legislature met, he was unanimously nominated by the free-soilers, as their candidate for Speaker. During the session, he was in his seat every day, always attentive to business.

After Mr. Webster made his seventh of March speech, an effort was made to instruct him to vote for the doctrines embodied in the resolutions pending before the legislature; but the proposition was resisted, and voted down by the Whig majority. General Wilson told the House that the people would repudiate that speech, and the men who indorsed it, and that at the coming election, the men who had deserted the cause of freedom would be crushed by the people. This prediction, which was received with defiance by the Whig leaders, was fulfilled, and no one in Massachusetts contributed more to its fulfillment than the man who made it.

In the summer of 1850, General Wilson called together, at the Adams House in Boston, the State Committee, and the leading men of the free-soil party, to the number of about seventy. He stated to the meeting that the people would make a coalition; that it would be successful if the committee would aid it; that Mr. Webster's seventh of March speech could be rebuked; the Fillmore administration condemned; a free-soiler sent to the United States Senate in place of Mr. Webster for the long term; and an anti-compromise Democrat for the short term; and in short, that by a coalition, Massachusetts could be placed in such a position that the anti-slavery men could control her policy. After a debate of five hours, in which Messrs. Marcus Morton, Samuel Hoar, J. G. Palfrey, C. F. Adams, R. H. Dana, Jr., and others took part, the meeting declined to sanction the coalition, only nine gentlemen, and they the youngest present, advocating the coalition. The people, however, made it, in spite of the disapprobation of the eminent men, and the State was carried against the Whigs, and Geo. S. Boutwell made Governor, and Charles Sumner and Robert Rantoul sent to the United States Senate.

In 1850, General Wilson was unanimously nominated for senator from Middlesex County by the free-soil and Democratic conventions, and elected by twenty-one hundred majority. When the legisture met, he was chosen President of the Senate. In 1851, he was reëlected and again chosen president. While President of the Senate, he was made

Chairman of the Committee to welcome President Fillmore to Massachusetts, and also Chairman of the Committee to welcome Kossuth.

In 1852, he was a delegate to the free-soil National Convention at Pittsburg, and was selected to preside over that body, and also made Chairman of the National Free-soil Committee. In the same year, he was unanimously nominated for Congress by the free-soilers of the eighth district, and, although the majority against the free-soilers in that district exceeded seventy-five hundred, he failed of an election by only ninety-three votes. A large portion of the free-soilers desired him that year to be a candidate for Governor, and most of the coalition Democrats likewise desired his nomination. In a public letter he peremptorily declined to be a candidate, notwithstanding which he received more than a third of the votes of the Free-soil State Convention at Lowell.

In March, 1853, General Wilson was elected to the Constitutional Convention by the town of Berlin, and also by his own town of Natick. He was not absent from the convention for an hour during the session, and the journal and report of the debates show the active part taken by him in its transactions. During the temporary illness of the president, Mr. Banks, he was chosen president *pro tem.* In September, 1853, he was nominated by the Free Democratic State Convention, as candidate for the office of Governor. Out of six hundred votes cast by the convention, he received all but three. At the time he was nominated, men of all parties conceded the probability of his election. But the letter of Caleb Cushing, denouncing, in behalf of the administration, the coöperation of Democrats and free-soilers in State affairs—the bitter hostility of conservatism toward the new constitution, and the Irish vote against it—all contributed to overthrow the State reform party, and to defeat General Wilson and his friends.

When the proposition was made in 1854 to abrogate the Missouri Compromise, the country was profoundly excited, and the opponents of slavery extension in all parties hoped to bring about the union of men who were ready to resist the slave-power. Believing that the time had come to effect the union of men who were opposed to the Kansas Nebraska Act, Gen. Wilson labored with unflagging zeal to accomplish that result, and for that end he visited Washington, in May, and consulted with the opponents of the bill, to repeal the prohibition of slavery in Kansas and Nebraska. Returning home, he avowed in the Free-soil State Convention, assembled in Boston on the 31st of May, the readiness of the free-soilers to abandon their organization, everything but their principles, to bring about the union of men who were ready to crush out the members from the North who had betrayed the people, and to sustain the faithful men of all parties who had been true to principle, and who were ready to resist hereafter the policy of the slavery propagandists. Speaking for the men of the free-soil party, he said they "were ready to go into the rear; if a forlorn hope was to be led, they would lead it; they would toil; others might take the lead, hold the offices, and win the honors. The hour had come to form one great Republican party, which should hereafter guide the policy and control the destinies of the Republic. A State Convention was called at Worcester on the 10th of August, with the view of uniting the people in one organization, and Gen. Wilson addressed the people in all sections of the State in favor of the fusion, in which he assured men of all political creeds that the men of the free-soil party would gladly yield to others the lead and the honors; all they asked was the acceptance of their doctrines of perpetual hostility to the aggressive policy of the slave power. But the leaders of the Whig party in Massachusetts, then in the pride of power, resisted all attempts to unite the people, and the convention at Worcester, on the 10th of August, failed to accomplish that decided result. Gen. Wilson, and other members of the free-soil party at this convention, again avowed their desire for union, for the sake of the cause of freedom, and their readiness to yield to men of other parties, everything but principle. The people desired fusion, and in spite of the efforts of the Whig leaders, they rushed into the councils of the American organization to effect that object. Gen. Wilson, finding that all efforts to unite the people in the Republican movement had been defeated by men who had personal ends to secure, urged his friends to unite in that rising organization, liberalize its platform and action, and make it a party for freedom. With the view of bringing about harmonious action among men who desired to unite the people, he accepted the nomination of the Republican party for Governor, and exerted every effort to conciliate and bring together men in favor of organizing a great party of freedom. Some of his political friends doubted the wisdom of his policy, as they did in 1850 the wisdom of the coalition with the Democrats; but that coalition placed Rantoul and Sumner in the Senate of the United States, and this union largely contributed to increase the influence of anti-slavery men, enabling them to choose a delegation to Congress, of true men, a majority of whom were free-soilers, and to elect the most radical anti-slavery legislature ever chosen in America.

In the elections of 1854, the Americans had in the free States coöperated with men of other parties in opposition to the pro-slavery policy of the Administration. But in November of that year, a national council assembled at Cincinnati, and through the management of southern men, anxious to win local power, and corrupt and weak politicians from the North, hungry for place, the American organization was placed in an equivocal attitude on the slavery question. The work of treachery to freedom commenced, and men who had labored to combine the opponents of slavery in one organization, as Gen. Wilson had done, were marked for swift destruction, and men who were ready to compromise away the cause of freedom, were to be the trusted leaders of the now nationalized American party.

The legislature of Massachusetts, which assembled in January, 1855, had to choose a United States senator in place of Mr. Everett, who had resigned and whose term expired on the 3d of March, 1859. General Wilson had publicly and privately declared that the slavery question was with him the paramount question, and in the spring and summer of 1854, while a member of the American organization, he had at all times openly labored to unite men of all parties for freedom. He had taken this position, and his declared opinions and acts were well known in and out of his State, and the men who were ready to sacrifice the anti-slavery cause, to adhere to the compromising policy of the past, were bitterly hostile to his elevation to the Senate. But the anti-slavery men in and out of the State were enthusiastic in his support. He was nominated in the caucus of the members of the legislature, by more than one hundred majority on the first ballot. While the election was pending, several gentlemen representing that portion of the party who wished to nationalize the organization, called upon him, and urged him to write something to modify his recorded opinions, and thus give the men who claimed to be national men, an opportunity to assent to his elevation. In answer to this request, he said he had not travelled a single mile, expended a single dollar, nor conversed with a single member to secure votes for his election;—that his opinions upon the slavery questions were the matured convictions of his life, and that he would not qualify them to win the loftiest position on earth. If elected, he should carry these opinions with him into the Senate, and if the party with which he acted proved recreant to freedom, he would, if he had the power, shiver it to atoms. His position was distinctly avowed and fully comprehended, and he was opposed to the end by members who dissented from his principles, and supported and chosen by men who concurred with him in opinion and policy. He received 234 to 130 votes in the House of Representatives, and 21 to 19 votes in the Senate, and took his seat in the Senate of the United States on the 8th of February, 1855.

When he arrived in Washington, leading politicians were assembled there from the South, endeavoring to organize a National American party, which should ignore the slavery issues, and contest the supremacy of the Democracy in the South. In his speech at Springfield, before the State Council, he thus described the efforts made to seduce him to assent to this policy:

"On my arrival at Washington, I saw at a glance that the politicians of the South—men who had deserted their northern associates upon the Nebraska issue, were resolved to impose upon the American party by the aid of doughfaces from New York and Pennsylvania, as the test of nationality, fidelity to the slave power. Flattering words from veteran statesmen were poured into my ears—flattering appeals were made to me to aid in the work of nationalizing the party whose victories in the South were to be as brilliant as they had been in the North. But I resolved that upon my soul the sin and shame of silence or submission should never rest. I returned home, determined to baffle if I could the meditated treason to freedom and to the North."

Two weeks after taking his seat, he addressed the senate upon Mr. Toucey's "bill to protect persons executing the fugitive slave act, from prosecution by State courts." Extracts from this speech show that his sentiments had undergone no change in Washington, under the pressing influences of political leaders:

"Now, sir, I assure senators from the South, that we of the free States mean to change our policy—I tell you, frankly, just how we feel and just what we propose to do. We mean to withdraw from these halls that class of public men who have betrayed us and deceived you; men who have misrepresented us, and not dealt frankly with you. And we intend to send men into these halls who will truly represent us and deal justly with you. We mean, sir, to place in the councils of the nation men who, in the words of Jefferson, 'have sworn on the altar of God eternal hostility to every kind of oppression of the mind and body of man.' Yes, sir, we mean to place in the national councils men who cannot be seduced by the blandishments, or deterred by the threats of power; men who will fearlessly maintain our principles. I assure senators from the South that the people of the North entertain for them and their people no feelings of hostility; but they will no longer consent to be misrepresented by their own representatives, nor proscribed for their fidelity to freedom. This determination of the people of the North has manifested itself during the past few months in acts not to be misread by the country. The stern rebuke administered to faithless northern representatives, and the annihilation of old and powerful political organizations, should teach senators that the days of waning power are upon them. This action of the people teaches the lesson, which I hope will be heeded, that political combinations can no longer be successfully made to suppress the sentiments of the people. We believe we have the power to abolish slavery in all the territories of the Union; that, if slavery exists there, it exists by the permission and sanction of the Federal Government, and we are responsible for it. We are in favor of its abolition wherever we are morally or legally responsible for its existence.

"I believe conscientiously, that if slavery should be abolished by the National Government in the District of Columbia, and in the territories, the fugitive slave act repealed, the Federal Government relieved from all connection with, or responsibility for the existence of slavery, these angry debates banished from the halls of Congress, and slavery left to the people of the States, that the men of the South who are opposed to the existence of that institution, would get rid of it in their own States at no distant day. I believe that if slavery is ever peacefully abolished in this country—and I certainly believe it will be—it must be abolished in this way.

"The senator from Indiana [Mr. Pettit] has made a long argument to-night to prove the inferiority of the African race. Well, sir, I have no contest with the senator upon that question. I do not claim for that race intellectual equality; but I say to the senator from Indiana that I know men of that race who are quite equal in mental power to either the senator from Indiana or myself—men who are scarcely inferior, in that respect, to any senators upon this floor. But, sir, suppose the senator from Indiana succeeds in establishing the inferiority of that despised race, is mental inferiority a valid reason for the perpetual oppression of a race? Is the mental, moral, or physical inferiority of a man a just cause of oppression in republican and Christian America? Sir, is this Democracy? Is it Christianity? Democracy cares for the poor, the lowly, the humble. Democracy demands that the panoply of just and equal laws shall shield and protect the weakest of the sons of men. Sir, these are strange doctrines to hear uttered in the Senate of republican America, whose political institutions are based upon the fundamental idea that 'all men are created equal.' If the African race is inferior, this proud race of ours should educate and elevate it, and not deny to those who belong to it the rights of our common humanity.

"The senator from Indiana boasts that his State imposes a fine upon the white man that gives employment to the free black man. I am not surprised at the degradation of the colored people of Indiana, who are compelled to live under such inhuman laws, and oppressed by the public sentiment that enacts and sustains them. I thank God, sir, Massachusetts is not dishonored by such laws! In Massachusetts we have about seven thousand colored people. They have, the same rights that we have; they go to our free schools, they enter all the business and professional relations of life, they vote in our elections, and in intelligence and character are scarcely inferior to the citizens of this proud and peerless race whose superiority we have heard so vauntingly proclaimed to-night by the senators from Tennessee and Indiana."

Returning home at the close of the session, he warned his personal friends and political associates that the American organization, which had acted with the anti-Nebraska men in the North, was to be seduced by the South, and betrayed by men in the North, who assumed to control its actions. On the 8th of May, he delivered an address before a large assemblage in the Metropolitan Theatre in New York, upon the development of the anti-slavery sentiment in America for twenty years, from 1835 to 1855. On this occasion he declared that:

"He owed it to truth to speak what he knew—that the anti-slavery cause was in extreme peril—that a demand was made upon us of the North to ignore the slavery question, to keep quiet, and go into power in 1856. If there were men in the free States who hoped to triumph in 1856 by ignoring the slavery issues now forced upon the nation by the slave propagandists, he would say to them, that the anti-slavery men cannot be reduced or driven into the organization of a party that ignores the question of slavery in Christian and Republican America. Let such men read and ponder the history of the Republic; let them contrast anti-slavery in 1835 and anti-slavery in 1855. Those periods are the grand epochs in the anti-slavery movement, and the contrast between them cannot fail to give us some faint conception of the mighty changes that twenty years of anti-slavery agitation have wrought in America. Anti-slavery in 1835 was in the nadir of its weakness; anti-slavery in 1855 is in the zenith of its power. Then, a few unknown, nameless men were its apostles and leaders; now, the most profound and accomplished intellects of America are its chiefs and champions. Then, a few proscribed and humble followers rallied around its banner; now, it has laid its grasp upon the conscience of the people, and hundreds of thousands rally under the folds of its flag. Then, not a single statesman in all America accepted its doctrines or defended its measures; now, it has a decisive majority in the national House of Representatives, and is rapidly changing the complexion of the American Senate. Then, every State in the Union was arrayed against it; now, it controls fifteen sovereign States by more than 300,000 popular majority. Then, the public press covered it with ridicule and contempt; now, the most powerful journals in America are its instruments. Then, the benevolent, religious and literary institutions of the land repulsed its advances, rebuked its doctrines and persecuted its advocates; now, it shapes, molds and fashions them at its pleasure, compelling the most powerful benevolent organizations of the western world, upon whose mission stations the sun never sets, to execute its decress, and the oldest literary institution in America to cast from its bosom a professor who had surrendered a man to the slave hunters. Then, the political organizations trampled disdainfully upon it; now, it looks down with the pride of conscious power upon the wrecked political fragments that float at its feet. Then, it was impotent and powerless; now it holds every political organization in the hollow of its right hand. Then, the public voice sneered at and defied it ; now it is the master of America and has only to be true to itself to grasp the helm and guide the ship of State hereafter in her course."

"This brief contrast," he said, "would show the men who hoped to win power by ignoring the transcendent issue of our age in America, how impotent would be the efforts of any class of men to withdraw the mighty questions involved in the existence and expansion of slavery on this continent, from the consideration of the people." To the idea of going into power by sacrificing the anti-slavery cause, he replied:

"Now, gentlemen, I say to you frankly, I am the last man to object to going into power [laughter], and especially to going into power over the present dynasty that is fastened upon the country. But I am the last man that will consent to go into power by ignoring or sacrificing the slavery question. [Applause.] If my voice could be heard by the whole country to-night—by the anti-slavery men of the country to-night of all parties, I would say to them, resolve it—write it over your door-posts—engrave it on the lids of your Bibles—proclaim it at the rising of the sun and the going down of the sun, and in the broad light of noon, that any party in America, be that party Whig, Democratic, or American, that lifts its finger to arrest the anti-slavery movement, to repress the anti-slavery sentiment, or proscribe the anti-slavery men, it surely shall begin to die—[loud applause]—it would deserve to die ; it will die ; and by the blessing of God I shall do what little I can to make it die."

This address was repeated in Boston, Worcester,

Springfield, Lowell, Dorchester, and other places in Massachusetts, and General Wilson was branded as an agitator, traitor, and disorganizer, by men who had been for six months secretly and darkly intriguing to betray the liberty-loving men who had given the American organization power in the free States. This feeling of hostility was heightened by the publication of his speech, delivered on the 16th of May, at Brattleborough, Vt., "On the position and duty of the American party." In this speech he said that

"The time has come for the advocates of the American movement distinctly to define their principles and their policy.

"If the American party is to achieve anything for good, it must adopt a wise and humane policy consistent with our Democratic ideas—a policy which will reform existing abuses and guard against future ones—which shall combine in one harmonious organization moderate and patriotic men who love freedom and hate oppression. Upon the grand and overshadowing question of American slavery, the American party must take its position. If it wishes a speedy death and a dishonored grave, let it adopt the policy of neutrality upon that question or the policy of ignoring that question. If that party wishes to live, to impress its policy upon the nation, it must repudiate the sectional policy of slavery and stand boldly upon the broad and national basis of freedom. It must accept the position that 'Freedom is national and slavery is sectional.'. It must stand upon the national idea embodied in the Declaration of Independence—that 'all men are created equal, and have an inalienable right to life, liberty, and the pursuit of happiness.' It must accept these words as embracing the great central national idea of

America, fidelity to which is national in New England and in South Carolina. It must recognize the doctrine that the Constitution of the United States was made 'to secure the blessing of liberty,'—that Congress has no right to make a slave or allow slavery to exist outside of the slave States, and that the Federal Government must be relieved from all connection with, and responsibility for slavery.

"In their own good time the Americans of Massachusetts have spoken for themselves. They have placed that old Commonwealth face to face to the slave oligarchy and its allies. Upon their banner they have written in letters of living light the words, 'No exclusion from the public schools on account of race or color.'—'No slave commissioners on the judicial bench.'—'No slave States to be carved out of Kansas and Nebraska.'—'The repeal of the unconstitutional fugitive slave act of 1850.'—'An act to protect personal liberty.' The men who have inscribed these glowing words upon their banner will go into the conflicts of the future like the Zouaves at Inkermann, 'with the light of battle on their faces,'—and if defeat comes, they will fall with their 'backs to the field, and their feet to the foe.'"

Early in June, 1855, the American National Council assembled at Philadelphia. General Wilson was a delegate, and his position in the Senate, and his avowed sentiments, opinions and policy, brought him at once into conflict with the men in and out of the council, who were intriguing to make the American organization an instrument of the slave power. An attempt was made to keep him out of the council, on account of the sentiments he had expressed, and to draw off the Massachusetts delegation from him;

but they stood by him, and thus baffled the designs of the plotters. On taking his seat in the council, he was at once recognized by friends and foes as the leader of the North—the representative of the anti-slavery men of the free States. The National Council sat for more than one week, and during that time it was the scene of stormy, exciting and angry discussion upon the slavery question. Early in the debate, a delegate from Virginia made a fierce personal attack upon him, quoting from his speeches, and denouncing him as the leader of the anti-slavery men of the North, who had come into the council to rule or to destroy. General Wilson promptly replied to this assault, and defiantly told the delegate from Virginia and his compeers, that "his threats had no terrors for free men—that he was then and there ready to meet argument with argument—scorn with scorn—and if need, be, blow with blow, for God had given him an arm ready and able to protect his head! It was time the champions of slavery in the South should realize the fact, that the past was theirs—the future ours." The debate went on, and on the 12th of June, General Wilson made an elaborate speech in reply to the assaults made upon the North and upon the anti-slavery men, by both southern and northern delegates. To the assaults made upon Massachusetts by some of the delegates from New York, he said: "When Massachusetts pleads to any arraignment before the nation, she will demand that her accusers are competent to draw the bill." To the men of the South who had denounced the action of Massachusetts, he replied:

"But gentlemen of talents and of character have undertaken here to arraign Massachusetts. To those gentlemen I have to say, that Massachusetts means to go to the very verge of her constitutional powers, to protect the personal rights of her people! She means to exercise her constitutional rights, for the security of the liberties of her people, against what she deems to be unconstitutional, inhuman and unchristian legislation; and I tell you frankly, if any constitutional powers are in doubt, she will construe them in favor of liberty; not in favor of slavery. In the future, if she errs at all, in the interpretation of her reserved rights, as a sovereign State, I trust she will go a little beyond the limits of State sovereignty, rather than fall short of marching up to those limits. The personal liberties of her people demand that she should do so.

"Massachusetts has the right, if she chooses, to remove from her judicial bench, any officers who shall consent to perform the duties imposed upon United States commissioners. She denies your right, gentlemen, to arraign her here or elsewhere for the exercise of her own constitutional powers. By the decision of the Supreme Court of the United States, Massachusetts has a right to forbid the use of her prisons —she has a right to forbid her officers from engaging in the extradition of fugitives from labor. She believes that every human being within her limits, has a right to the benefits of the writ of *habeas corpus*, and to a jury trial. She proposes to test the question by the judicial authorities. Her 'offence hath that extent, no more.' Massachusetts stands upon the State rights doctrines of Virginia and Kentucky, of 1798 and 1799. She raises no standard of nullification or rebellion—she will submit to the decisions of those tribunals authorized to expound the judicial powers of the Government.

"The gentleman from Alabama (Judge Hopkins), has hinted to us that the Southern States may find it necessary to protect themselves against this action of Massachusetts, by legislation that shall touch her material interests. Threats of that kind, sir, have no terrors for Massachusetts. Her people will laugh to scorn all such idle threats, by whomsoever made. Massachusetts, with one million of intelligent people, with free schools, free churches, free labor, is competent to take care of her own material interests. 'Her goods are for sale—not her principles.' If gentlemen from the South expect to intimidate Massachusetts by such threats, I tell them here and now, that we scorn, spurn and defy your threats."

Of the proposed national platform he said:

"The adoption of this platform commits the American party unconditionally to the policy of slavery—to the iron dominion of the Black Power. I tell you, sir, I tell this convention, that we cannot stand upon this platform in a single free State of the North. The people of the North will repudiate it, spurn it, spit upon it. For myself, sir, I here and now tell you to your faces, that I will trample with disdain on your platform. I will not support it. I will support no man who stands upon it. Adopt that platform, and you array against you everything that is pure and holy—everything that has the elements of permanency in it—the noblest pulsations of the human heart—the holiest convictions of the human soul—the profoundest ideas of the human intellect and the attributes of Almighty God! Your party will be withered and consumed by the blasting breath of the people's wrath! There is an old Spanish proverb, which says that 'the feet of the avenging deities are shod with wool.' Softly and silently these avenging deities are advancing upon you. You will find that 'the mills of God grind slowly, but they grind to powder.'

"When I united with the American organization in March, 1854, in its hour of weakness—I told the men with whom I acted that my anti-slavery opinions were the matured convictions of years, and that I would not modify or qualify my opinions or suppress my sentiments for any consideration on earth. From that hour to this, in public and in private, I have freely uttered my anti-slavery sentiments, and labored to promote the anti-slavery cause, and I tell you now, that I will continue to do so. You shall not proscribe anti-slavery principles, measures or men, without receiving from me the most determined and unrelenting hostility. It is a painful thing to differ from our associates and friends—but when duty, a stern sense of duty, demands it, I shall do so. Reject this majority platform—adopt the proposition to restore freedom to Kansas and Nebraska, and to protect the actual settlers from violence and outrage—simplify your rules—make an open organization—banish all bigotry and intolerance from your ranks—place your movement in harmony with the humane progressive spirit of the age, and you may win and retain power, and elevate and improve the political character of the country. Adopt this majority platform—commit the American movement to the slave perpetualists and the slave propagandists, and you will go down before the burning indignation and withering scorn of American freemen."

But the pro-slavery platform was adopted, and most of the delegates from the North retired from the National Council. A meeting was at once held, over which General Wilson presided. This meeting adopted a protest against the action of the council, and announced their final separation from the national organization. The American organization was shivered to atoms, and no man contributed more to that result than General Wilson; and in doing it he but redeemed the words he had uttered while his election to the Senate was pending. The New York "Tribune," referring to the action of the council, said:

"The antecedents of Mr. Wilson naturally made him the particular object of hostility to the slave-drivers in the convention; and one of the earliest displays after the body was organized, was a grossly personal attack upon him by a delegate from Virginia. But the assailants had now met an antagonist who was not to be cowed or silenced, and the response they received was of a character to induce them not to repeat their experiment. We have the unanimous testimony of many northern members of the convention to the signal gallantry and effect of Mr. Wilson's bearing, and to the bold, virile and telling eloquence of his speeches. While all have done so well in bringing about results so gratifying, it may be invidious to particularize; but a few names among the northern members, who were devoted from the start to the work of creating a unity and a strength of *northern backbone,* should justly be exposed to the public appreciation and honor that they deserve. First stands Henry Wilson of Massachusetts, preëminent as the leader in the whole movement. He was handsomely sustained by all his associates, and the numerous insidious efforts of the enemy to separate them from him, only attached them the more closely to his side. He has the highest honor in this contest, exhibited the greatest political ability, and broke down many strong prejudices against him, both among Massachusetts men who were witnesses to his conduct, and among the delegates of the other States, North and South. No man went into that council with more elements of distrust and opposition combined against him ; no one goes out of it with such an enviable fame, or such an aggregation to his honor. He is worthy of Massachusetts, and worthy to lead the new movement of the people of that State, which the result here so fitly inaugurates."

General Wilson, during the summer and autumn of 1855, visited thirteen States, travelled more than twenty thousand miles, consulted with leading men of all parties, and addressed tens of thousands of people in favor of the fusion of men of all parties for freedom. In the State council of the Americans of Massachusetts, at Springfield, on the 7th of August, he made an elaborate speech on the "necessity of the fusion of parties," in which he invoked the members to sustain the resolution announcing the readiness of the Americans "to unite and coöperate with" men of other parties, in forming a great party of freedom. On that occasion he said:

"The gathering hosts of northern freemen, of every party and creed, are banding together to resist the aggressive policy of the Black Power. Freedom, patriotism, and humanity demand the union of the freemen of the Republic, for the sake of liberty now perilled. Religion sanctions and blesses it.

"How and where stands Massachusetts? Shall she range herself in line, front to the Black Power, with her sister States? or shall she maintain the fatal position of isolation? Here and now, we, the chosen representatives of the American party of this Commonwealth, are to meet that issue, to solve that problem.

"The American party of Massachusetts, dashing other organizations into powerless fragments, had grasped the reins of power, placed an unbroken delegation in Congress pledged to the policy of freedom, ranged this ancient Commonwealth front to front with the slave power, and written, with the iron pen of history, upon her statutes, declarations of principles and pledges of acts hostile to the aggressive policy of the slaveholding power. When the Black Power of the imperious South, aided by the servile power of the faltering North, imposed upon the national American organization its principles, measures and policy, the representatives of the American party of this Commonwealth, spurned the unhallowed decrees, turned their backs, forever, upon that prostituted organization, and their action received the approving sanction of this State council by a vote approaching unanimity. The American party, as a national organization, is broken and shivered to atoms. By its own act the American party of Massachusetts has severed itself from all connection with that product of southern domination and northern submission.

"The American party of Massachusetts has, during its brief existence, uttered true words and performed noble deeds for freedom. The past at least is secure. Whatever may have been its errors of omission or commission, the slave and the slave's friends will never reproach it. Holding, as it does, the reins of power, it has now a glorious opportunity to give to the country the magnanimous example of a great and dominant party, in the full possession of consummated power, freely yielding up that power, for the holy cause of freedom, to the equal possession of other parties, who are willing to coöperate with it upon a common platform. Here and now, we, its representatives, are to show by our acts whether we can rise above the demands of partisan policy, to the full comprehension of the condition of public affairs—to the full realization of the obligations which fidelity to freedom now imposes upon us.

"If the representatives of the American party reject this proposition for fusion, I shall go home once more with a sad heart—but I shall not go home to sulk in my tent—to rail and fret at the folly of men; I shall go home, sir, with a resolved spirit and iron will, determined to hope on and to struggle on, until I see the lovers of universal and impartial freedom banded together in one organization—moved by one impulse. For seven years I have labored to break up old organizations, and to make new combinations, all tending to the organization of that great party of the future, which is to relieve the government from the iron dominion of the Black Power.

"Sir, gentlemen may defeat this proposed fusion here to-day, but they cannot control the action of the people. A fusion movement will be made under the lead of gentlemen of the Whig, Democratic and Free-soil parties, of talents and character. The movement will be in harmony with the people's movements in the North. Sir, such a movement will put a majority of the men, who voted with you last autumn, in a false position before the country, or drive them from your ranks. I cannot speak for others, but I tell you frankly, that I cannot be placed in a false position—I cannot, even for one moment, consent to stand arrayed against the hosts of freedom now preparing for the contest of 1856. I tell you frankly that whenever I see a formation in position to strike effective blows for freedom, I shall be with it in the conflict—whenever I see an organization in position antagonistic to freedom, my arm shall aid in smiting it down."

The proposition for a union of the people was lost by a small vote, and the twenty-one years' amendment adopted by a small majority. Against the twenty-one years proposition, General Wilson said:

"Sir, the American movement is not based upon bigotry, intolerance or proscription. If there is anything of bigotry, intolerance or proscription in the American movement—if there is any disposition to oppress or degrade the Briton, the Scot, the Celt, the German or any one of another clime or race, or to deny to them the fullest protection of just and equal laws, it is time such criminal fanaticism was sternly rebuked by the intelligent patriotism of the State and country. I deeply deplore, sir, the adoption of the twenty-one years amendment. It will weaken the American movement at home and in other States, especially in the West, and tend to defeat any modification whatever of the naturalization laws. I warn gentlemen, who desire the correction of the evils growing out of the abuses of the naturalization laws, against the adoption of extreme opinions. I tell you, gentlemen of the council, that this intense nativism kills—yes, sir, it kills and is killing us, and unless it is speedily abandoned, will defeat all the needed reforms the movement was inaugurated to secure, and overwhelm us all in dishonor. Every attempt, by whomsoever made, to interpolate into the American movement, anything inconsistent with the theory of our democratic institutions—anything inconsistent with the idea that 'all men are created equal'—anything contrary to the commands of God's Holy Word that 'the stranger that dwelleth with you shall be unto you as one born among you, and thou shalt love him as thyself,'—is doing that which will baffle the wise policy which tries to reform existing evils and to guard against future abuses."

General Wilson engaged with his accustomed industry and energy in the practical business, and in the exciting debates of the memorable session of 1855–6. In February, he made a speech on the affairs of Kansas, replete with facts not then familiar to the country. This speech went through three editions, and nearly 200,000 copies were circulated through the free States. In April, General Wilson made a speech in favor of receiving the petition of the Topeka Legislature for admission into the Union, and on this occasion in reply to the taunts of Mr. Douglas about "Amalgamationists," he said:

"Mr. President, the senator from Illinois tells us, with an air of proud assurance, that the State he represents does not believe the negro the equal of the white man; that she is opposed to placing that degraded race upon terms of equality; that she had a right to enact her black laws; and that if we of Massachusetts do not like those acts, she does not care. Illinois, he tells us, does not wish the blood of the white race to mingle with the blood of the inferior race—Massachusetts can do otherwise if she chooses. Let me tell the honorable senator from Illinois, that these taunts, so often flung out about the equality of races, about amalgamation, and the mingling of blood, are the emanations of low and vulgar minds. These taunts usually come from men with the odor of amalgamation upon them. Sir, I am proud to live in a commonwealth where every man, black or white, of every clime and race, is recognized as a man, standing upon terms of perfect and absolute equality before the laws. Yes, sir, I live in a commonwealth that recognizes the sublime creed embodied in the Declaration of Independence—a commonwealth that throws over the poor, the weak, the lowly, upon whom misfortune has laid its iron hand, the protection of just and equal laws.

Sir, the people of Massachusetts may not believe that the African race,

"Outcast to insolence and scorn,"

is the equal to this Anglo-Saxon race of ours in intellectual power ; but they know no reason why a man, made in the image of God, should be degraded by unjust laws, because his Creator has given him a weak body or a feeble mind. Sir, the philanthropist, the Christian, the true Democratic statesman, will, see in the fact that a man is weak, ignorant, and poor, the reason why the State should throw over him the panoply of just and equal laws."

In the latter part of May, 1856, Mr. Sumner was assailed in his seat in the Senate chamber by Mr. Brooks of South Carolina, and beaten over the head with a cane until he fell unconscious upon the floor, covered with blood. When the assault was made, General Wilson was in the room of Speaker Banks engaged in conversation with several members of the House. Returning to the Senate Chamber, he found his friend and colleague almost unconscious in the hands of his friends. He aided in the sad task of bearing him to his chamber and placing him on his couch of pain. That night the Republican members met at the house of Mr. Seward, and commissioned General Wilson to call the attention of the Senate to the assault upon his colleague, which duty he performed next day in a few very appropriate words. On motion of Mr. Seward, a committee was appointed, and on the morning of the 27th, Mr. Slidell, Mr. Toombs, Mr. Douglas and others rose to make some personal explanations concerning the statement made to the committee by Mr. Sumner. The floor and galleries were crowded, and every word was listened to with the most intense interest. General Wilson rose to defend his absent colleague, who was confined to his room, as he declared, from the effects "of *a brutal, murderous, and cowardly assault.*" He was instantly interrupted by an exclamation from Mr. Butler, and cries of order increased the intense excitement which prevailed in the crowded chamber. Threats of personal violence were made by Mr. Brooks' friends, and several members of both houses assured General Wilson that they would stand by him in any emergency. That evening, after the adjournment of Congress, he was compelled to leave Washington for Trenton, to address the Republican State convention of New Jersey. On his return, on the morning of the 29th, he was called upon by General Lane, of Oregon, and a challenge from Mr. Brooks placed in his hands. General Wilson promptly responded by placing in the hands of General Lane, through his friend, Mr. Buffinton, the following note:

WASHINGTON, *May* 29, 10½ *o'clock.*

"HON. P. S. BROOKS,

"SIR: Your note of the 27th inst. was placed in my hands by your friend General Lane, at twenty minutes past ten o'clock to-day.

"I characterized, on the floor of the Senate, the assault

upon my colleague as 'brutal, murderous, and cowardly.' I thought so then, I think so now. I have no qualifications whatever to make in regard to those words.

"I have never entertained or expressed in the Senate or elsewhere, the idea of personal responsibility in the sense of the duellist.

"I have always regarded duelling as the lingering relic of a barbarous civilization, which the law of the country has branded as a crime. While, therefore, I religiously believe in the right of self-defence in its broadest sense, the law of my country and the matured convictions of my whole life alike forbid me to meet you for the purpose indicated in your letter.

"Your obedient servant,

"HENRY WILSON."

This prompt and emphatic response, declining to fight a duel, but at the same time avowing his readiness to maintain the right of self-defence, was most enthusiastically approved and applauded by the people and presses of the North, and he received many letters, from men of the highest character, warmly commending his noble and dignified course.

On the 13th of June. General Wilson made a full and elaborate reply to Mr. Butler, and in defence of Mr. Sumner. This speech and his speeches on the bill to admit Kansas, his speech in defence of the acts of Col. Fremont, and against using the army to enforce the acts of the territorial legislature of Kansas, were largely circulated through the country.

On the adjournment of Congress, General Wilson

entered into the Presidential campaign, and gave all his energies to secure the triumph of the Republican cause.

During the sessions of 1856–7–8 and 1858–9, General Wilson was in constant attendance upon Congress, and his duties, owing to the prolonged absence of his colleague, were very arduous and pressing. In those sessions he took his full share of labor in the committee rooms, on the floor of the Senate, and on matters of legislative action. He took part in the debates during these sessions, upon all questions of importance, and on most of the questions before the Senate, he delivered elaborate speeches. Those upon the affairs of Kansas exhibit an amount of information, concerning that territory, surpassed by no other member of either House of Congress, and his speeches on the Treasury Note bill, the expenses of the Government, the revenue collection appropriations, the tariff, the President's Message, and the Pacific Railroad, are remarkable for fullness and accuracy of facts, and clearness and force of statement. His speech in March, 1850, in reply to Mr. Hammond of South Carolina, is one of the most effective speeches ever delivered in Congress, in defence of free labor. It is full of facts and points of great power, and few speeches ever made in Congress have had a wider circulation, or received warmer approval, in the free States.

Mr. Hammond characterized the manual laborers as "slaves"—the "mud-sills" of society. This extract is quoted from General Wilson's reply:

"Mr. President, the senator from South Carolina tells us that 'all the powers of the world cannot abolish' 'the thing' he calls slavery. 'God only can do it when he repeals the fiat, "the poor ye have always with you;" for the man who lives by daily labor, and your whole class of hireling manual laborers and operatives, are essentially slaves! Our slaves are black; happy, content, unaspiring; yours are white, and they feel galled by their degradation. Our slaves do not vote; yours do vote, and, being the majority, they are the depositaries of all your political power; and if they knew the tremendous secret, that the ballot-box is stronger than an army with banners, and could combine, your society would be reconstructed, your government overthrown, and your property divided.'

"'The poor ye have always with you!' This fiat of Almighty God, which Christian men of all ages and lands have accepted as the imperative injunction of the common Father of all, to care for the children of misfortune and sorrow, the senator from South Carolina accepts as the foundation-stone, the eternal law, of slavery, which 'all the powers of earth cannot abolish.' These precious words of our Heavenly Father, 'the poor ye have always with you,' are perpetually sounding in the ears of mankind, ever reminding them of their dependence and their duties. These words appeal alike to the conscience and the heart of mankind. To men blessed in their basket and their store, they say 'property has its duties as well as its rights!' To men clothed with authority to shape the policy or to administer the laws of the State, they say, 'lighten by wise, humane, and equal laws, the burdens of the toiling and dependent children of men!' To men of every age and every clime they appeal, by the

Divine promise that 'he that giveth to the poor lendeth to the Lord!' Sir, I thank God that I live in a commonwealth which sees no warrant in these words of inspiration to oppress the sons and daughters of toil and poverty. Over the poor and lowly she casts the broad shield of equal, just, and humane legislation. The poorest man that treads her soil, no matter what blood may run in his veins, is protected in his rights and incited to labor by no other force than the assurance that the fruits of his toil belong to himself, to the wife of his bosom, and the children of his love.

"The senator from South Carolina exclaims, 'The man who lives by daily labor, your whole class of manual laborers, are essentially slaves'—'they feel galled by their degradation!' What a sentiment is this to hear uttered in the councils of this democratic Republic! The senator's political associates who listen to these words which brand hundreds of thousands of the men they represent in the free States, and hundreds of their neighbors and personal friends as 'slaves,' have found no words to repel or rebuke this language. This language of scorn and contempt is addressed to senators who were not nursed by a slave; whose lot it was to toil with their own hands—to eat bread earned, not by the sweat of another's brow, but by their own. Sir, I am the son of a 'hireling manual laborer' who, with the frosts of seventy winters on his brow, 'lives by daily labor.' I, too, have 'lived by daily labor.' I, too, have been a 'hireling manual laborer.' Poverty cast its dark and chilling shadow over the home of my childhood, and want was there sometimes—an unbidden guest. At the age of ten years—to aid him who gave me being, in keeping the gaunt spectre from the hearth of the mother who bore me—I left the home of my boyhood, and went to earn my bread by 'daily labor.' Many a weary mile have I travelled

"'To beg a brother of the earth
To give me leave to toil.'

"Sir, I have toiled as a 'hireling manual laborer' in the field and in the workshop; and I tell the senator from South Carolina that I never 'felt galled by my degradation.' No, sir—never! Perhaps the senator who represents that 'other class which leads progress, civilization, and refinement,' will ascribe this to obtuseness of intellect and blunted sensibilities of the heart. Sir, I was conscious of my manhood; I was the peer of my employer; I knew that the laws and institutions of my native and adopted States threw over him and over me alike the panoply of equality; I knew, too, that the world was before me, that its wealth, its garnered treasures of knowledge, its honors, the coveted prizes of life, were within the grasp of a brave heart and a tireless hand, and I accepted the responsibilities of my position all unconscious that I was a 'slave.' I have employed others, hundreds of 'hireling manual laborers.' Some of them then possessed, and now possess, more property than I ever owned; some of them were better educated than myself—yes, sir, better educated, and better read, too, than some senators on this floor; and many of them, in moral excellence and purity of character, I could not but feel, were my superiors. I have occupied, Mr. President, for more than thirty years, the relation of employer and employed; and while I never felt 'galled by my degradation' in the one case, in the other I was never conscious that my 'hireling laborers' were my inferiors. That man is a 'snob' who boasts of being a 'hireling laborer,' or who is ashamed of being a 'hireling laborer;' that man is a 'snob' who feels any inferiority to any man because he is a 'hireling laborer,' or who assumes any superiority over others because he is an employer. Honest labor is honorable; and the man who is ashamed that he is or was a 'hireling laborer' has not manhood enough to 'feel galled by his degradation.'

"Having occupied, Mr. President, the relation of either employed or employer for a third of a century; having lived in a commonwealth where the 'hireling class of manual laborers' are 'the depositaries of political power;' having associated with this class in all the relations of life; I tell the senator from South Carolina, and the class he represents, that he libels, grossly libels them, when he declares that they are 'essentially slaves!' There can be found nowhere in America, a class of men more proudly conscious or tenacious of their rights. Friends and foes have ever found them

'A stubborn race, fearing and flattering none.'

"Ours are the institutions of freedom; and they flourish best in the storms and agitations of inquiry and free discussion. We are conscious that our social and political institutions have not attained perfection, and we invoke the examination and the criticism of the genius and learning of all Christendom. Should the senator and his agitators and lecturers come to Massachusetts on a mission to teach our 'hireling class of manual laborers,' our 'mud-sills,' our 'slaves,' the 'tremendous secret of the ballot-box,' and to help 'combine and lead them,' these stigmatized 'hirelings' would reply to the senator and his associates, 'We are freemen; we are the peers of the gifted and the wealthy; we know the "tremendous secret of the ballot-box;" and we mold and fashion these institutions that bless and adorn our proud and free Commonwealth! These public schools are ours, for the education of our children; these libraries, with their accumulated treasures, are ours; these multitudinous and varied pursuits of life, where intelligence and skill find their reward, are ours. Labor is here honored and respected, and great examples incite us to action. All around us in the professions, in the marts of commerce, on the exchange, where merchant-princes and capitalists do congregate; in these manufactories and workshops, where the products of every clime are fashioned into a thousand forms of utility and beauty; on these smiling farms, fertilized by the sweat of free labor; in every position of private and of public life, are our associates, who were but yesterday "hireling laborers,' "mud-sills," "slaves." In every department of human effort are noble men who sprang from our ranks—men whose good deeds will be felt and will live in the grateful memories of men when the stones reared by the hands of affection to their honored names shall crumble into dust. Our eyes glisten and our hearts throb over the bright, glowing and radiant pages of our history that records the deeds of patriotism of the sons of New England who sprang from our ranks and wore the badges of toil. While the names of Benjamin Franklin, Roger Sherman, Nathaniel Greene and Paul Revere live on the brightest pages of our history, the mechanics of Massachusetts and New England will never want illustrious examples to incite us to noble aspirations and noble deeds. Go home, say to your privileged class, which, you vauntingly say, "leads progress, civilization and refinement," that it is the opinion of the "hireling laborers" of Massachusetts, if you have no sympathy for your African bondmen, in whose veins flows so much of your own blood, you should at least sympathize with the millions of your own race, whose labor you have dishonored and degraded by slavery! You should teach your millions of poor and ignorant white men, so long oppressed by your policy, the "tremendous secret that the ballot-box is stronger than an army with banners!" You should combine and lead them to the adoption of a policy which shall secure their own emancipation from a degrading thralldom!'"

Early in January, 1859, Gen. Wilson was reëlected United States Senator for six years from March 3, 1859. He had in the Senate 35 to 5 votes, and in the House of Representatives 199 to 36 votes. Before the people and in the legislature, he was without a competitor in the ranks of his own party; and the unity of sentiment in favor of his reëlection was a noble tribute of which any public man might justly be proud.

JEFFERSON DAVIS.

JEFFERSON DAVIS is a native of Kentucky. His father took him, when he was an infant, to Mississippi Territory, about the year 1806. His father was moderately wealthy and gave his son an excellent education. He had the ordinary course at the schools, and then entered Transylvania University College, Kentucky. There he remained till his father removed him to West Point as a cadet. This was in 1822, and in 1828 he left it with honor as brevet second lieutenant, and was at once placed in active service. He served in the Indian war of the times so ably as to gain almost immediately a first lieutenant's commission. The famous Indian chief, "Black Hawk," became his prisoner, and a strong friendship was struck up between the lieutenant and his prisoner, which lasted till the death of the latter.

In 1835, Mr. Davis, sickened of military life without the excitement of actual engagement with an enemy, and retired from the service, settling down upon a cotton plantation in Mississippi. For nearly ten years he remained on his plantation in quiet, cultivating cotton and his intellect at the same time, for he was during all these years of rural life a great student and reader. He was contentedly preparing himself for the future occasion which should call for his services. In 1843, he took the stump for Mr. Polk, and such was his ability before the people that they sent him to Congress in 1845. When he had been in Washington but a few months, the war with Mexico broke out, and his constituents raised a regiment of volunteers, who elected Mr. Davis as their colonel. He immediately resigned his seat in Congress, and went with his regiment to join General Taylor in Mexico. The history of Col. Davis' career in Mexico is full of interest, but we cannot stay to elaborate it. At Buena Vista he won laurels of glory, in the parlance of the soldier. Says a friend of his:

"His men—though volunteers—showed a steadiness which equalled anything that might have been expected of veteran troops; and they were handled in so masterly a way, that, if the glory of that day were to be assigned to any one corps rather than any other, they would probably bear away the palm. Every one remembers the proud appeal of Colonel Davis to another regiment of volunteers, who were finding the fire rather warm, to 'Stay and re-form behind that wall'—pointing to his Mississippians. Throughout the war, he and his brave riflemen loom up at intervals whenever the fire grows hot or the emergency grave, and never without good effect. They were armed with a peculiar rifle, now best known as the Mississippi rifle, chosen by their colonel himself; it was scarcely less deadly than the Minié. Their colonel set the example of intrepidity and recklessness of personal injury: at Buena Vista he was badly wounded at an early part of the action; but he sat his horse steadily till the day was won, and refused even to delegate a portion of his duties to his subordinate officers."

The term of service for which his regiment was enlisted having expired, his medical advisers insisted upon his going home and curing himself of his wounds. He did not stay long, however; for that very year—in the late autumn—he was appointed United States Senator by the Governor of Mississippi to fill a vacancy, and when the legislature of the State came together, it elected him to the same high office for the ensuing six years.

In the Senate he at once took a high position. He was made Chairman of the Military Committee of the Senate, a position he has held during his entire term of senatorial services, and which he has honored. In the long and excited debates of 1849–50, and 1850–51, Mr. Davis took a prominent part, and always what is termed an ultra-sectional position. He was the champion of the extreme South, and made some of the ablest speeches of the entire slavery debate.

In September, 1851, Mr. Davis was nominated by the Democrats of Mississippi, as their candidate for Governor. He at once resigned his seat in the

Senate. He lost an election by a thousand votes—and retired to his plantation.

Upon the nomination of Franklin Pierce to the Presidency, he took the stump for him in several of the more doubtful southern States, and with great success. His popularity before the people as a speaker was great, and his success was in due proportion.

Mr. Pierce rewarded Mr. Davis for his eminent services in the campaign by the offer of the Secretaryship of War—an office which he was peculiarly qualified to fill. He was quite successful as Secretary of War, though his unfortunate quarrel with General Scott (about the merits of which we are incompetent to pronounce an opinion), damaged his popularity with a portion of his friends. When the Pierce administration went out, Mr. Davis was reëlected United States Senator, and he has latterly been looked upon as a Democratic leader in the Senate.

In his personal appearance in the Senate-room, Mr. Davis has few equals. Tall, upright, stern, and with the bearing of a prince, he at once commands the admiration of the stranger so far as his personal appearance is concerned. His military manners have followed him from the camp into the Senate. We say this in no offensive sense, though it is true that the senator often unintentionally offends by the quickness, the savageness, and the irritability of his style and speech. This is not intentional, and though it now and then gives offence, it at the same time gives great force to the sentiment which the senator may be uttering at the time. He has a peculiar voice, keyed high, yet musical, and his words come flowing out like so many cannon-balls with the force of gunpowder behind them.

The political position of Mr. Davis cannot be misunderstood. He is ultra-southern. Not a disunionist, at all events; but a disunionist in a certain event. He stands by the extreme southern men—occupies an extreme southern position for a man who claims yet to stand by the national Democratic party. His views upon the non-intervention doctrines of Mr. Douglas, we shall quote that we may not do him injustice. He is an enthusiastic and consistent advocate of utter free trade. Nothing short of absolute free trade will suit him or satisfy him. He is also opposed to the Homestead bill, and all like appropriations of the public lands. He is in favor of the acquisition of Cuba, but opposed the Senate resolution—proposed—giving Mr. Buchanan power to make war upon the southern republics when he should think the occasion demanded it.

If Mr. Davis' position be thought to be extremely southern, it must be remembered that he is an honest, upright man—much more so than some who clamor after office; and that such a man can be trusted generally, in spite of his prejudices, to deal fairly even with his opponents. An honest man, however ultra his position, if he have intellect, is safer to be trusted with a high office, than the mere twaddling politician, who will execute the party's bidding, however iniquitous it may be.

In the great "non-intervention debate" of the Senate, in February, 1859, Mr. Davis said:

"Now, the senator asks will you make a discrimination in the territories? I say yes, I would discriminate in the territories wherever it is needful to assert the right of a citizen: wherever it is proper to carry out the principle, the obligation, the clear intent and meaning of the Constitution of the United States. I have heard many a siren's song on this doctrine of non-intervention; a thing shadowy and fleeting, changing its color as often as the chameleon, which never meant anything fairly unless it was that Congress would not attempt to legislate on a subject over which they had no control; that they would not attempt to establish slavery anywhere nor to prohibit it anywhere; and such was the language of the compromise measures of 1850 when this doctrine was inaugurated. Since that, it has been woven into a delusive gauze, thrown over the public mind, and presented as an obligation of the Democratic party to stand still; withholding from an American citizen the protection he has a right to claim; to surrender their power; to do nothing; to prove faithless to the trust they hold at the hands of the people of the States. If the theory of the senator be correct, and if Congress has no power to legislate in any regard upon the subject, how did you pass the fugitive slave law? He repeats, again and again, that you have no power to legislate in regard to slavery either in the States or in the territories, and yet the fugitive slave law stands on the statute-book ; and although he did not vote for it, he explained to the country why he did not, and expressed his regret that his absence had prevented him from recording his vote in favor of it.

"From the plain language of the Constitution, as I have read it, how is it possible for one still claiming to follow the path of the Constitution, to assert that Congress has no power to legislate in relation to the subject anywhere? He informs us, however, that by the Kansas-Nebraska bill, the full power of the inhabitants of a territory to legislate on all subjects not inconsistent with the Constitution, was granted by Congress. If Congress attempted to make such a grant; if Congress thus attempted to rid themselves of a trust imposed upon them, they exceeded their authority. They could delegate no such power. The territorial legislature can be but an instrument, through which the Congress of the United States execute their trust in relation to the territories. Therefore it was, that notwithstanding the exact language of that bill which the senator has read, the Congress of the United States did assume, and did exercise, the power to repeal a law passed in that very territory of Kansas, which they clearly could not have done if they had surrendered all control over its legislation. Whether the senator voted for that report or not, I do not know ; I presume he did ; but whether he did or not, does not vary the question, except so far as it affects himself. The advocates of the Kansas-Nebraska bill were generally the men who most promptly claimed the repeal of those laws, because they said they were a violation of those rights which every American citizen possessed under the Constitution.

"But the senator says territorial laws can only be set aside by an appeal to the Supreme Court of the United States. If so, then they have a power not derived from

Congress; they are not the instruments of Congress. But in the course of the senator's remarks, and quite inconsistent with this position, he announced that they possessed no power save that which they derived from the organic act and the Constitution. They can derive no power from the Constitution save as territories of the United States, over which the States have given the power of a trustee to the Congress; and being the delegate of the Congress, they have such powers as Congress has thought proper to give, provided they do not exceed such powers as the Congress possesses. How, then, does the Senator claim that they have a power to legislate which Congress cannot revise; and yet no power to legislate at all save that which they derive from their organic act?

"My friend from Alabama presented a question to the senator from Illinois, which he did not answer. It was, whether a law pronounced unconstitutional by the Supreme Court was still to remain in force within the territory, Congress failing to provide any remedy which would restore the right violated by that unconstitutional act? The senator answers me from his seat, 'clearly not.' Then I ask him, what is the remedy? The law is pronounced unconstitutional, and yet the right which it has violated is not restored; the protection which is required is not granted; the law which deprived him of the protection, though it may be declared unconstitutional, is not replaced by any which will give him the adequate protection to hold his property. Then what is the benefit he derives from the decision of the Supreme Court? The decision of the Supreme Court is binding upon the Congress; but this squatter-sovereignty legislation, seeming to be outside of the Constitution, outside of the legislation of the Federal Government, erects itself into an attitude that seems to me quite inappropriate.

"I concede to the Congress the power, through the instrumentality of a territorial legislature, to legislate upon such subjects as Congress itself has the right to make laws for ; no more than that. More than that the senator cannot claim, unless he can show to us that philosophical problem of getting more out of a tub than it contains ; its contents being measured, to find something more which can be taken out of it. If he will not—and I suppose he will not—contend that Congress can delegate more power than it possesses, how does he get the power in the territorial legislature to pass laws which will interfere with the rights of a citizen choosing to migrate to a territory ? It is the common property of the people of the States. Every citizen has a right to go there, and to carry with him whatever property is recognized by the Constitution ; the common law of the States forming the Union. Congress has no power to prohibit it ; is bound to see that it is fully enjoyed. Then, I ask the senator, where does he derive the power for the territorial legislature to do it ? for he has planted himself now on the ground that they derive their authority from the organic act."

At a subsequent stage of the debate, the subjoined colloquy occurred between Mr. Pugh, of Ohio, who had the floor, and Mr. Davis :

"Mr. Davis.—With the permission of the senator from Ohio, I will ask him whether he understood the senator from Virginia to assert that the Constitution of the United States would give the right to carry this property into the limits of a State where it is prohibited ?

"Mr. Pugh.—No, sir ; but I say that this proposition is nothing, unless it goes to that extent.

"Mr. Davis.—In the absence of my friend from Virginia, I would say that his theory, I believe, agrees with mine ; and certainly does not go to that extent. It is that the

Constitution makes it property throughout the United States. It can, therefore, be taken and held wherever the sovereign power of a State has not prohibited it. When it reaches the territory of a sovereign State where its introduction is inhibited, it there stops ; except for the reserved right to recover a fugitive, and for the right of transit, which belongs to every citizen of the United States. That is the decision of the Supreme Court.

"MR. PUGH.—I repeat my assertion : if the Constitution of the United States gives this form of property its peculiar protection, as gentlemen assert, and the right to carry it, it is carried into every State over the constitution and laws of the State ; for the Constitution of the United States is supreme above the constitutions and laws of the States ; and it means that, or it means nothing. There is no distinction ; there can be none made ; and my colleague put the very question which proved the fallacy of the whole proposition. But senators say there is no sovereignty in the territories. I agree to that ; but why do we deceive ourselves about words ? There is no such language as sovereignty in the Constitution of the United States. Senators say it requires a power of sovereignty to exclude slavery, and the senator from Mississippi has just now spoken of the sovereignty of the State which excludes slavery. He says it requires sovereign power to exclude slavery. Well, how is that sovereignty to be expressed ?

"MR. DAVIS.—When a State, being a sovereign, by its organic law excludes that species of property, the act is final. There is no sovereignty in the Constitution, as the senator states, and why ? Because the Constitution is a compact between sovereigns creating an agent with delegated powers; and sovereignty is an indivisible thing. They gave functions of sovereignty from their plenary power. Sovereignty remained with the people of the States.

"MR. PUGH.—Then I understand the senator that the

sovereignty can only speak through a constitution, and that it is in the constitution of a State only that the power to admit or exclude slavery is to be exercised. Why, sir, until the year 1820 not a State of this Union, in her constitution, either admitted or excluded slavery, and I do not believe Virginia did until 1850 or 1851. None of the States did it until Missouri when she came into the Union, and she put it into her constitution, not upon the idea that that was peculiarly the place, but for the express purpose of disarming her legislature. It was an ordinary legislative power, nothing else in the world; known and recognized as such and admitted as such by every State in the Union. New York abolished slavery by law, Pennsylvania abolished slavery by law, and in the States where the institution continued, it was fostered, protected, and recognized by ordinary acts of legislation.

"Mr. Davis.—I am sorry to interrupt the senator again, and I believe this will be the last time. The first instance he will find was that of Massachusetts, who, in her bill of rights, at the Revolutionary era, made a declaration which her supreme court held to be the abolition of slavery; and I think he will find that it has generally been acted on in that way; but he has not the right to assume anything more than I stated. I stated a mode."

JAMES L. ORR.

COL. ORR is of Irish extraction, his ancestors on the paternal and maternal side coming originally from Ireland. His grandfather, a native of North Carolina, was a Revolutionary soldier. Christopher Orr, his father, was a country merchant of considerable means, and who expended them liberally upon the education of his children. James L. Orr was born May 12, 1822, at Craytonville, Anderson District, South Carolina. He began his education at a common school, but was soon sent to the Anderson Academy, at the same time, however, assisting his father in keeping his books. When he was eighteen years old, he was sent to the University of Virginia, where his proficiency in his studies was so great, that he attracted the attention of his tutors, who predicted a promising career for the young student. In 1841, he left college and spent two years in pursuing a course of general reading, of the greatest importance to him in after life.

In 1843, he studied law, was admitted to the bar. He began the practice of law at home, in Anderson, the same year establishing a village newspaper and editing it. It was called the "Anderson Gazette." In 1844, when but twenty-two years of age, his neighbors and friends elected him to the State Legislature, where he began his political career in a quiet, unostentatious manner. Still, he took a very decided position—one which gave an indication of his future policy. It was this: he delivered a speech in opposition to the doctrine of nullification, in reference to the tariff of 1812. He also took democratic ground in favor of the election of Presidential electors of the people. They were then, and are now in South Carolina, elected by the legislature.

In 1848, Mr. Orr became a candidate for Congress. His chief opponent was a Democrat, a lawyer of wealth and talents, and of course the contest was simply one of personal popularity, as both gentlemen held the same political sentiments. After a very lively contest, Mr. Orr was elected by 700 majority over his Democratic competitor. He entered Congress at a time when the country was convulsed with the slavery question, and though such men as Webster, Clay, Calhoun, Cass, and the like, were in Congress, he very soon attracted the attention of the experienced legislators of that time. Not by egotistic speeches, forcing himself, as some men do, upon the attention of Congress and the country, but by delivering, at judicious times, speeches which were full of solid ability. While he was a firm defender of slavery and what are called "the constitutional rights of the South," he condemned the agitation of the question of slavery, and arrayed himself against the ultraists of his section of the country. Col. Orr's constituents were so well pleased with his conduct that they have left him in it till he was, in December, 1857, elected speaker of the House of Representatives.

When the compromise measures were passed, South Carolina for a time seemed to favor a secession from the Union. A Constitutional Convention had been called and a large majority of the delegates were pledged to favor secession. Col. Orr, however, come out very boldly and eloquently against their policy. A General Convention of the disaffected people was held in Charleston, in 1851, and Col. Orr attended as a delegate from the Anderson District. In the Convention he took strong ground against disunion, and introduced resolutions embodying his opinions on that subject. But out of 450 members, only 30 came to his support. But Col. Orr was undaunted by the majority of numbers against him. He appealed to the people by voice and pen, and as the result he and a companion in his disunion views were elected to the proposed Southern Congress over two secession candidates. An apparent admirer of Col. Orr, speaking of this contest, says:

"That the crisis was one full of alarm and danger must be admitted even by those furthest from the scene, and most disposed to deny both the right and power of a State to secede; and that Mr. Orr, in the very opening of a brilliant political career, hazarded his future hopes and prospects to a sense of right and duty, entitles him to the regard of every true lover of the Union. His triumph was highly honorable to himself, and fixed him more firmly than ever in the esteem and affections of his constituents."

The same writer remarks:

"The Congressional career of Mr. Orr, which a want of space prevents us from noticing more in detail, has been both a brilliant and a useful one. Always sustaining his positions with eloquence and force of argument, and exhibiting great fairness in debate, he has commanded attention, and exercised a powerful influence over the questions of the day. His habits of thorough investigation and analysis, and his tenacious adherence to his convictions of right, have frequently placed him at the head of important committees; and his reports are among the ablest in our legislative records. As chairman of the Committee of the Whole on the State of the Union, during the discussion of the most important and exciting measures, he displayed so much promptness, firmness, and intelligence in his decisions that he won the confidence and respect of men of all parties; and at the commencement of last Congress he was almost unanimously selected by the Democrats as their candidate for Speaker. His party was, however, in the minority, and his election failed. When the present session of Congress opened, Mr. Orr was nominated, without opposition, and elected its presiding officer. So far he has justified the expectations of his friends and of the party which placed him in the chair. In the fulfillment of the duties of his present position Mr. Orr will doubtless add honorably to the reputation he now enjoys. He is too wise a man not to perceive that while fidelity to party was the best ladder for him to rise to his present height, impartial neutrality will now serve his fame and ambition better."

Upon the whole, Mr. Orr made an admirable Speaker to the Thirty-fifth Congress. If he was not always rigidly impartial, the exceptional cases were rare, and when he was swerved from the straight line of duty by his sectional prejudices.

In November, 1855, to go back a little—Col. Orr published a letter in reference to the duty of South Carolina toward the Democratic party of the North. The people of that State were then, as they seem almost always to be, in a state of high excitement on the slavery question. Many leading politicians counselled secession and non-action in reference to the Presidential canvass. But Col. Orr took different ground. In his letter to Hon. C. W. Dudley, dated Anderson, Nov. 23, 1855, he said:

"A convention is merely a method of finding out what

the popular opinion is, and giving to it a more conspicuous and imposing expression. It has been steadily and uniformly pursued by the Democracy of all the States (except our own) for fifteen years or more, and the selection of delegates, manner of voting and nominating, has been defined by a usage well understood and acquiesced in, as if regulated by law. Hence, we know that such a convention will assemble in Cincinnati in May next, and that it will nominate candidates for the Presidency and Vice Presidency—adopt a platform of principles—and it is nearly certain that the nominees will receive the votes of the Democratic party of every State in the Union. Shall the Democracy of this State send delegates? It is our privilege to be represented there, and at the present time I believe it to be a high and solemn duty to meet our political allies, and to aid, by our presence and councils, in selecting suitable nominees and constructing a platform, which will secure our rights and uphold the Constitution.

"There has never been a time since the convention policy was adopted—if, indeed, there has been such a time since the government was inaugurated—when the success of the Democratic party in the electoral college was so vitally important as now. If that party should be defeated in the election before the people, every patriot's mind must be filled with gloomy forebodings of the future. The indications now are, that the opposition to the Democratic party, made up of Know Nothings, Abolitionists, and Fusionist, will run two or more candidates: if the Democracy fail to secure a majority in the electoral college over all elements of opposition, then the election must be made, according to the Constitution, by the House of Representatives. Can we safely trust the election of our rights to that body? The House is now elected, and we *know* that a decided majority of the House are members of the Know Nothing, Fusion and Whig parties; and if the election be devolved on them, the Democratic party will be certainly defeated, and perhaps a Fusionist promoted to the Presidency. Are the people of South Carolina so indifferent to their relations to the Federal Government, that they will quietly look on and see such an administration as we have had since the 4th of March, '53—an administration that has faithfully and fearlessly maintained the Constitution in its purity—supplanted by Know Nothingism or Black Republicanism? That is the issue to be decided in the next presidential election, and that, too, in the electoral college; for if we fail there, then we know now with absolute certainty that we must be defeated before the House. Was it, then, ever so important before that the Convention should be filled with discreet, patriotic men; that there should be the fullest representation of every man devoted to the Democratic faith, and opposed to Fusion and Know Nothingism; that they should commune freely together, and nominate a candidate who will command the confidence of the entire party.

* * * * * * *

"We have heard much of southern union being necessary to our safety. We now have it in our power, by cordial co-operation with our southern sisters, to secure it—to secure it on such a basis as will permanently preserve our institutions. We can here make our demand, and with a united South, we can offer it to the true men of the North. If we act wisely and present such an ultimatum, I doubt not that thousands, perhaps millions, at the North, will espouse and maintain it; for it is a platform of the Constitution, and there are hosts of conservative men who I know are prepared to maintain the Constitution of our fathers.

"Will we reject it with silent contempt—adhere to our isolation, and stubbornly refuse to fraternize with her, and all the balance of our southern sisters? Who doubts that all the South will be represented there? and can it be said, truthfully, that our voice can be of no avail or weight, when the ultimatum shall be laid down? If we send delegates, who can say that our votes may not secure a reliable nominee and a sound platform? Will the instructions of Georgia to her delegates be more or less potent with the indorsement of all or of only a portion of the South?

"If, indeed, fanaticism is in the ascendant in the North, and cannot be overcome, then what initiative step toward a southern Union, for the last resort, can be more effective than to unite all the South on the Georgia platform and instructions? Our influence in counsel and in action will be increased, whenever we show a hearty disposition to harmonize with our sisters in the South. Have we not heretofore kept aloof from their consultations in every instance, save in the Nashville Convention?—and that was a movement which did not derive any popularity in the South from being suspected of having originated in South Carolina. Sooner or later we must learn the important truth, that the fate and destiny of the entire South is identical. Isolation will give neither security nor concert. When we meet Virginia and Georgia, Alabama and Mississippi, in consultation, as at Cincinnati, it is the supremacy of Pharisaism to flippantly denounce such association as either dangerous or degrading. North Carolina, Missouri, Florida, and Texas, will be there represented; and are we too exalted or conceited to meet them at the same council board?

"We shall meet there many liberal men from the North; those who in their section have done good service against political abolitionism. When we insist upon our platform with firmness, and they see we only make a demand of our constitutional rights, they will concede it; and when they go home they will prosecute the canvass in good faith, upon the principles enunciated at the Convention. Concert among ourselves, with the aid of the conservative men at the North, may enable us to save a constitutional Union; if that cannot be preserved, it will enable us to save ourselves and our institutions. Are we alone to have unoccupied seats, when such grave matters are to be decided by the Cincinnati Convention?

"Suppose the Democracy of this State should decide not to send delegates, and the other States of the South should follow her example, who would be voted for? Could the party, *even at the South*, without some concert, which could only be secured by meeting, rally upon the same man? No well-informed person would venture an affirmative answer; what would be the result? The Democratic party would certainly be defeated, and the Know Nothing, or Black Republican party, would as certainly be successful. Our policy, then, would inevitably bring upon us defeat; and if we are to be saved from a free-soil President, it is only to be done by the party in the other States assembling and making a nomination in which we refuse to participate. Even those who are opposing the sending of the delegates, I doubt not, rejoice in the hope that the other States, despite our impracticable example, will meet and nominate candidates.

* * * * * *

"The northern Democrats aided us to bring into the Union Texas, a magnificent slave-holding territory—large enough to make four slave States, and strengthened us more in that peculiar interest than was ever before done by any single act of the Federal Government. Since then they have amended a very imperfect fugitive slave law, passed in 1793, and have given us now a law for the recovery of fugitive slaves, as stringent as the ingenuity of man could devise. Since then they have aided us by their votes in establishing the doctrine of non-intervention with slavery by Congress in the territories. Since then they have reduced the odious tariff of 1842, and fixed the principle of imposts on the revenue, not the protective basis. Since then they have actually repealed the Missouri restriction, opened the territories to settlement, and enabled us, if the South will be true to herself, and aid in peopling Kansas, to form another slave State.

"In 1843, a man would have been pronounced insane, had he predicted that slavery would be introduced there by the removal of congressional restrictions. Since then they have adopted the the Virginia and Kentucky resolutions and Madison's report—the very corner-stone of State rights—as a part of the Democratic platform. They have by their votes in Congress and Convention given all these pledges to the Constitution since 1843; and if we could then fraternize with them, what change has transpired that justifies the delegates in that Convention, at least, in refusing now to fraternize with northern and southern Democrats?"

The reader will easily see Col. Orr's position from this letter. He is a southern Democrat, and, as such, a defender of slavery and slavery extension, a free trader, and an opponent of all homestead bills, but he does not go with the most ultra class of Southern politicans; in short, he is "a National Democrat." He stands by the Democratic organization of the country, so long as it stands by the South and her institutions as well as it has done in the past. Upon the new issues of intervention for slavery in the territories he has not yet spoken, but he was, of course, a rigid Lecomptonite. But during the debate on the Kansas-Nebraska bill he spoke very decidedly. He said: "The legislative authority of a territory is invested with no vote for or against laws. *We* think they ought to pass laws in every territory, when the territory is open to settlement, and slaveholders go there, to protect slave property. But if they decline to pass such laws, what is the remedy? *None, sir.* If the majority of the people are opposed to the institution, and if they do not desire it ingrafted upon their territory, all they have to do is simply to decline to pass laws in the territorial legislature for its protection."

In Congress, Col. Orr has generally ranged himself with the compromising democracy. He is not born of the old aristocratic stock of South Carolina planters, but was the son of a worker—a country merchant. This fact has never been lost sight of by a portion of the citizens of South Carolina, and they have been, some of them at least, his bitter enemies for years. It is not impossible but Col. Orr, for this reason, has taken a more "national" view of politics, and has refused to go out of the Union for the sake of the slaveholding aristocracy.

In his personal appearance Col. Orr is not, perhaps, prepossessing; though his great, black eye and fine open face show the force and power of his intellect. He is large in person, and not particularly graceful in his actions or appearance. He has a certain dignity, however, which enforces attention if he is the orator of the occasion, and obedience if he is the presiding officer.

JOHN MINOR BOTTS.

We have no extended sketch of Mr. Botts to present to the reader, but a few leading facts in reference to the political man.

Mr. Botts is a native of Dumfries, Prince William County, Virginia, and was born in September, 1802. As early as 1834, he joined the Whig party, and in 1839, he came to Congress as a Whig. He was known in the House as a follower of Mr. Clay, or rather a supporter of Mr. Clay and his peculiar doctrines. Mr. Botts, in other words, was in favor of a highly protective tariff, the distribution of the public lands, and internal improvements. He is to-day in favor of these measures of what he would call reform. So strong was he in his devotion to the tenets of the Whig party, that when President Tyler disappointed his friends by his tariff policy, Mr. Botts, though a friend of years, at once terminated the friendship. He could not hold in respect the man who, it seemed to him, had betrayed his friends.

Mr. Botts was opposed to the Kansas-Nebraska act and to the passage of the Lecompton bill. Nevertheless he is a slaveholder and a defender of the institution as it now exists in Virginia. But he is not a believer in the finality of the present system, nor is he afraid to express his opinions of slavery. This will be seen at once by the perusal of a letter to the "Richmond Whig," from Mr. Botts, from which we quote. It is dated April 18, 1859:

"I have recently received many letters from different parts of the State, asking for a copy of my Powhatan speech, delivered in 1850, which it is impossible for me to furnish, as I have only some half dozen copies left. As the best means of supplying the information so earnestly sought by those friends who are anxious to ascertain *what horrible sentiments I uttered on the subject of slavery*, which have been recently, to a great extent, substituted for the 'free negro' misrepresentation, I have concluded to publish, for the benefit of the Imposition party in particular, everything in that speech that relates to the question of slavery; garbled extracts of which have already appeared in a small portion of the press of that party—many of them, seeming to think there was no great amount of capital to be made out of it, have declined to notice it. The following is the portion objected to. I said:

"'There are, sir, two parties in our country, distinct from all the rest, of whom I wish to say a word. The one in the North, called 'Abolitionists,' and the other, in the South, known as 'Disunionists.' I am not sure for which of the two parties I have the least sympathy or respect; and I am not sure to which attaches the largest share of the responsibility for the chief difficulties with which the nation has been lately afflicted.

"The Abolitionists seem to estimate the value of this Union (and to hold as a condition and a price for its continuance) by the *abolition of African slavery*. While the ultra men of the South, or disunionists, seem to regard the *perpetuation* and *extension* of slavery as the chief bond that can hold them and the Union together. For neither of these parties have I any sympathy. I hold to the Union for far different, and, I trust, higher and nobler purposes. It is for the *perpetuation of American Freedom*, rather than the *abolition* or *perpetuation of African Slavery*. I am one of those who think slavery, in the abstract, is much to be deprecated; and whilst I think that, as at present organized in the southern States, it is a humanizing, civilizing, and Christianizing institution, as must all agree who will take the pains to compare the present condition of our slaves with the original African race, yet I regard it as a great calamity that it should have been entailed upon us; and I should look upon that man as the first and greatest benefactor to his country, whose wisdom could point out to us some practical and satisfactory means by which we could, through our own instrumentality, and without interference from our neighbors, provide for the ultimate emancipation and removal of all the slaves in the country. I speak of this as a desirable thing, especially to the owners of slaves, who, I think, are the chief sufferers, but at the same time I fear it is perfectly Utopian to attempt it; but I have seen too much difference between the enterprise, the industry, and the prosperity of the free and the slave States, to doubt the advantage we would derive from it if it could be accomplished.'

"Now, there it is; let them make the most of it. I will add, that I said it all at mature age, after full and careful deliberation, honestly believing and thinking all that it contains. I have seen no reason for *modification, recantation*, or *equivocation*. What I thought and said then, I think and repeat now, *in the most emphatic terms*; and hold, that he who objects to the sentiments conveyed, to be consistent, must not only be in favor of reopening the African slave trade at this time, but must take the position, that if no such thing as slavery had ever been known to or introduced amongst us, he would now favor its introduction for the first time ; for if its original introduction is not to be deprecated, but justified and approved, why would he not advocate a traffic that holds so high a place in his judgment and regard ? I do not know how many there are in this State, or in the South, who set themselves up as advocates of this revolting trade, nor do I care ; I have only to say, that I am not one of them, and that, as a *humanized, civilized* and *christianized*, member of the community, I should be utterly *ashamed* of myself, if I could *entertain* any other opinions than those I have expressed ; and I should deserve the scorn of all men, if I could permit any condition of the public mind to induce me so far to *debase* myself as to render me capable of expressing any other, for the purpose of catering to a morbid, vitiated, and corrupt taste, or to an affected and artificial sentimentality on the subject of slavery. These were then, and are now, my honest convictions, and I think all who have participated in the clamor that has been attempted to be gotten up, for the opportunity afforded me of proclaiming them from the house-tops, to the *humanized, civilized,* and *christianized* world ; and I hope the Imposition press, throughout the State, will publish them, and that their candidates for gubernational and subordinate honors may read this my last declaration on the subject, wherever they may speak.

" In another part of that speech I said :

" ' What I would ask and *demand* of the North, is that they shall not interfere with slavery as it exists under the Constitution ; that they shall not touch the question of the slave trade between the States ; that they shall carry out the true intent and meaning of the Constitution in reference to the restitution of fugitive slaves. These are the *true issues* between the North and the South ; and I would go as far as he who goes furthest in exacting them, ' at all hazards, and to the last extremity." And what I would ask of the South is, not to suffer itself to be led off, without due consideration, upon false issues, presented by intemperate or over-zealous politicians, many of whom delight in, and live upon, agitation and excitement, and many more, perhaps, who owe their ephemeral fame and position to a *pretended, exclusive championship for southern rights.* Southern honor does not depend upon making unreasonable and untenable demands. The interference *with*, or abolition *of* slavery, where it exists, is one thing; the extension of it, where it does not exist, is a very different thing! Let us claim no more than we are entitled to under the Constitution; and then, what we do claim, let us stand by, like men who "know their rights, and, knowing, dare maintain them."'

"I have seen no reason to recant what I said here, either; these are the sentiments I now entertain, as I did when they were delivered before the people of Powhatan. What fault do they find with this? Do they indorse it or repudiate it? If they indorse it, even-handed justice requires them to say so. If they condemn it, justice to themselves, as they are resolved to make war on me, requires that they should point out wherein they differ from me.

"In this connection it may be proper to add, for the information of all who feel an interest in my record, one short paragraph from my African Church speech, in 1856, relating to the same subject; and from the several extracts herewith furnished, I think few will have any difficulty in ascertaining my position on the slavery question. Here is the passage referred to:

"'My position on the question of slavery is this; and, so far from wishing to conceal it, I desire it should be known to all. Muzzles were made for dogs, and not for men; and no press and no party can put a muzzle on my mouth, so long as I value my freedom. I make bold, then, to proclaim that I am no slavery propagandist. I will resort to all proper remedies to protect and defend slavery where it exists, but I will neither assist in nor encourage any attempt to force it upon a reluctant people anywhere, and still less will I justify the use of the military power of the country to establish it in any of the territories. If it finds its way there by legitimate means, it is all well ; but never by force, through any instrumentality of mine. I am myself a slaveholder, and all the property my children have in the world is slave property, inherited from their mother ; and he who undertakes to connect my name, or my opinions, with abolitionism, is either a knave or a fool, and not unfrequently both. And this is the only answer I have to make to them. I have not connected myself with any sectional party or sectional question ; and so help me God, I never will.'"

JAMES H. HAMMOND.

THE moderate political views which Gov. Hammond, of South Carolina, has within a couple of years given publicity to, has given him a somewhat national reputation among the adherents of the Democratic party. He came to Congress as a politician of the Southern Rights school, and it was generally supposed that he would be found acting with the ultra wing of the Southern party in Congress. He brought with him the reputation of a scholar and an orator, and mingled at once in the Lecompton fray. He took sides with the administration against Mr. Douglas, though it was noticed at the time that the senator had very little to say about the Lecompton Constitution and the real issue then before Congress. His speeches were upon the general question of slavery.

The new senator from South Carolina attracted the universal attention of Congress and the strangers then present in Washington, and the impression he made was generally a happy one. His manners were quiet, unostentatious, gentlemanly. His style of speech was smooth, pleasant, and sometimes eloquent. As a man he was liked. Genial in his nature and pleasant in his conversation, he soon made warm friends at the capital—even among some of the very men whom he had in his South Carolina home regarded as little less than monsters in human shape. Senator Hammond at first tried his lance with the Illinois Giant, but either from personal considerations, or other, he soon desisted. To show Gov. Hammond's position on the slavery question in the winter of 1847–8, we quote a few passages from his celebrated speech delivered in the Senate in the Lecompton debate. We have, in the following passage, his opinion of squatter sovereignty:

"If what I have said be correct, then the will of the people of Kansas is to be found in the action of her Constitutional Convention. It is immaterial whether it is the will of a majority of the people of Kansas *now*, or not. The convention was, or might have been, elected by a majority of the people of Kansas. A convention, elected in April, may well frame a constitution that would not be agreeable to a majority of the people of a new State, rapidly filling up, in the succeeding January; and if legislatures are to be allowed to put to vote the acts of a convention, and have them annulled by a subsequent influx of immigrants, there is no finality. If you were to send back the Lecompton Constitution, and another was to be framed, in the slow way in which we do public business in this country, before it would reach Congress and be passed, perhaps the majority would be turned the other way. Whenever you go outside of the regular forms of law and constitutions to seek for the will of the people, you are wandering in a wilderness—a wilderness of thorns.

"If this was a minority constitution, I do not know that

that would be an objection to it. Constitutions are made for minorities. Perhaps minorities ought to have the right to make constitutions, for they are administered by majorities. The Constitution of this government was made by a minority, and as late as 1840 a minority had it in their hands, and could have altered or abolished it; for, in 1840, six out of the twenty-six States of the Union held the numerical majority. In all countries and in all time, it is well understood that the numerical majority of the people could, if they chose, exercise the sovereignty of the country; but for want of intelligence, and for want of leaders, they have never yet been able successfully to combine and form a stable popular government. They have often attempted it, but it has always turned out, instead of a popular sovereignty, a *populace* sovereignty; and demagogues, placing themselves upon the movement, have invariably led them into military despotism.

"I think that the popular sovereignty which the senator from Illinois would derive from the acts of his territorial legislature, and from the information received from partisans and partisan presses, would lead us directly into *populace*, and not popular sovereignty. Genuine popular sovereignty never existed on a firm basis except in this country. The first gun of the Revolution announced a new organization of it, which was embodied in the Declaration of Independence, developed, elaborated, and inaugurated forever in the Constitution of the United States. The two pillars of it were Representation and the Ballot-box. In distributing their sovereign powers among the various departments of the Government, the people retained for themselves the single power of the ballot-box; and a great power it was. Through that they were able to control all the departments of the Government. It was not for the people to exercise political power in detail; it was not for them to be annoyed with the cares of government; but, from time to time, through the ballot-box, to exert their sovereign power and control the whole organization.

This is popular sovereignty, the popular sovereignty of a legal constitutional ballot-box; and when spoken through that box, the 'voice of the people,' for all political purposes, 'is the voice of God;' but when it is heard outside of that, it is the voice of a demon, the *tocsin* of the reign of terror."

Speaking of the South and slavery, he said:

"If we never acquire another foot of territory for the South, look at her. Eight hundred and fifty thousand square miles. As large as Great Britain, France, Austria, Prussia, and Spain. Is not that territory enough to make an empire that shall rule the world? With the finest soil, the most delightful climate, whose staple productions none of those great countries can grow, we have three thousand miles of continental shore line, so indented with bays and crowded with islands, that, when their shore lines are added, we have twelve thousand miles. Through the heart of our country runs the great Mississippi, the father of waters, into whose bosom are poured thirty-six thousand miles of tributary streams; and beyond we have the desert prairie wastes, to protect us in our rear. Can you hem in such a territory as that? You talk of putting up a wall of fire around eight hundred and fifty thousand square miles so situated! How absurd.

"But, in this territory lies the great valley of the Mississippi, now the real, and soon to be the acknowledged, seat of empire of the world. The sway of that valley will be as great as ever the Nile knew in the earlier ages of mankind. We own the most of it. The most valuable part of it belongs to us now; and, although those who have settled above us are now opposed to us, another generation will tell a different tale. They are ours by all the laws of nature; slave labor will go over every foot of this great valley where it will be found profitable to use it; and some of those who may not use it are soon to be united with us by such ties as will make us one and inseparable. The iron horse will soon be clattering over the sunny plains of the South, to bear the products of its upper tributaries to our Atlantic ports, as it now does through the ice-bound North. There is the great Mississippi, a bond of union made by Nature herself. She will maintain it forever."

* * * * * *

"In all social systems, there must be a class to do the menial duties, to perform the drudgery of life—that is, a class requiring but a low order of intellect and but little skill. Its requisites are vigor, docility, fidelity. Such a class you must have, or you would not have that other class which leads progress, civilization, and refinement. It constitutes the very mud-sill of society and of political government; and you might as well attempt to build a house in the air, as to build either the one or the other, except on this mud-sill. Fortunately for the South, she found a race adapted to that purpose to her hand—a race inferior to her own, but eminently qualified, in temper, in vigor, in docility, in capacity, to stand the climate to answer all her purposes. We use them for our purpose, and call them slaves. We found them slaves, by the 'common consent of mankind,' which, according to Cicero, '*lex naturæ est*'—the highest proof of what is Nature's law. We are old-fashioned at the South yet; it is a word discarded now by 'ears polite;' I will not characterize that class at the North with that term; but you have it; it is there; it is everywhere; it is eternal."

Upon going home to his South Carolina plantation, a change seems to have come over the mind of the senator—or he was greatly misunderstood while at Washington. In a speech, delivered at Brownwell Court House, South Carolina, October 27, 1858, he astonished some of his neighbors as well as distant friends and enemies, by the enunciation of peculiarly moderate views for a South Carolina Democrat. Let us quote a few paragraphs. First upon Disunion. Says Senator Hammond:

"But I will not detain you longer with what belongs to the past. The present and the future are what concern us most. You desire to know my opinion of the course the South should pursue under existing circumstances. I will give you, frankly and fully, the results of my observations and reflections on this all-important point. The first question is, Do the people of the South consider the present Union of these States as an evil in itself, and a thing that it is desirable we should get rid of under all circumstances? There are some, I know, who do; but I am satisfied that an overwhelming majority of the South would, if assured that this government was hereafter to be conducted on the true principles and construction of the Constitution, decidedly prefer to remain in the Union rather than incur the unknown costs and hazards of setting up a separate government. I think I say what is true when I say that, after all the bitterness that has characterized our long warfare, the great body of the southern people do not seek disunion, and will not seek it as a primary object, however promptly they may accept it as an alternative, rather than submit to unconstitutional abridgments of their rights. I confess that for many years of my life I believed that our only safety was in the dissolution of the Union, and I openly avowed it. I should entertain and without hesitation express the same sentiments now, but that the victories we have achieved, and those I think we are about to achieve, have inspired me with hope, I may say the belief, that we can fully sustain ourselves in the Union, and control its action in all great affairs."

Upon the African Slave Trade thus speaks the senator:

"We have it proposed to reopen the African slave trade and bring in hordes of slaves from that prolific region to restore the balance. I once entertained that idea myself; but, on further investigation, I abandoned it. I will not now go into the discussion of it further than to say that the South is itself divided on that policy, and, from appearances, opposed to it by a vast majority, while the North is unanimously against it. It would be impossible to get Congress to reopen the trade. If it could be done, then it would be unnecessary, for that result could only be brought about by such an entire abandonment by the North and the world of all opposition to our slave system that we might safely cease to erect any defences for it. But if we could introduce slaves, where could we find suitable territory for new slave States? The Indian Reserve, west of Arkansas, might make one; but we have solemnly guaranteed that to the remnants of the red race. Everywhere else, I believe, the borders of our States have reached the great desert which separates the Atlantic from the Pacific States of this Confederacy. Nowhere is African slavery likely to flourish in the little oasis of that Sahara of America. It is much more likely, I think, to get the Pacific slope and to the north in the great valley than anywhere else outside of its present limits. Shall we, as some suggest, take Mexico and Central America to make slave States? African slavery appears to have failed there. Perhaps, and most probably, it will never succeed in those regions. If it might, what are we to do with the seven or eight millions of hardly semi-civilized Indians and the two or three millions of Creole Spaniards and Mongrels who now hold those countries? We would not enslave the Indians! Experience has proved that they are incapable of steady labor, and are therefore unfit for slavery. We would not exterminate them, even if that inhuman achievement would not cost ages of murder and incalculable sums of money. We could hardly think of attempting to plant the black race there, superior for labor, though inferior, perhaps, in intellect, and expect to maintain a permanent and peaceful industry, such as slave labor must be to be profitable, amid those idle, restless, demoralized children of Montezuma, scarcely more civilized, perhaps more sunk in superstition, than in his age, and now trained to civil war by half a century of incessant revolution. What, I say, could we do with these people or these countries to add to southern strength? Nothing. Could we degrade ourselves so far as to annex them on equal terms, they would be sure to come into this Union free States all. To touch them in any way is to be contaminated. England and France, I have no doubt, would gladly see us take this burden on our back if we would secure for them their debts and a neutral route across the Isthmus. Such a route we must have for ourselves, and that is all we have to do with them. If we can not get it by negotiation or by purchase, we must seize and hold it by force of arms. The law of nations would justify it, and it is absolutely necessary for our Pacific relations. The present condition of those unhappy States is certainly deplorable, but the good God holds them in the hollow of his hand and will work out their proper destinies."

Upon the Cuban question:

"We might expand the area of slavery by acquiring Cuba, where African slavery is already established. Mr. Calhoun, from whose matured opinions, whether on constitutional principles or southern policy, it will rarely be found safe to depart, said that Cuba was 'forbidden fruit' to us unless plucked in an exigency of war. There is no reasonable grounds to suppose that we can acquire it in any other way; and the war that will open to us such an occasion will be great and general, and bring about results that the keenest intellect cannot now anticipate. But if we had Cuba, we could not make more than two or three slave States there, which would not restore the equilibrium of the North and South; while, with the African slave trade closed, aud her only resort for slaves to this continent, she would, besides crushing our whole sugar culture by her competition, afford in a few years a market for all the slaves in Missouri, Kentucky and Maryland. She is, notwithstanding the exorbitant taxes imposed on her, capable now of absorbing the annual increase of all the slaves on this continent, and consumes, it is said, twenty to thirty thousand a year by her system of labor. Slaves decrease there largely. In time, under the system practised, every slave in America might be exterminated in Cuba as were the Indians. However the idle African may procreate in the tropics, it yet remains to be proven, and the facts are against the conclusion, that he can in those regions work and thrive. It is said Cuba is to be 'Africanized' rather than that the United States should take her. That threat, which at one time was somewhat alarming, is no longer any cause of disquietude to the South, after our experience of the Africanizing of St. Domingo and Jamaica. What have we lost by that?"

And finally upon his own position as a National Democrat:

"And this leads me to say that having never been a mere party politician, intriguing and wire-pulling to advance myself or others, I am not learned in the rubric of the thousand slang, unmeaning and usually false party names to which our age gives birth. But I have been given to understand that there are two parties in the South, called 'National' and 'State Rights' Democrats. The word 'national' having been carefully excluded from the Constitution by those who framed it, I never supposed it applicable to any principle of our government; and having been surrendered to the almost exclusive use in this country of the federal consolidationists, I have myself repudiated it. But if a southern 'National Democrat' means one who is ready to welcome into our ranks with open arms, and cordiality embrace and promote according to his merits every honest free State man who reads the

Constitution as we do, and will coöperate with us in its maintenance, then I belong to that party, call it as you may, and I should grieve to find a southern man who does not.

"But, on the other hand, having been all my life, and being still, an ardent 'State Rights' man—believing 'State Rights' to be an essential, nay, the essential, element of the Constitution, and that no one who thinks otherwise can stand on the same constitutional platform that I do, it seems to me that I am, and all those with whom I act habitually are, if Democrats at all, true 'State Rights Democrats.' Nothing in public affairs so perplexes and annoys me as these absurd party names, and I never could be interested in them. I could easily comprehend two great parties, standing on two great antagonistic principles which are inherent in all things human; the right and the wrong, the good and the evil, according to the peculiar views of each individual; and was never at a loss to find my side, as now, in what are known as the Democratic and Republican parties of this country. But the minor distinctions have, for the most part, seemed to me to be factitious and factious, gotten up by cunning men for selfish purposes, to which the true patriot and honest man should be slow to lend himself. For myself and for you, while I represent you, I shall go for the Constitution strictly construed and faithfully carried out. I will make my fight, such as it may be, by the side of any man, whether from the North, South, East or West, who will do the same; and I will do homage to his virtue, his ability, his courage, and, so far as I can, make just compensation for his toils, and hazards, and sacrifices. As to the precise mode and manner of conducting this contest, that must necessarily, to a great extent, depend upon the exigencies that arise; but, of course, I could be compelled by no exigency, by no party ties or arrangements, to give up my principles, or the least of those principles which constitute our great cause."

Senator Hammond entered the Senate with the reputation of a southern "Fire-eater," but before a year had passed by, he had taken ground with the most conservative northern Democrat, on Cuba, the African slave trade, and the general question of the annexation of foreign territory to this Union. Here was an apparent change which very naturally excited the criticisms of the ultra southern politicians.

Gov. Hammond is a native of Newberg District, South Carolina, where he was born, November 15, 1807. His parents were natives of the State of New York. He graduated at Columbia College, S. C., practised law from 1828 to 1830, afterward became editor of the "Southern Times," came to Congress a single term in 1835 and when the two years were over, made the trip of Europe. In 1841, he was made a militia general—yet something of an honor in South Carolina—and a year later was elected Governor of the Palmetto State. After a single term he retired to his extensive estate upon the Savannah River, where he remained in quiet, raising cotton and reading books till in 1857 he was elected by the State legislature to represent, in part, South Carolina in the United States Senate.

In his personal appearance Senator Hammond is prepossessing. He is of medium height, has a fine, open façe, sparkling black eyes, and black hair—what there is left—a broad forehead and the manners of a pleasant gentleman.

HOWELL COBB.

Mr. Cobb is a native of Cherry Hill, Georgia, where he was born, in September, 1815. His father was in affluent circumstances, and the family one of distinction. He was educated at Franklin College, Georgia, where he graduated at the age of nineteen, in the year 1834. His uncle, Howell Cobb, after whom he was named, was in Congress during the war of 1812, and still later a cousin was U. S. senator. So the young man had examples in his own family of political distinction which were calculated to fire his ambition.

In 1834, Mr. Cobb was married, which was set down, we dare say, by his elderly friends as a very imprudent step, for he was but nineteen and had no profession; nevertheless, he established his household gods at that time, and two years after was admitted to the bar. The very next year he was made solicitor general of the western part of Georgia, so finely had he succeeded in his profession. For the next three years he applied himself very closely to the duties of his profession, and being naturally shrewd and quick-witted, he at once attained unusual success. To this day, in Upper Georgia, Mr. Cobb has a reputation unsurpassed by no local favorite.

Early in life, Mr. Cobb was known as a Jackson or Union man, in the thick of the nullification agitation. Either from education or nature, he seems from the first to have had a repugnance for ultraism, and has therefore never agreed with that class of southern politicians usually termed Fire-eaters.

In 1842, Mr. Cobb was elected to Congress, where he, in a short time, rose to a prominent position as one of the party leaders among the Democratic members. He was especially great on parliamentary questions, and was in his way a party oracle in these matters. Though he never sympathized with the disunionists of the South, he has been a consistent as well as an ardent supporter of the institution of negro slavery. His entire course in Congress showed his strong and persistent opposition to any of the movements of the friends of freedom. He voted against the right of petition on the 3d of May, 1844, and made a strong speech in favor of utter free trade. Mr. Cobb also favored the Mexican war. In 1849, he underwent a severe contest in Georgia. While in Congress he supported the famous compromise measures, which secured to him the opposition and enmity of the southern fire-eaters. The greatest contest of his life ensued. The Union Democrats put him in nomination for Governor of Georgia, and he took the stump and was elected by a tremendous majority. In 1855, he was reëlected to Congress and was soon known as a Buchanan man. He labored for Mr. Buchanan's nomination, and when he was nominated canvassed the county in favor of his election. This secured, Mr. Cobb was rewarded for his services by a seat in the Cabinet, and as he was thought to be peculiarly fitted for the Treasury Department, he was made Secretary of the Treasury.

As a member of the Cabinet, Mr. Cobb used his influence in favor of the Lecompton bill and made war upon Mr. Douglas. During the winter of 1858–9 his recommendations on the tariff question were thought to indicate a change of opinion. Formerly he was in favor of free trade, and lacking that, he was in favor of the nearest possible approach to it. But in his communications to Congress as Secretary of the Treasury, Mr. Cobb admitted that the revenues of the country were not sufficient for its expenses, and he recommended a revision of the tariff to meet the emergency. It is not probable, however, under present circumstances, that he would favor any change in the tariff.

As a man—socially speaking, we mean—Mr. Cobb is a favorite. Good natured and intelligent, he is surrounded by scores of friends, who like him all the better for the fact that he has been independent enough in his political career to make enemies.

JOHN C. BRECKINRIDGE.

Perhaps no public man has more friends or fewer enemies than Mr. Breckinridge; but his modesty, or caution, is so great, that but few particulars of his history have ever got into print. His high position has attracted the eyes of the nation as well as the Senate to him, and he has been unanimously pronounced, both by political friend and foe, to be an impartial presiding officer, and a pleasant and upright man. His personal appearance is unusually prepossessing, and his social bearing is such as to win him scores of friends.

Mr. Breckinridge was born near Lexington, Kentucky, January 21, 1821, and is the grandson of John Breckinridge, who was United States Senator and Attorney General. He was educated at Central College, Danville, and studied law at Transylvania Institute. After his professional education was complete, he emigrated to Iowa, but the frontier life did not suit him, and he returned to Kentucky, where there was a better field for the display of his talents. Soon after his return, he married Miss Birch of Georgetown, Kentucky, and settled down in

Lexington in the practice of his profession. When the Mexican war broke out, he volunteered at once to take a part in it, and was elected Major of the Third Regiment of Kentucky volunteers. The regiment came to the scene of strife so late that they did not see much active service.

Upon Mr. Breckinridge's return from Mexico, he was elected to the State legislature, and in 1851, after an exciting contest with General Leslie Coomb, he was elected to Congress. In 1853, a still fiercer canvass ensued; but he was reëlected to the House by a heavy majority. One of his first acts was to deliver a eulogy upon Henry Clay, a political opponent.

In the Thirty-third Congress, an unpleasant scene occurred between Mr. Breckinridge and Mr. Cutting of New York, upon the Kansas and Nebraska act. Mr. Cutting, though a Democrat, refused to support that measure, while Mr. Breckinridge supported it with considerable zeal.

The debate occurred March 27, 1854, and we quote from a report of it:

"The House of Representatives, Monday, resolved itself into committee of the whole on the Custom House bill, Mr. Hamilton in the chair; but the chairman decided that before that bill could be taken up, all those preceding it must first be set aside; and that the first business in order was the consideration of the bill making appropriations for the civil and diplomatic expenses of the Government for the year ending June 30, 1855. Mr. Houston moved that the committee take up the bill named by the Chair, which was agreed to.

"Mr. Cutting then arose and replied to the remarks made by Mr. Breckinridge on Thursday last. He adverted to his course in moving that the Senate Nebraska bill be committed to the committee of the whole on the state of the Union, and said that at that time he gave his reasons for the act, and declared that there was no gentleman on this floor who was to be regarded as a stronger and more zealous advocate of the great principle which the measure was said to contain —that of non-intervention—than he was. But the bill required amendment and discussion before it could receive that support to which, in his opinion, it was entitled. After this subject had been disposed of, and after the elapse of some two days, a gentleman from a slaveholding State, who had had no lot or parcel in its discussion, as a volunteer merely, came into the House, and thought it not incompatible with his character as a leading member to undertake to assail his motives; though it was true that he disclaimed any intention of attacking them. The gentleman [Mr. Breckinridge] came into the House, with concentrated wrath and bitterness, to assail him for having, in his place, and under his responsibility as a member, stated his views frankly as to the direction this bill ought to take.

"The gentleman had charged him with being a secret enemy of the bill, and, while professing friendship for it, as having taken a course which would end in its destruction. When did the gentleman from Kentucky ever hear him say he was friendly to the bill? The gentleman was present, and heard him declare his opposition to it in the shape in which it came from the Senate, and the belief that not only himself, but a majority of the House, would be found against it. Had not the gentleman sufficient perspicuity of understanding to know the difference between the principles involved in a measure and a bill which professed to carry them out? And when he [Mr. C.] declared in this House frankly and openly, before the question on the motion to commit was put, that he was against the bill, but in favor of the principles which it professed to enact, how came the gentleman to undertake to declare that he [Mr. C.] had declared himself a friend of the bill, against the record, against the reports that appeared everywhere?

"The gentleman had complained that by the motion to commit he [Mr. C.] had consigned this measure to the tomb of the Capulets. If this were so, and this bill could never again be brought before the House, why did the gentleman submit to an hour's argument to prove that it ought to pass? It was time wasted, time thrown away. No gentleman acquainted with the orders of the calendar could for a moment believe that sending this bill to the committee of the whole would prevent action on it this session. The gentleman had said that there were scores and scores of bills before it on the calendar. Now, what was the fact? There were some eighteen or nineteen bills and resolutions, all told, large and small, of great and little degree, ahead of it on the calendar, including appropriation bills, which were subject to the control of the committee of ways and means. Then why, with this fact staring the gentleman in the face, did the gentleman undertake, for the purpose of making an assault on him, to declare that there were scores upon scores of bills before this measure on the calendar? By what authority did the gentleman, who had a supposed connection with the Administration, complain of him, a friend of the measure, of undertaking to send it to a tomb, where there was a mountain piled upon it, for the purpose of creating a false impression in the public mind?

"For the course he had seen proper to pursue he had been assailed in papers of this city (one of them, the "Union," it was said, conducted by the clerk of this House), and by other presses. How was it that he, a friend of the measure, had been selected as a victim to drive off those who had given the principle their support? Was it to assassinate the friends who had stood with him on this subject?

"Mr. Breckinridge.—Does the gentleman intend to apply that remark to me?

"Mr. Cutting.—Not unless you consider yourself a portion of the Union newspaper.

"Mr. Breckinridge.—I was at that moment taking a note, and heard the word. I would ask whether the gentleman applied the remark to me?

"Mr. Cutting.—I did not. I am the only one charged with being an assassin.

"He had been subject to the continual attacks of New York papers, which, while opposing this measure, were enjoying the patronage of the Administration.

"In the course of his remarks, he said that there was but one single ground upon which the Democracy of the North could stand, and that was the principle of non-intervention. If this was found in the bill, he should vote for it; and the reason why he wished it referred was for the purpose of examining into the matter, that there might be a distinct and plain understanding between the different sections of the country, as to the character of the act, so that there might be no misunderstanding upon the subject of the principles contained in it.

"Mr. Breckinridge said that he had forborne to interrupt the gentleman; but whilst his remarks were fresh in his mind he wished to reply.

"Mr. Cutting yielded, and no objection was made to Mr. B.'s proceeding.

"Mr. Breckinridge said that he had listened to the gentleman from New York, who had not met a single position which he took the other day. He had been amazed at the manner in which a man of intellectual ingenuity had twisted and distorted words and opinions out of their proper connections.

"He explained that the reason why he permitted two days to elapse before he replied to the gentleman, was because the gentleman himself, after making his speech the other day on the motion to commit, put down the hatchway of the previous question, so that he was denied an opportunity of responding to him.

"He had said, and he now repeated, that with the gentleman's motives he had nothing to do; he had made and should make no attack upon them. When he spoke of the movement of the gentleman, he characterized it as one the effect of which would be to kill the bill, and said that after the question was decided, he was surrounded by every abolitionist in the hall, and received their congratulations for the course he had pursued. He did not intend to charge the gentleman with intentionally playing the part of an assassin; but said, and could not take it back, that the act, to all intents, was like throwing one arm around it in friendship, and stabbing it with the other—to kill the bill.

"The gentleman from New York had said that there were but eighteen or nineteen bills before the Nebraska bill on the calendar?

"MR. ENGLISH.—There are fifty bills before the Senate bill.

"MR. CUTTING.—Before the House bill?

"MR. BRECKINRIDGE.—I will nail the gentleman to the counter there. 'Before the House bill?' says he. 'Why, I give up that we will never reach the Senate bill, but we will reach the House bill.' But did not the gentleman say that his object in moving to commit the bill was that he might discuss the bill and examine the Badger proviso? And is not the Badger amendment contained in the Senate bill? Thus it would be seen that the bill which the gentleman moved to commit for the purpose of examining into could never be reached.

"The meaning of the gentleman's remarks about the press was, that he (Mr. B.) had acted in concert with papers in this city to drive the gentleman from the support of the bill. Was it not a low ambition for a man to take a course against a measure because another was for it? Did the gentleman suppose that twenty Administrations could ever drive him (Mr. B.) from his position? Even if the Administration were against the bill, he (Mr. B.) would go for it. They should never influence him in this respect. He had no more connection with the Administration than any other gentleman on this floor.

"The gentleman had said that he (Mr. B.) was the last individual whom he supposed would have made an assault on him, because in the hour of his greatest need the Hards came to his assistance. This innuendo was so deep that he could not understand it, and therefore asked for an explanation.

"MR. CUTTING replied, that he had been informed that during the canvass in Kentucky, it having been intimated that the gentleman's friends needed assistance to accomplish his election, his friends in New York made up a subscription of some $1,500, and transmitted it to Kentucky, to be em-employed for the benefit of the gentleman, who is now the peer of Presidents and Cabinets. [Laughter.]

"MR. BRECKINRIDGE.—And not only the peer of Presidents and Cabinets, but the peer of the gentleman from New York, fully and in every respect.

"MR. BRECKINRIDGE, resuming, said that the gentleman should have known the truth of what he uttered before he pronounced it on this floor. He (Mr. B.) was not aware that any intimations were sent from Kentucky that funds were needed to aid in his election, nor was he aware that they were received. He did not undertake to say what the fact might be in regard to what the gentleman had said, but he had no information whatever on that fact. He (Mr. B.) came here not by the aid of money, but against the use of money. [Applause.] The gentleman could not escape by any subtlety, or by any ingenuity, a thorough and complete exposure of any ingenious device to which he might resort for the purpose of putting gentlemen in a false position, and the sooner he stopped that game, the better.

"MR. CUTTING said that he had given the gentleman an opportunity of indulging in one of the most violent, inflammatory, and personal assaults that had ever been known upon this floor; and he would ask, how could the gentleman disclaim any attack upon him when he followed it up by declaring that his (Mr. C.'s) intention and motive was to destroy a measure for which he professed friendship?

"MR. BRECKINRIDGE asked the gentleman to point to the occasion when he made such a remark.

"MR. CUTTING submitted to the committee that the whole tenor and scope of the speech of the gentleman from Kentucky was an attack upon his motives in moving to commit the bill. It was in vain for the gentleman to attempt to escape by disclaiming it; the fact was before the committee. But he would say to the gentleman that he scorned his imputation. How dare the gentleman undertake to assert that he had professed friendship for the measure, with a view to kill it, to assassinate it by sending it to the bottom of the calendar? And then, when he said that the committee of the whole had under its control the House bill upon this identical subject, which the committee intended to take up, discuss, amend, and report to the House, the gentleman skulked behind the Senate bill, which had been sent to the foot of the calendar!

"MR. BRECKINRIDGE.—I ask the gentleman to withdraw that last word.

"MR. CUTTING.—I withdraw nothing. I have uttered what I have said in answer to one of the most violent and most personal attacks that has ever been witnessed upon this floor.

"MR. BRECKINRIDGE.—Then, when the gentleman says I skulk, he says what is false.

"THE CHAIR.—The gentleman is not in order.

"MR. CUTTING.—I do not intend upon this floor to answer the remark which the gentleman from Kentucky has thought proper to employ. It belongs to a different region. It is not here that I will desecrate my lips with undertaking to retort in that manner.

"Mr. C. then declared that in moving to commit the bill, his object was to get it in such a shape as would be satisfactory to the country, and put at rest the outcries of fanaticism which now prevailed throughout the land.

"He desired peace and harmony, and would suggest to gentlemen who were anxious for the passage of the bill, that it was not the best mode of accomplishing their object by assailing those who proclaimed themselves favorable to its principles and its great cardinal outlines. It seemed to him, if gentlemen desired the success of the bill, it would answer a better purpose if they would turn their batteries upon its enemies, rather than attempt to destroy those who were its friends."

The result was, that the preliminaries of a duel were arranged, but fortunately, by the interposition of friends, an amicable adjustment of the difficulty was arrived at.

When Mr. Pierce was in power, he offered Mr. Breckinridge the Spanish mission, but he refused it. In 1856, he was put upon the Democratic ticket and elected Vice-President of the United States.

The official position of Mr. Breckinridge has been such as to render his position on some of the present political issues somewhat doubtful. He is, of course, a believer in the old Democratic creed, and is a moderate supporter of the South and her institutions. It was generally understood at Washington, during the Lecompton struggle, that he sided with the President against Mr. Douglas—in other words, was in favor of the bill. He was a warm supporter of Mr. Douglas in 1854, and his great measure, the Kansas act. In the last session of Congress, Mr. Breckinridge gave his casting vote to postpone the consideration of the Homestead bill, which gives an indication of his hostility to the measure. He is a very fair politician, of unspotted integrity as a man, and is possessed of talents of high order, such as fit him to occupy with ability any office within the gift of the people.

JOHN C. FREMONT.

The leadership of Mr. Fremont in a Presidential campaign has doubtless made his name and history familiar to all intelligent men, but the fact that he is a prominent candidate for the Presidency in 1860, makes it proper to give in this volume an outline sketch of his life. Aside from this, such men as Fremont, whether Presidential candidate or not, whether President or not, are the great, daring, characteristic, men of our times, and their deeds should always be held in remembrance.

Mr. Fremont is a native of Savannah, Georgia, where he was born, June 21, 1813. At an early age he entered the law office of John W. Mitchell, of Charleston, where he gave such indications of talent, that Mr. Mitchell bestowed unusual pains upon his education, placing him under the care of an excellent teacher, Dr. Robertson, a Scotch gentleman, who carried him through the classics. At the age of sixteen, young Fremont was confirmed in the Protestant Episcopal church. In 1833, the sloop-of-war Natchez entered the port of Charleston and was ordered from there to South America. Fremont, just twenty years old, got the situation of teacher of mathematics aboard of her, and made a cruise of two and a half years. Upon his return, he was made professor of mathematics and appointed to the frigate Independence. He afterward made one of a corps of topographical engineers to explore a route of a railway from Charleston to Cincinnati. It was here that Fremont got his first experience of camp life. He went next to the Upper Mississippi on a similar undertaking.

In 1841, Mr. Fremont was ordered to examine the Desmoines River, in Iowa—then a wilderness; and when it was performed, he returned to marry Jessie Benton, the young daughter of Thomas H. Benton. The next year he projected his first great exploring expedition to the Rocky Mountains, setting out from Washington, May 2, 1842. The results of the expedition were great and made a deep impression upon the Government and nation, and a second expedition was ordered, much more complete in preparation than the first. The party left Kansas in May, 1843, and did not get back to the United States until August of 1844. The tour was full of dangers and thrilling incidents, and the results were still more striking than those of the first expedition. Col. Benton sketched the expedition in a few eloquent words, as follows:

"'The Government deserves credit for the zeal with which it has pursued geographical discovery.' Such is the remark which a leading paper made upon the discoveries of Fremont, on his return from his second expedition to the great West; and such is the remark which all writers will make upon all his discoveries who write history from public documents and outside views. With all such writers the expeditions of Fremont will be credited to the zeal of the Government for the promotion of science, as if the Government under which he acted had conceived and planned these expeditions, as Mr. Jefferson did that of Lewis and Clark, and then selected this young officer to carry into effect the instructions delivered to him. How far such history would be true in relation to the first expedition, which terminated in the Rocky Mountains, has been seen in the account which has been given of the origin of that undertaking, and which leaves the Government innocent of its conception; and, therefore, not entitled to the credit of its authorship, but only to the merit of permitting it. In the second, and greater expedition, from which great political as well as scientific results have flowed, their merit is still less; for, while equally innocent of its conception, they were not equally passive to its performance—countermanding the expedition after it had begun—and lavishing censure upon the adventurous young explorer for his manner of undertaking it. The fact was, that his first expedition barely finished, Mr. Fremont sought and obtained orders for a second one, and was on the frontier of Missouri with his command, when orders arrived at St. Louis to stop him, on the ground that he had made a military equipment which the peaceful nature of his geographical pursuit did not require! as if Indians did not kill and rob scientific men as well as others, if not in a condition to defend themselves. The particular point of complaint was that he had taken a small mountain howitzer, in addition to his rifles ; and which, he was informed, was charged to him, although it had been furnished upon a regular requisition on the commandant of the arsenal at St. Louis, approved by the commander of the military department (Colonel, afterward General Kearney). Mr. Fremont had left St. Louis, and was at the frontier, Mrs. Fremont being requested to examine the letters that came after him, and forward those which he ought to receive. She read the countermanding orders and detained them ! and Fremont knew nothing of their existence, until after he had returned from one of the most marvellous and eventful expeditions of modern times—one to which the United States are indebted (among other things) for the present ownership of California, instead of seeing it a British possession. The writer of this view, who was then in St. Louis, approved of the course which his daughter had taken (for she had stopped the orders before he knew it) ; and he wrote a letter to the department condemning the recall, repulsing the reprimand which had been lavished upon Fremont, and demanding a court martial for him when he should return. The Secretary of War was then Mr. James Madison Porter, of Pennsylvania ; the chief of the topographical corps the same as now (Colonel Abert), himself an office man, surrounded by West Point officers, to whose pursuit of easy service, Fremont's adventurous expedition was a reproach ; and in conformity to whose opinions the secretary seemed to have acted. On Fremont's return, upward of a year afterward, Mr. William Wilkins, of Pennsylvania, was Secretary of War, and received the young explorer with all honor and friendship, and obtained for him the brevet of captain from President Tyler. And such is the inside view of this piece of history—very different from what documentary evidence would make it.

"To complete his survey across the continent, on the line of travel between the State of Missouri and the tide-water region of the Columbia, was Fremont's object in this expedition; and it was all that he had obtained orders for doing; but only a small part, and to his mind, an insignificant part, of what he proposed doing. People had been to the mouth of the Columbia before, and his ambition was not limited to making tracks where others had made them before him. There was a vast region beyond the Rocky Mountains—the whole western slope of our continent—of which but little was known; and of that little, nothing with the accuracy of science. All that vast region, more than seven hundred miles square—equal to a great kingdom in Europe—was an unknown land—a sealed book, which he longed to open, and to read. Leaving the frontier of Missouri in May, 1843, and often diverging from his route for the sake of expanding his field of observation, he had arrived in the tide-water region of Columbia in the month of November; and had then completed the whole service which his orders embraced. He might then have returned upon his tracks, or been brought home by sea, or hunted the most pleasant path for getting back; and if he had been a routine officer, satisfied with fulfilling an order, he would have done so. Not so the young explorer, who held his diploma from nature, and not from the United States Military Academy. He was, at Fort Vancouver, guest of the hospitable Dr. McLaughlin, Governor of the British Hudson Bay Fur Company; and obtained from him all possible information upon his intended line of return—faithfully given, but which proved to be disastrously erroneous in its leading and governing feature. A southeast route, to cross the great unknown region diagonally through its heart (making a line from the Lower Columbia to the Upper Colorado of the Gulf of California), was his line of return; twenty-five men (the same who had come with him from the United States) and a hundred horses, were his equipment; and the commencement of winter the time of starting—all without a guide, relying upon their guns for support; and, in the last resort, upon their horses—

such as should give out! for one that could carry a man, or a pack, could not be spared for food.

"All the maps up to that time had shown this region traversed from east to west—from the base of the Rocky Mountains to the bay of San Francisco—by a great river called the *Buena Ventura:* which may be translated, the *Good Chance.* Governor McLaughlin believed in the existence of this river, and made out a conjectural manuscript map to show its place and course. Fremont believed in it, and his plan was to reach it before the dead of winter, and then hibernate upon it. As a great river, he knew that it must have some rich bottoms, covered with wood and grass, where the wild animals would collect and shelter, when the snows and freezing winds drove them from the plains: and with these animals to live on, and grass for the horses, and wood for fires, he expected to avoid suffering, if not to enjoy comfort, during his solitary sojourn in that remote and profound wilderness.

"He proceeded—soon encountered deep snows, which impeded progress upon the highlands—descended into a low country to the left (afterward known to be the Great Basin, from which no water issues to any sea)—skirted an enormous chain of mountain on the right, luminous with the glittering white snow—saw strange Indians, who mostly fled—found a desert—no Buena Ventura; and death from cold and famine staring him in the face. The failure to find the river, or tidings of it, and the possibility of its existence seeming to be forbid by the structure of the country, and hibernation in the inhospitable desert being impossible, and the question being that of life and death, some new plan of conduct became indispensable. His celestial observations told him that he was in the latitude of the bay of San Francisco, and only seventy miles from it. But what miles! up and down that snowy mountain which the Indians told him no men could cross in the winter—which would have snow upon it as deep as the trees, and places where people would slip off, and fall half a mile at a time ;—a fate which actually befell a mule, packed with the precious burden of botanical specimens, collected along a travel of two thousand miles. No reward could induce an Indian to become a guide in the perilous adventure of crossing this mountain. All recoiled and fled from the adventure. It was attempted without a guide—in the dead of winter—accomplished in forty days—the men and surviving horses, a woeful procession, crawling along one by one—skeleton men leading skeleton horses—and arriving at Sutter's Settlement in the beautiful valley of the Sacramento ; and where a genial warmth, and budding flowers, and trees in foliage, the grassy ground, and flowing streams, and comfortable food, made a fairy contrast with the famine and freezing they had encountered, and the lofty Sierra Nevada which they had climbed. Here he rested and recruited ; and from this point, and by way of Monterey, the first tidings were heard of the party since leaving Fort Vancouver.

"Another long progress to the south, skirting the western base of the Sierra Nevada, made him acquainted with the noble valley of the San Joaquin, counterpart to that of the Sacramento ; when crossing through a gap, and turning to the left, he skirted the Great Basin ; and by many deviations from the right line home, levied incessant contributions to science from expanded lands, not described before. In this eventful exploration, all the great features of the western slope of our continent were brought to light—the Great Salt Lake, the Utah Lake, the Little Salt Lake ; at all which places, then deserts, the Mormons now are ; the Sierra Nevada, then solitary in the snow, now crowded with Americans, digging gold from its flanks ; the beautiful valleys of the Sacramento and San Joaquin, then alive with wild horses, elk, deer, and wild fowls, now smiling with American cultivation ; the Great Basin itself, and its contents ; the Three

Parks; the approximation of the great rivers which, rising together in the central region of the Rocky Mountains, go off east and west, toward the rising and the setting sun—all these, and other strange features of a new region, more Asiatic than American, were brought to light and revealed to public view in the results of this exploration.

"Eleven months he was never out of sight of snow; and sometimes, freezing with cold, would look down upon a sunny valley, warm with genial heat; sometimes, panting with the summer's heat, would look up at the eternal snows which crowned the neighboring mountain. But it was not then that California was secured to the Union—to the greatest power of the new world—to which it of right belonged; but it was the first step toward the acquisition, and the one that led to it. The second expedition led to a third, just in time to snatch the golden California from the hands of the British, ready to clutch it. But of this hereafter. Fremont's second expedition was now over. He had left the United States a fugitive from his Government, and returned with a name that went over Europe and America and with discoveries bearing fruit which the civilized world is now enjoying."

In 1845, the third expedition of Col. Fremont was made—principally intended to explore the Great Basin and country of Oregon and California.

"He approached these settlements in the winter of 1845-6. Aware of the critical state of affairs between the United States and Mexico, and determined to give no cause of offence to the authorities of the province, with commendable prudence he haulted his command on the frontier, one hundred miles from Monterey, and proceeded alone to that city to explain the object of his coming to the commandant general, Castro, and to obtain permission to go to the valley of the San Joaquin, where there was game for his men and grass for his horses, and no inhabitants to be molested by his presence. The leave was granted; but scarcely had he reached the desired spot for refreshment and repose, before he received information from the American settlements, and by express from our Consul at Monterey, that General Castro was preparing to attack him with a comparatively large force of artillery, cavalry and infantry, upon the pretext that, under the cover of a scientific mission, he was exciting the American settlers to revolt. In view of this danger and to be in a condition to repel an attack, he then took a position on a mountain overlooking Monterey, at a distance of about thirty miles, intrenched it, raised the flag of the United States, and with his own men, sixty-two in number, awaited the approach of the commandant general.

"From the 7th to the 10th of March, Colonel Fremont and his little band maintained this position. General Castro did not approach within attacking distance, and Colonel Fremont, adhering to his plan of avoiding all collisions, and determined neither to compromise his Government nor the American settlers, ready to join him at all hazards, if he had been attacked, abandoned his position, and commenced his march for Oregon, intending by that route to return to the United States. Deeming all danger from the Mexicans to be past, he yielded to the wishes of some of his men who desired to remain in the country, discharged them from his service, and refused to receive others in their stead, so cautious was he to avoid doing anything which would compromit the American settlers or give even a color of offence to the Mexican authorities. He pursued his march slowly and leisurely, as the state of his men and horses required, until the middle of May, and had reached the northern shore of the greater Tlamath Lake, within the limits of the Oregon territory, when he found his further progress in that direction obstructed by impassable snowy mountains and hostile Indians, who, having been excited against him by General Castro, had killed and wounded four of his men, and left him no repose either in camp or on his march. At the same time, information reached him that General Castro, in addition to his Indian allies, was advancing in person against him with artillery and cavalry, at the head of four or five hundred men ; that they were passing around the head of the Bay of San Francisco to a rendezvous on the north side of it, and that the American settlers in the valley of the Sacramento were comprehended in the scheme of destruction meditated against his own party.

"Under these circumstances, he determined to turn upon his Mexican pursuers, and seek safety both for his own party and the American settlers, not merely in the defeat of Castro, but in the total overthrow of the Mexican authority in California, and the establishment of an independent government in that extensive department. It was on the 6th of June, and before the commencement of the war between the United States and Mexico could have there been known, that this resolution was taken ; and, by the 5th of July, it was carried into effect by a series of rapid attacks, by a small body of adventurous men, under the conduct of an intrepid leader, quick to perceive and able to direct the proper measures for accomplishing such a daring enterprise.

"On the 11th of June, a convoy of 200 horses for Castro's camp, with an officer and 14 men, were surprised and captured by 12 of Fremont's party. On the 15th, at daybreak, the military post of Sonoma was also surprised and taken, with nine brass cannon, 250 stand of muskets, and several officers and some men and munitions of war.

"Leaving a small garrison at Sonoma, Colonel Fremont went to the Sacramento to rouse the American settlers ; but scarcely had he arrived there, when an express reached him from the garrison at Sonoma, with information that Castro's whole force was crossing the bay to attack that place. This intelligence was received in the afternoon of the 23d of June, while he was on the American fork of the Sacramento, 80 miles from the little garrison at Sonoma ; and, at two o'clock on the morning of the 25th, he arrived at that place with 90 riflemen from the American settlers in that valley. The enemy had not yet appeared. Scouts were sent out to reconnoitre, and a party of 20 fell in with a squadron of 70 dragoons (all of Castro's force which had crossed the bay), attacked and defeated it, killing and wounding five, without harm to themselves ; the Mexican commander, De la Torre, barely escaping with the loss of his transport boats and nine pieces of brass artillery, spiked.

"The country north of the bay of San Francisco, being cleared of the enemy, Colonel Fremont returned to Sonoma on the evening of the 4th of July, and on the morning of the 5th, called the people together, explained to them the condition of things in the province, and recommended an immediate declaration of independence. The declaration was made, and he was selected to take the chief direction of affairs.

"The attack on Castro was the next object. He was at Santa Clara, an intrenched post on the upper or south side of the Bay of San Francisco, with 400 men and two pieces of field artillery. A circuit of more than a hundred miles must be traversed to reach him. On the 6th of July the pursuit was commenced, by a body of 160 mounted riflemen, commanded by Colonel Fremont in person, who, in three days, arrived at the American settlements on the Rio de los Americanos. Here he learnt that Castro had abandoned Santa Clara, and was retreating south toward Ciudad de los Angeles (the city of the Angels), the seat of the Governor General of the Californias, and distant 400 miles. It was instantly resolved on to pursue him to that place. At the moment of departure, the gratifying intelligence was received that war with Mexico had commenced ; that Monterey had been taken by our naval force, and the flag of the United States there raised on the 7th of July; and that the fleet would coöperate in the pursuit of Castro and his forces. The flag of independence was hauled down, and that of the United States hoisted, amidst the hearty greetings and to the great joy of the American settlers and the forces under the command of Colonel Fremont.

"The combined pursuit was rapidly continued; and on the 12th of August, Commodore Stockton and Colonel Fremont, with a detachment of marines from the squadron and some riflemen, entered the City of the Angels, without resistance or objection; the Governor General, Pico, the Commandant General, Castro, and all the Mexican authorities, having fled and dispersed. Commodore Stockton took possession of the whole country as a conquest of the United States, and appointed Colonel Fremont Governor, under the law of nations; to assume the functions of that office when he should return to the squadron.

"Thus, in the short space of sixty days from the first decisive movement, this conquest was achieved by a small body of men, to an extent beyond their own expectation; for the Mexican authorities proclaimed it a conquest, not merely of the northern part, but of the whole province of the Californias.

"The Commandant General, Castro, on the 9th of August, from his camp at the Mesa, and next day 'on the road to Sonora,' announced this result to the people, together with the actual flight and dispersion of the former authorities; and at the same time, he officially communicated the fact of the conquest to the French, English, and Spanish Consuls in California; and to crown the whole, the official paper of the Mexican government, on the 16th of October, in laying these official communications before the public, introduced them with the emphatic declaration, 'The loss of the Californias is consummated.'

"The whole province was yielded up to the United States, and is now in our military occupancy. A small part of the troops sent out to subject this province will constitute, it is presumed, a sufficient force to retain our possession, and the remainder will be disposable for other objects of the war."

We shall not stop to examine the Stockton and the Kearney controversies, the Monroe duel, nor the troubles which beset the gallant explorer and officer. Suffice it to say, that out of all he came with clean hands, and an unspotted reputation. Though a court martial, asked for by himself, sentenced him to be dismissed the service for disobedience of orders, or rather for not selecting the proper officer in California to obey, the President remitted the penalty. Too proud to hold an office in any army of any nation under such circumstances, Col. Fremont tendered his resignation as Lieutenant Colonel in the United States army.

It was the old story of the triumph of Red Tapism and dull routine over genius and services of transcendent importance; but, however Col. Fremont might fare before a board of jealous officers, the people took his cause up, and make him a hero. From all parts of the land, and from countries over the sea, letters of congratulation and admiration of his scientific explorations, poured in upon him.

In October, 1848, Mr. Fremont set out upon his *fourth* trip over the Rocky Mountains, which proved to be the most dangerous and fearful of all. Though 120 mules were frozen in one night, and some of his comrades were starved, he had succeeded in reaching California. The trip was made entirely at his own expense, but its results were given in the journals at the time for the benefit of the nation.

The year previous to his fourth Overland Expedition, Col. Fremont had, for $3,000, bought the since famous "Mariposa Estate," which will eventually make him a very wealthy man, if he succeeds in establishing his rights in California.

In 1849, General Taylor appointed Fremont Commissioner to run the boundary line between the United States and Mexico; but while he was deliberating upon an acceptance or declination, the new legislature of California, assembled at San Jose, elected him United States Senator. In the Senate his course was distinguished by great industry and indefatigable exertion in favor of his constituents, and it was much regretted by those who knew the youthful senator, that he chose the short term, so that his term of office expired in March, 1851. In the Constitutional Convention in California, Col. Fremont had taken a very decided part against slavery, and in Congress his course had been so unpartisan that he lost the support of his party, and a reëlection was out of the question. His subsequent history is known to every man. He was nominated in 1856 by the Republican party as its candidate for the Presidency, and polled a tremendous vote. The enthusiasm in his favor in the East and the Northwest, was intense, and in the opinion of many, nothing but the intervention of a third candidate—Mr. Fillmore—prevented his election.

Mr. Fremont, *as a politician*, is little known to the country, for he has had little to do with politics, and is uncorrupted. He is, however, known to favor, first of all things, a Pacific railroad, is opposed to lawless filibusterism, and thoroughly in favor of the supremacy of free labor over slave labor. He unhesitatingly indorsed the Philadelphia platform, and can always be relied on to oppose the schemes of the slavery-propagandists.

As *a man*, Col. Fremont is known to the country to be fearless, brave, devoted to fulfilling all his duties, and ready to brave the frowns of millions, if necessary, in redeeming a pledge. Such a man can be *trusted*, whether in or out of office.

THE END.

www.ingramcontent.com/pod-product-compliance
Lightning Source LLC
LaVergne TN
LVHW010148110826
845151LV00002B/456

* 9 7 8 1 4 2 5 5 3 6 9 8 5 *